HARD COUNTRY

HARD COUNTRY

A Golden Bay Life

ROBIN ROBILLIARD

RANDOM HOUSE
NEW ZEALAND

R. V. Robilliard

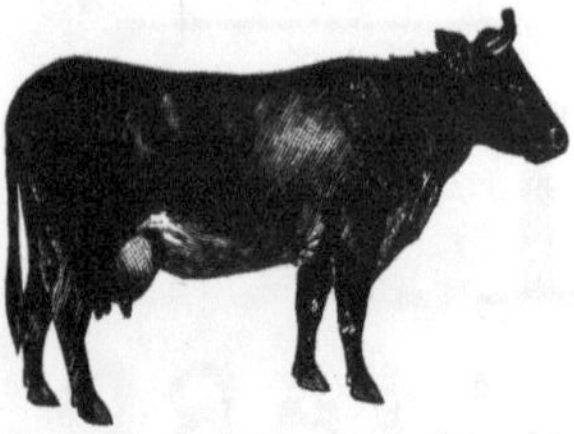

The poem on page 255, from *These Small Fields* by Frank Soper, is reproduced with the permission of the poet.

A RANDOM HOUSE BOOK published by Random House New Zealand
18 Poland Road, Glenfield, Auckland, New Zealand

For more information about our titles go to www.randomhouse.co.nz

A catalogue record for this book is available from the National Library of New Zealand

Random House New Zealand is part of the Random House Group
New York London Sydney Auckland Delhi Johannesburg

First published 2014, reprinted 2014

ISBN 978 1 77553 663 5
eISBN 978 1 77553 664 2

Please note that some names have been changed. Some material has previously been published in the *Auckland Weekly News*.

Design: Megan van Staden
Front cover photographs: Robin Robilliard
Back cover photograph: Writer and traveller, 1982. The *Nelson Mail* Collection.

Printed in Australia by Griffin Press

To Garry, my husband, and our children
Timothy, Sally and Michael, with love.

ROCKLANDS

PREFACE

The Takaka Hill is my Rubicon. It's the mountainous barrier that isolates Golden Bay, in the north-west corner of New Zealand's South Island, from the rest of the country.

What was I doing here?

Well, I'd married someone as independent as myself. We were not going to work for other people any longer than we had to. And so it was that in 1957, within a year of our marriage, and with a six-week-old baby, Garry and I had taken on what was undoubtedly some of the worst land in the country. Some 1500 mountainous acres of gorse, scrub and bracken, aptly named Rocklands, now belonged to us.

It was all we could afford.

But what a place it was. Rocky slopes rose so steeply they seemed to touch the sky. On the northern slopes of the Pikikirunga Range, our back boundary bordered the Abel Tasman National Park. Sparrow hawks soared at the skyline, the untouched bush thrived, and the beautiful view back down to the ocean took our breath away.

It was wonderful for the soul, but dreadful for farming.

With a slum dwelling to live in, and not a viable fence on the property, we learned the farm had bankrupted its three previous owners. All had been unable to make a living on the unforgiving land.

And so Garry began a lifetime of punishing toil on the land. I simply had no choice but to get on with it as well. If we had given up the struggle, I believe neither of us would have ever recovered from the failure. It was to be an existence that would either make me or break me.

I'D BEEN BROUGHT UP IN HAWKE'S BAY, surrounded by prosperous sheep stations and gracious homesteads. It was a life that had certain rules, certain ways of assessing people.

Were they one of us, or not?

But in Golden Bay, I was to learn, people are judged on what they had achieved in their life. No one here asks, 'Who was your mother, dear?' It's what you do that counts. And extraordinary things happen in this isolated but beautiful region. Outsiders say that the people of Golden Bay are like no one else.

Perhaps it's all due to that towering Takaka Hill. Severe boundaries of mountain on three sides and the sea on the fourth meant that, in Golden Bay's early years, supplies were brought in by boat, and its produce – wool, pigs and butter – departed the same way. The first road over the Takaka Hill was built in the early 1900s, replacing the old bridle track with its knee-deep mud puddles. It was improved using relief labour in the 1930s Depression, but even then the new road was hardly a breeze. There is no alternative road out.

I think the isolation made so many of us dig deep into ourselves to find hidden talents, a drive, a focus to do extraordinary things we may never have achieved if we'd lived in an easier environment with countless distractions. It has created a close, hard-working community, people who rely on themselves and each other to get through.

Golden Bay's first settlers may have named the region for the gold they came to prospect, but once the gold ran out they put in the backbreaking work to carve farms from the bush. By the 1870s the lawlessness of the prospecting days had passed, and the settlers were a self-contained, respectable community with a library, a garden society, several schools and regular musical concerts. Generations of sheep farmers continued to struggle on the rocky hills, with dairy faring better on the fertile pastures on the flats. Much was expected of children as they worked alongside their parents on the land. The courage needed to keep going in the face of poverty and hardship on those desperate hills was immense.

I'VE OFTEN ASKED MYSELF, OVER THE LAST almost 60 years in the Bay, where I would have preferred to have spent that large part of my life. There were times, many, when I would have said 'anywhere but here', but I eventually came to realise that this is the place that suits me. It allows me to be myself like nowhere else I know – as long as I can escape sometimes.

And who would ever have believed it possible in 1957, when I first crossed the mighty barrier of the Takaka Hill, aged 23, that I would one day have the opportunity to travel to faraway places as a journalist, giving me a creative outlet and much-needed education, with seclusion once home to get the writing done.

Above all, our tortuous landscape, on which my brave husband slogged out his guts over a lifetime, has proved an ideal environment for our three children to grow up in – unspoilt, with character and guts. I'm humbled by their work ethic and sense of character.

It took me a while, but I did come to realise that I have been fortunate indeed, not only in my husband, but in the incredible friends we have made, and the life that can be lived in this very beautiful place.

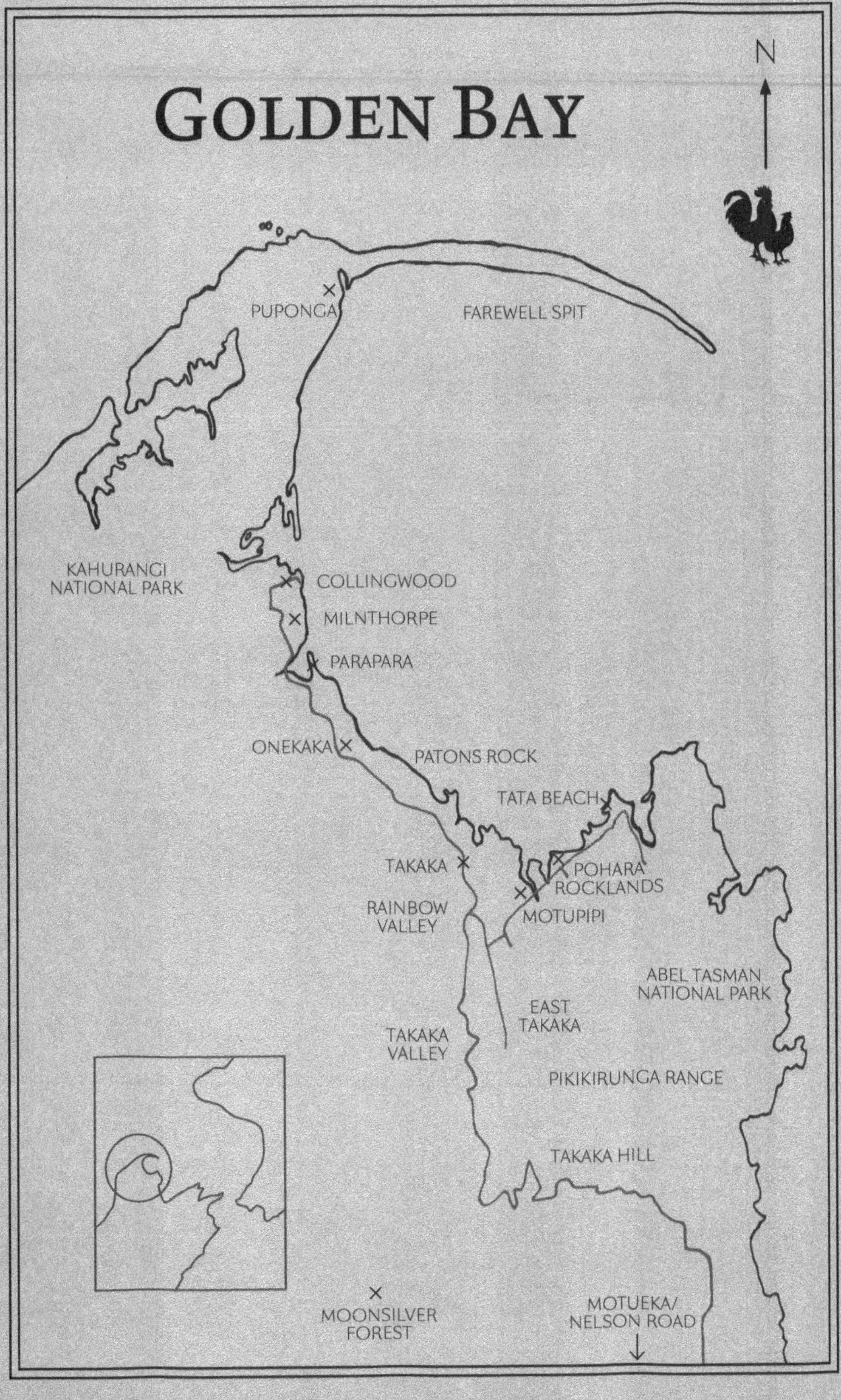
GOLDEN BAY
N
PUPONGA
FAREWELL SPIT
KAHURANGI
NATIONAL PARK
COLLINGWOOD
MILNTHORPE
PARAPARA
ONEKAKA
PATONS ROCK
TATA BEACH
TAKAKA
POHARA
ROCKLANDS
MOTUPIPI
RAINBOW
VALLEY
ABEL TASMAN
NATIONAL PARK
EAST
TAKAKA
TAKAKA
VALLEY
PIKIKIRUNGA RANGE
TAKAKA HILL
MOONSILVER
FOREST
MOTUEKA/
NELSON ROAD

CHAPTER 1

We had driven our ex-army truck, loaded to its gun turrets with our bedraggled worldly goods, through the gate, when I remembered the eggs. 'Stop! We'll have to go back! We've left the eggs behind!'

This was serious. Once we'd signed up for a derelict farm in the remote north-west corner of the South Island, I'd searched every corner of the pine plantation on the North Canterbury farm which my husband Garry was managing, for eggs from our few hens.

Nine dozen had been preserved in Vaseline as a hedge against initial starvation, as we faced survival as farm owners without the security of wages.

'I'm not going back,' said Garry. 'We've said our goodbyes.'

Reluctantly I had to agree, but was unable to prevent the tears, caused as much from exhaustion as the egg fiasco. It was only six weeks since Tim's birth, which had been a difficult one.

At the time, in 1957, we were both in our early twenties, and for the first year of our marriage we'd lived on a prosperous sheep and cattle property in Waipara, an hour's drive from Christchurch. The house was a dream. We had free meat and electricity, and a car allowance on top of wages. But we longed for a farm of our own. With us it was an obsession, all the more compulsive because we didn't have the wherewithal to even look at a decent property.

With the arrival of the Saturday newspaper we turned first to *Farms for Sale*. Anything sounding rough or isolated enough to suit our pockets would find Garry visiting the stock firm involved, trying to look 10 years older, and therefore a better loan risk. But he always received the same answer – no – and we soon learnt that without sufficient capital Canterbury's high land prices were an impossible barrier.

Undaunted, we spent our Sundays travelling around advertised farms, exploring sour, weed-infested country with little shacks for dwellings. But we couldn't even afford to breathe the air above these expensive properties.

With our first child on the way, there was no complacent, placid atmosphere as we prepared for his arrival. Instead we found ourselves even more desperate to have a log cabin, or even a canvas tent on 10 acres of bush – anything, so long as it was our own.

We'd spent our honeymoon searching the neglected wastes of Northland without success, hoping to find a farm we could afford. Now, hearing there was an abundance of infertile – and therefore more reasonably priced – land in Nelson's back country, we took a tent to Kaiteriteri Beach for our annual leave, and settled there to spy out the territory.

Our days were spent being driven at white-knuckle speed over pot-holed back-country roads by youthful employees of stock firms, who had been delegated to show us the province's cheapest farms. But even the worst of these scrub-infested properties, depressingly poked up cold, narrow gullies, were beyond our budget.

At length, more to get rid of us than anything else, our driver suggested we could look for ourselves over *The Hill*. If we were interested. The capitals were implied.

'What hill?' we enquired innocently.

'The Takaka Hill,' he replied.

We'd never heard of it. 'Why wouldn't we be interested?' I asked suspiciously.

'Well,' said the young man, 'the road over the Takaka Hill isn't everyone's cup of tea. In fact,' he added, 'I've heard that there are people on the other side who've never been over it!'

'And what is on the other side?' Garry asked.

'A region called Golden Bay; a huge area of wild and rugged bush-covered mountains, with predominantly dairy farms in the valleys, and long stretches of beach which are mostly empty. Only about three thousand people live there.'

'Any sheep farming?' we asked, to hear that the poverty, roughness and scant carrying capacity of most of the hill country makes it of little value for sheep farming.

Of course we were going to look.

Perhaps there was a chance for us?

THE NEXT DAY – VERY SLOWLY – we took our old coupé up the infamous Takaka Hill. The narrow road climbed steeply round continuous tortuous bends, and as we climbed the weather became thicker, cloudier and wetter. Cars approached from above with their lights on. A marble factory appeared near the road, creaking eerily in the mist. From here on up it was a ghostly world of dead and lifeless trees and weird, grey rocks scattered on the ground, like petrified stumps on a moonscape. A signpost to Canaan only added to the surreal atmosphere.

And then, in one breathless moment, we came out of the gloom at the top of the Hill and could look down the other side. It was now late afternoon, with the sun lighting up a glitter of blue sea in the far distance. A different world lay at our feet, a paradise of incomparable scenery.

As if from an aeroplane we looked down some 900 metres, to lush green paddocks in a triangular-shaped valley, with steep ranges framing each side. To the west they were bush-clad and undeveloped, climbing higher and higher in folds, back to snow-covered mountains. The eastern range, stretching towards the sea, was shaped like gigantic lumps of dough, predominantly covered in secondary growth. Here and there was scattered evidence of tamed pastoral land.

As we sped along the valley with increasing excitement, we saw small, well-painted houses and cow sheds. The warm glow of the sun, the citrus trees and subtropical growth in the gardens demonstrated the rich abundance of the valley floor, where huge totara trees gave a park-like appearance to farms flanking the river.

Impatiently we sought out a land agent in the small township of Takaka, but on hearing how little capital we had the salesman's enthusiastic patter soon faltered. 'I really can't show you anything,' he admitted. 'Except,' he added as an afterthought, noting our disconsolate faces, 'there is one hell of a run-down place, where the owners are so desperate to sell they're prepared to leave two-thirds of the price on the land as a first mortgage. But I have to warn you, it's a grim proposition. I don't suppose you'd be interested?'

'Show us,' said Garry and I, in unison.

AND SO WE CAME TO VIEW the property aptly named Rocklands. Knowing we couldn't afford to be fussy, we each took a deep breath and looked open-mouthed at a mountainous, rocky terrain smothered in bracken, gorse, hawthorn, barberry and manuka. The only grass to be seen was a small patch flanking the drive, which ran between two rough, small cottages. The homestead and the only flat paddocks were not part of the sale.

What was for sale was 1500 acres, on the northern slopes of the Pikikirunga Range, where rocky slopes reared up so steeply they seemed to be part of the sky, disappearing into an ethereal mist. The height of the back boundary was close to 800 metres, bordering the Abel Tasman National Park. The property was carrying 500 ewes and 14 cattle – if we could find them. There wasn't a viable fence on the place.

It was a sight to daunt any sensible person, and we noticed other buyers weren't exactly panting up the drive. Indeed, we were later to learn the property had a history of bankrupting its owners, the land reverting each time back to the same mortgagors. Each time it happened, the property was in an even more run-down state.

But this was our only chance. We were grateful the owners were willing to leave money in the place. Nobody else had wanted to lend us money.

Both stubbornly independent, neither Garry nor I wanted to work for other people. We wanted to build our own future. We talked briefly together and decided. 'We'll buy the place.'

And so, with that hasty, uninformed and naïve decision, we committed ourselves to trying to survive on rotten land in the remote north-west tip of the South Island.

Why did we do it? All my life I had wanted to own a sheep farm. The happiest days of my childhood had been spent at Waiwhenua, my maternal grandparents' sheep station in the foothills of the Kaweka Ranges in Hawke's Bay, where my mother Elinor had grown up.

Garry, born in Christchurch, had been expected to take over his father's city-based accountancy firm. Right from childhood, however, he had also been determined to farm. His father would send him on school holidays to work for his toughest farming clients, hoping that the hardship of farm work and the grubbiest chores would deter his bright elder son. It didn't work. His parents would drive out to collect Garry at the end of a holiday job to find a happy, bright-eyed boy, either covered in oil greasing a tractor, mucking out a cow bail, or with a shed of daggy sheep still to crutch.

WITH THE TAKE-OVER DATE FOR ROCKLANDS still six months ahead, we settled back at our North Canterbury job to await the birth of our baby, and for Garry to haunt clearing sales to buy farm tools. He bought a truck at a government disposal sale where prospective buyers weren't permitted to lift the bonnet of any vehicle, let alone check if the engine would start.

But in George, as we called the former military truck, we had struck gold. Thirty years later that old Dodge was still going.

On our first wedding anniversary, 29 June 1957, Timothy de Garis Robilliard was born, and the title deeds for Rocklands were signed, neither without considerable drama.

The family lawyer had done his research on Rocklands and informed my in-laws that this was 'poor, useless land' and we 'shouldn't touch it with a barge pole'.

We ignored the advice. We weren't going to cancel the sale.

'You must be mad!' we were told daily by family and friends. 'You haven't an ounce of business sense between you!'

'You can't live west of the Wairau River,' an aunt declared. 'Nobody we know lives there!'

And finally, when they realised we weren't changing our minds: 'You made your bed, now lie in it!'

Indeed, it was a proud and excited new father and farm owner who arrived in George to collect Tim and me from the hospital. So excited, in fact, that Garry placed our infant son in his carrycot on the deck of the truck.

'Hey!' I yelled. 'Tim can't ride there!'

Now I think of it, perhaps this was a signal to the wife and any offspring of the new Rockland's owner that we were going to have to be tough.

THREE WEEKS LATER WE WERE READY to leave North Canterbury for our Golden Bay farm. With chaos reigning everywhere, due to my inexperience as a housewife and mother, let alone as a packer of our worldly goods, there seemed to be more lying around that couldn't be packed until the last minute than was shut away in crates.

Both grandmothers came to help with the final packing, but at 11 a.m. on the day of departure we were still there, having a frustrating time of it.

Ray, from the next-door farm, arrived to help. He'd guessed we might need a hand when we hadn't passed his gate several hours earlier, where his family were all lined up to wave to us. Taking one look at Garry trying to fit a sofa, easy chairs and a table into the small space left on the truck deck, our kind neighbour sprang into action.

I stood helplessly by and watched the strange procession of furniture being carried out by my toiling husband, and being brought back effortlessly under Ray's one arm. Having lost an arm during the war, the remaining limb had gained phenomenal strength.

'What's going on?' I asked Ray, as he walked past clutching a table.

'No room for half these things, Robby,' he said. 'Garry is just wasting his time trying to get everything loaded.'

'But that's my kitchen table,' I wailed. 'And that's our sofa!'

'Can't help that. There's no room!'

It's no wonder the nine dozen eggs were forgotten.

The truck was eventually packed to the height of the cab with chests, trunks, beds, washing machine, fridge, blanket bundles and countless cardboard cartons. Stuffed into every cranny were loose articles such as brooms, buckets, farm tools, saddles, a baby's bath and a preserving pan. Draped over the cab roof, like a floppy sun hat, was our mattress, topped with Tim's bassinet. A dozen hens were penned in a crate beside the three sheepdogs at the back of the deck.

At last the moment came to squeeze ourselves into the cab. I found myself jammed over the gears, sitting on a pile of nappies, knees rubbing my nose, sandwiched between Garry at the wheel and Tim in his carrycot.

Heart-rending goodbyes were said to the two grandmothers, who both privately thought we were off to our doom, and we made an earnest attempt to thank Ray, who waved us off cheerfully, no doubt highly relieved to see the end of such bedlam.

George was eased carefully out the gate, from where we had known comfort and security for the first year of our married life, to turn north at the Waipara Junction, for the start of the slow, cumbersome drive to Rocklands. Our exodus to Golden Bay had begun.

The load was securely roped, but that didn't prevent the rattling and crashing of the multitude of loose articles, accompanied by the screech of the truck's overloaded deck on tyres as we cornered the hills.

Many eyes were turned on us as we drove up the east coast. From every passing car and astonished bystander we received a smiling wave. Whining and cackling hysterically at the back, our dogs and hens announced, to anyone who hadn't yet noticed, that we were about to pass by. The amusement we caused helped to take my mind off any concerns I had about leaving a comfortable home and the security of wages.

We spent a night en route with elderly friends in Blenheim. And it was going to be a long time before I stopped thinking nostalgically about the welcome we tired refugees received in that elegant home; with my first experience of an electric blanket, and with even the bathroom floor carpeted. In turn, our hosts' astounded neighbours were still talking many years later about this rough-looking truck turning up, letting sheepdogs loose for a run in the posh leafy street, and hens announcing at dawn they'd laid an egg or two!

On reaching Nelson late the next morning, Garry made an

important visit to Loan and Mercantile, the stock firm, to plead for a loan to purchase Rocklands' sheep and cattle.

The manager knew Rocklands well. 'It'll be a hell of a hurdle,' he said. 'There's everything to do on it. It's been run right back.' But he agreed his firm would finance the stock, as an advance against any wool or stock we would sell.

We pressed on westward to tackle the mighty Takaka Hill. For us, the Hill signified the end of social and light-hearted entertainment, the parties and weddings of our friends, and the concerts and plays in big city theatres. The other side of the range held the adventure of growing up, and a test of our ingenuity.

At the top of the mountain pass we paused to let an over-heated George take a rest. 'Nearly there,' said Garry.

Darkness was already encroaching on the view. 'Come on,' I said, 'let's get going. I want to get home.'

An hour later we wearily entered our long drive, where the night's kind blanket obscured the rugged country we now owned. 'Here we are,' said Garry. 'Our land at last.'

How splendid it sounded.

Our first task, after letting the dogs loose, was to plug in our ancient fridge, which we'd been warned could lose its gas if it was disconnected too long. We couldn't afford for that to happen. We hauled it to the nearest connection, which turned out to be the only receptor for a three-point plug in the cottage. The switch was turned on, and – *voilà!* – with a cough and a rattle the old fridge purred into action.

That first night we sat on packing cases to eat a sandwich, and talked of the sheep we would graze and the cattle we would fatten. We didn't realise then that the hungry land, so unlike farms we knew on the east coast, would grow every kind of weed more easily than it would grow grass. We had yet to learn that in this wet, humid climate gorse, barberry, hawthorn, manuka and bracken would flourish. Unless tonnes of fertiliser were applied, and fences provided sufficient subdivision, there was little hope of taming this land.

No wonder the place had been on the market for years. Who would take it on? Only people who were young, poor, optimistic and adventurous. Only foolish people like us, we told each other, and laughed. We agreed it was the challenge we wanted. This was the life for us!

WE WOKE NEXT MORNING TO PELTING RAIN on the iron roof. I had never heard so much rain fall so fast before. Busily placing buckets under the leaks, we watched in astonishment as rain fell in sheets, and heard the laughing chatter of the creek between the cottage and the drive, which had been dry when we arrived. In our innocence we expected the downpour to cease at any moment, as the vendors had told us it only rained at night in this part of the world. How gullible we were was brought home to us when it was still raining 10 days later.

Regardless of the weather, Garry was off at dawn each day to seek out our sheep. Those he found were tucked up and miserable, most with half their fleeces pulled off. Finding remnants of fences smothered in bracken, he cleared them as best he could and attempted to make use of them.

When it had first been cleared of bush a hundred years earlier, Rocklands had grown coxsfoot grass so high that it blocked the farm gates, which were now rotting on the ground. Watering places were practically non-existent, with most of the troughs silted up and any fluming long since rotted away. The bracken fern was so high it brushed against Garry's chest as he pushed through on foot. Once he became lost in the thick gorse, and was unable to find a way out for some time.

The cottage had been built out of sap timber, to house a shepherd, 80 years earlier. Now it was borer-ridden, with two small bedrooms, a dark little sitting room with one sash window, a kitchen with a dreaded wood range, one small cupboard and a soggy lino-covered bench top.

Wallpaper hung in strips from the hessian linings of the bedrooms. The floors were warped and buckled, with the occasional patch of greenery breaking through. The bathroom was a lean-to at the back and the loo was outside, almost hidden in a tangle of vines. Trying to unpack, I walked round and round with articles in my hands, searching for somewhere to place them. Inevitably they were put back into their crates.

Sugar, flour and bread were kept in tin trunks, which also served as seating. Clothes were kept in suitcases under our bed, as were linen and crockery. To prepare a meal I had to dive into the trunks, the lids often crashing down on my head. At first there was the added puzzle of remembering which trunks held what, and with no system as to where the baby clothes were kept, Tim was clothed in some extraordinary garments.

Our water supply came from an antiquated system – basically just a pipe in a marshy creek, which blocked up when it rained. As a result, the water wasn't clean and no washing stayed white for long. If I held a glass of water up to the light I could see little things in it.

'It's a bit primitive,' Garry conceded. 'After the civilised homes you're used to, you must be shocked.'

I assured him I wasn't. Until, that is, I discovered there were no drains from the kitchen sink or the bath. The contents of both splashed down, to lie in stinking pools under the floorboards.

But I decided I would keep a stiff upper lip. *Don't look back*, I told myself. *It's the journey not the goal that is remembered.* A sense of humour would see me through the rough spots. If I shed a few tears, it was only little Tim who knew about it, as I snuggled his baby warmth against me for comfort.

But on the first fine day my heart lifted, as I turned my back on our tortuous land and gazed at the view to the north.

Our long drive led my eye towards the green pastures of neighbouring dairy farms. Beyond that, twinkling and blue in the sunshine, stretched the calm waters of Golden Bay.

The cottage was sheltered by protecting arms of native bush. Rata trees over 25 metres high, totara and rimu, nikau and ponga – a paradise for the native birds that sang so gaily this wonderful morning. Pukeko strode across our one patch of grass, looking as if they owned the place. A sole white heron alighted 20 metres away, a rare and special welcome.

What did it matter if there were spiders, mice, unlined walls and rotting floorboards inside, when outside there was this intoxicating peace and colour?

Not for anything did I want us to work for someone else. I wanted to build our own future.

And so began endless years of hard, physical work for my husband. One man alone.

Chapter 2

Throughout my life, from early childhood, I had one vision in mind: to be able to create another Waiwhenua, the beloved sheep station of my maternal grandparents, where my happiest days had been spent as a child. I never tired of hearing my mother's reminiscences of her childhood, growing up with two sisters and three brothers, of tennis, swimming and riding, and their teasing of long-suffering governesses and nannies.

To visit Waiwhenua I would travel in the newspaper car, which made a twice-weekly three-hour journey to the Waiwhare crossroads, having diverted up every side road, speeding and sliding around gravel-road corners. 'I'm going to be sick,' I'd announce, and the driver would leap out to hold my head over the grass.

Uncle John would be waiting at Waiwhare to collect me, plus mail, newspapers and supplies ordered from Hastings. Now it was only 16 more kilometres to near the end of River Road. Uncle John would be silent. He never said much, usually tired from working so hard. He and Aunt Dinah and my ever-more cousins lived in the farm cottage, about a kilometre from the Waiwhenua homestead.

At last comes the final bend – and the sight of my favourite house on earth. I stand on the veranda, ears humming in the sudden silence, as Aunt Bet unpeels my scarf and coat and Granny smothers my face with kisses.

Formality reigns over dinner in the dining room – ties and jackets are required for the males of the family and a change of dress for the women. Horace, my grandfather, understands whatever weird impulse makes an Englishman dress for dinner in the jungle. His father had left the Manor House in Preston, in the county of Rutland, to take up land in Hawke's Bay.

The table is lit with candles – there is no electricity in this back-country area. I am glad of the dusky light, so I can copy my elders' actions.

It's Aunt Bet who takes me upstairs to my bedroom, with the silver-topped bottles on the dressing table, and the little round window through which I will look first thing next morning to see the shepherds riding off to their work, and hear the distant bleat of sheep and the murmuring of cattle.

Other nights I climb the stairs alone. The long hall is dark and full of lurking dangers, so I run with my candle, spattering grease, until I can leap onto my bed. I don't admit I'm scared on this nightly journey. I want to be the least trouble possible, so I'll be invited to stay again and again.

BREAKFAST IS PORRIDGE, THE REAL STUFF, which has to be soaked overnight, and bacon and eggs for Grandad. Meals are passed through the servery hatch, beyond which the current cook, if they are fortunate enough to have one, is not to progress. In the same way, Grandad has never been known to set a foot in the kitchen.

Aunt Bet lectures me about Lizzy, the young maid. 'You may hear her going about her work singing pop songs,' she says, 'but you are not to copy her. Lizzy's taste in music is extremely common.' It was typical of my aunt to add, 'But you are not to tease her for this. She is a cheerful young person and cannot be expected to know better.'

There was no question that Aunt Bet could be a bit bossy, but she was the world's most family-loving person. An unshakeable rock of loyalty. It was always unmarried Aunt Bet who was the practical person in the homestead, constantly called home from some more exciting job whenever there was a domestic crisis, such as a lack of help in the house. And 'help' is increasingly hard to get, often arriving on Tuesday's mail car only to depart on Thursday's car once they became aware of Waiwhenua's isolation.

Granny breakfasts in bed, wrapped in a cashmere shawl

with library books scattered about, some of them in French. She throws them aside as I dive resolutely, breath held, into the folds of her soft Viyella nightdress.

Now there is hope that she will read to me, from one of the books in the nursery. And sometimes my cousins, Tony and Mike, will arrive from the cottage to leap between the sheets, muddy feet and all, to hear the story. More often than not, Granny will make it up.

I sit quietly, taking in every word of my grandmother's fantastic and funny stories. The boys are far more responsive, laughing, urging our grandmother on, but it's me who asks the questions.

'If I'm lucky, Granny, will the fairies come tonight?'

'Perhaps,' my grandmother replies. 'We will keep a sharp lookout. They're very shy.' Fairies are well respected in Ireland, so of course Granny, born in Ireland from an Anglo-Irish family, believes in them.

Indeed, if you ask me the quality I love most in another human being, I will say *magic*. That is why my maternal grandmother was such a beloved person in my childhood. And in later years, when I was traversing the world as a journalist, it was always the *magic* people I met who resonated most, and whom I remember best to this day.

'Shall I put my pinny on?' I ask my aunt, when I am at Waiwhenua, and just six years old.

'Why do you want to put on a penny, Robin?'

'No, pinny!' I say, eyes brimming in my effort to be understood. 'Mummy gave me a pinny to wear when I'm being helpful.'

'Oh! Well then, of course.'

I put on my pinny and fill the wood boxes and scrub the backyard, where the cow-boy has spilt milk and the wind has scattered pine needles.

'What can I do now?' I ask, as each job is finished.

Granny praises me to Grandad at lunch time. 'Robin has been such a help.'

'Hmph!' is Grandad's response. He doesn't say much – or he might give a throaty chuckle of appreciation.

The men on the station, the farm workers, eat in a room off the kitchen. I hear the jolly talk and teasing yelled through the hatch to the maid. I ask if I can eat some meals in the kitchen and share the fun. Grandad won't hear of such a thing.

'It can't do any harm,' Granny tells him.

'But it will harm the maid,' Grandad says.

FOR THE MOST PART I AM LEFT to entertain myself, but I am never at a loss for things to do. First I visit the former schoolroom with its sliding cupboard doors, which holds the books my mother and her siblings enjoyed. Most of Dickens, *Tom Brown's School Days*, *Little Women*, *Doctor Dolittle*, *Pollyanna*.

There are also soft-covered journals from England, which are useful to read while I walk to the end of River Road, to visit the Noell family at Te Konini. It's a three-kilometre journey, so I need something to read as I walk. On the hills to the right of me is the pine plantation boundary of Tunanui Station, from where my father, as an English cadet for Sir Andrew Russell, used to ride across the gorge to court my mother.

The Noell family consists of three spinster sisters – Stella, Kate and Ada – a bachelor brother Stan, and their elderly mother. The sisters endeavour to outdo each other by each pressing on a visitor a cake she has personally baked, and each has a separate teapot. It's quite usual for several members of the Noell family not to be speaking to the others.

My real treat is to ride with Kate across the Tutaekuri River to collect the Noells' weekly mail, clinging for dear life to the mane of my horse as it scrambles up the near-vertical shingle scree on the Rissington side of the gorge.

Once the original carriage track from Napier, it was along this same riverbed that my mother's eldest brother, Leslie, then a medical student at Otago, drove his father's car to and fro across the river. My grandparents were receiving medical attention in America at the time. He did it for a lark, and wrote off the car.

AUNT BET MAKES ME JAM SANDWICHES WRAPPED in newspaper, and off I go for hours – to explore stony gullies, or, best fun of all, slide down dry hills on a tin tray.

Granny keeps the key of the storeroom. When I suggest she must be very rich to buy so much lavatory paper, there are peals of laughter from Granny, but no disclaimer.

In fact Waiwhenua was heavily mortgaged, following the global Depressions of the 1920s and '30s. With aerial top-dressing non-existent until after World War Two, it was a struggle to maintain the land. It had been Granny's little 'ships from Ireland' – payments inherited from her Anglo-Irish Ascendancy ancestors as bits of estates were sold – which had paid for her children's education at private schools.

Granny also laughs, and repeats the story often, how I once suggested she must have got around in an ox-cart when she was young. Had I presumed she lived in the Middle Ages?

It's strange, isn't it, that as I dig deep to remember my childhood, it's the times my eyes filled with emotional tears that are the easiest to remember. Even when they swam from the joy of causing laughter, or being praised, as happened so often for me at Waiwhenua.

When Granny washes my hair, patiently combing out the tangles, she tells me I am pretty. 'Just like Princess Elizabeth.' I know this isn't true. I am a plain child, but my eyes swim with gratitude.

But Granny is perturbed by my full bottom lip. 'Next time my ship comes in from Ireland, you and I will go to the Mayo clinic in America,' she tells me. 'I'll have my nose straightened and we'll get your lip fixed.' In the meantime, I have formed a habit of sleeping with a little finger curled beneath my lip, to squash it up. In the daytime I walk round with a lip-firming grin. It becomes a habit. Strangers give me startled smiles in return!

Above all, Granny has taught me to believe in myself. 'One day your name will go up in lights,' she tells me. A ridiculous notion, but I believe it.

At a circle of daisies in a paddock, a fairy ring, Granny tells me to make a wish. 'Please,' I entreat the fairies, 'let me have a farm of my own when I grow up.'

So HERE WE WERE, WITHIN A YEAR of our marriage, owners of a farm called Rocklands. Well, it was hardly a farm in the statistical sense. It was far from being an economic unit, with crippling stock losses, falling wool, beef and lamb prices, stubborn debt, and the unending battle against fern.

'They'll be lucky to last six months,' the locals said.

It was land that had to be farmed every step of the way. Long neglected, it took an immediate revenge. But undeterred, stubborn, and ever-optimistic, Garry disappeared into the wilderness each day to pit himself against country, which to me began to seem cruelly reluctant to give anything back.

Our stock were forced to make their own pasture by a process called fern-crushing, simple enough on good land, but full of difficulty in marginal country. It began with a burn-off of bracken, followed by sowing whatever quality of grass seed could be afforded, which in our case was often little more than floor sweepings.

The moment young fern shoots appeared, sheep were driven onto the paddock, to subsist on the fern shoots and keep them in check, until the grass took over. That was the theory. But in our wet climate the ferns flourished. The old sheep died and the young refused to live. Fresh sheep would be introduced to boost numbers, and the process repeated – the ground in effect having to be stamped, rammed and bullied into grass.

It was a Herculean task for a man with no ready money and a growing family to support. We couldn't afford to employ labour, and there was no money to buy a tractor. As Garry once remarked facetiously, 'It looks like a slasher and axe job for the rest of our lives!'

But my brave husband worked on – burning, sowing, crushing, resurrecting buried fences, spreading out stock to the best advantage to hold the land he had won back. Uphill all the way, for year after year after year. For decades. And never, not once, did he ever admit defeat, regret we had bought Rocklands, or indeed be anything but optimistic. He remained ruthlessly focused.

The best help I could be was to make sure we lived on as little as possible. But there were times when I looked up at our mountainous land and hated it, because of the sacrifices it demanded. When I discovered that rats had eaten my trousseau linen, I declared that I would have a nervous breakdown, but for the fact that we couldn't afford it! Not very funny at the time, but in retelling it became a family joke.

Instead I tried to be reassured by Garry's enthusiasm, his dream for us to stand free and live our days and years on a rocky landscape on the outer edge of the world. As so many people doubted we would be successful, we were both, in our own ways, determined to prove them wrong.

This common aim over the difficult years – admittedly somewhat desperately on my part – continued to unite us. But if we had known what we were to face, would we have bought Rocklands, no matter how tempting it was, after we had searched other poor land in New Zealand for something, anything, we could afford?

Yes. Because independence was vitally important to both of us, no matter how rotten the property. I guess, looking back, that managing to survive without bankruptcy, as had driven our three predecessors off Rocklands, is the real success story.

CHAPTER 3

In a way, I had been training for Rocklands most of my life. My first 18 years were spent amidst the squatocracy of Hawke's Bay. It was a lifestyle stuck in a time warp, with a class system that emulated that of the British. Elinor, my mother, as a daughter of a sheep-station owner, was part of this world, but Campbell, my English-born father, had a terrible contempt for convention if he felt the values were false.

He was the rebellious product of a public school education in England and religiously conservative parents, who were unable to show their four children any love and affection. A succession of sadistic nannies had been employed to deal with their three sons and a daughter.

My father's memoirs, handwritten in exercise books he called 'The Blathers', tell of the pleasure he took in biting one nurse's bottom when she was leaning over the nursery fire. There were three sorts of sin, this nanny had told her charges: 'Little sins, bigger sins, and taking off your shoes without untying the laces.'

He would later complain bitterly that no Englishman or -woman at that time would have dreamt of employing anyone untrained or unintelligent to look after their horses or dogs. 'Yet time and again fools, sadists or incompetents were allowed to bring up their children.' He was unable to remember a single occasion when his parents came upstairs to say goodnight to their offspring.

'What!' was the usual way this paternal grandfather expressed disapproval. 'What! You don't like rice pudding? Think of the millions in India who would be grateful for such food.' When his children groaned about the necessity to attend church with their parents on Sundays he would exclaim: 'What! You enjoy all these good things for six days of the week, and grumble about giving thanks on the seventh?'

Most of my father's early memories were of conflict and revenge, such as refusing to get on a tram because he preferred to walk, and of getting under his bed and clutching the bed legs to escape the clutches of a stout, enraged nurse, who was reaching out and breathing heavily.

But it was Bigshotte, the prep school to which my father was sent, aged seven, that remained the rawest wound in his psyche. He was packed off, with a label round his wrist, and the train guard tipped to let him off at the right station on the other side of England. This small boy had gone without even the comfort of a farewell hug from his mother.

Bitterly homesick, he wet his bed nightly for weeks. It was during World War One, when the only staff available were those unsuitable for the forces. 'Third-rate men' according to my father.

Time spent at Old Mill House, however, the family home set on 40 acres in the North Downs in Kent, was an enormous compensation. It was thanks to the close network of winding lanes in the surrounding countryside that my father became infused with his life-long addiction to cycling, exploring and map-reading.

But with growing discord between Campbell and his father, plans were made to send him to New Zealand within days of his leaving Tonbridge, his public school. The New Zealand government was offering scholarships to public-school boys to attend Ruakura Agricultural College, to study farming and settle in the country.

My father couldn't remember objecting in any way to leaving home and the land of his birth, or not following his brothers and sister to Cambridge. Indeed, once in New Zealand, released from the restrictions and conventions of England, he reacted like a stabled horse let loose in a field. He was 'enabled to be himself', was how he described it.

On graduation from Ruakura he was invited to Government House for Christmas, as the guest of Sir Charles and Lady Alice

Fergusson. He was appointed an honorary aide-de-camp, the Governor General having come to admire the young man's ability to spark off stimulating conversation at otherwise boring official gatherings.

Of course it amused my father no end to be sitting on some sort of royal box making small talk, no doubt of an argumentative nature. He adored Lady Alice. All his life he had kicked like a mule at people who disapproved of him, but here was someone who *liked* him.

The holiday over, Campbell was driven by a vice-regal chauffeur to his first job, as a cadet for Sir Andrew Russell at Tunanui station in Hawke's Bay.

My mother's home, Waiwhenua, was some further 40 kilometres west by road, but a far shorter distance if riding across country. For Campbell, having made a good impression on the Sheild family at Waiwhenua with his good looks and riding ability, it wasn't hard to persuade 17-year-old Elinor to accept his proposal.

Their married life began in 1931, on the vast, scrub-covered pumice lands of Galatea in the Bay of Plenty. Campbell, still in his early twenties, was employed by the government to manage tractor drivers, fencers and stockmen, to develop land for farm settlement. Hard-working and capable, he loved the life. For recreation there were deer and wild pigs to hunt, and trout to fish in the rivers.

Then, in the lowest ebb of the world-wide Depression, a telegram arrived from the government, instructing Father to lay off all workers. He alone was to be retained, with the offer of a farm on which to settle. He was tempted, but this wasn't Elinor's world, with the dry-throated smell of the district's geysers whenever the southerly wind gusted over the fern-covered hills. Above all, she felt cut off from people of her own kind, although she had entered loyally into Galatea's activities and made one or two lasting friends.

Indeed, Campbell hesitated to commit himself to a farm which would entail a mortgage. All over the country, farmers, like broken reeds, were walking off their land as the banks foreclosed. His dominant reason for coming to New Zealand had been to farm, but the heartbreaking impact of the Depression made him reluctant to owe money to a bank for the rest of his life. Instead he chose to establish an agricultural contracting business in Hawke's Bay.

While Elinor was happy to be back among the people with whom she had grown up, the provincial social life was of no interest to my father. The elegant garments he had brought out from England – the tails, plus-fours and tennis flannels – all grew moth-eaten. Intellectually inclined, Campbell read widely, studied Maori history, native plants and birds, and developed an intimate association with both the historian Arnold Toynbee and Herbert Guthrie-Smith, the great naturalist of Tutira.

Born in 1934, I was five when we moved to a 40-acre property, eight kilometres from the market town of Hastings. My father named it Galatea, after the Bay of Plenty region where he'd worked.

Opposite our front gate was an old quarry filled with water, where I would row an old boat I had found, reading a book underneath an umbrella if it was raining. I was always happy on my own. If I needed playmates I had Ruth, a farmer's daughter, five years older than me, with an equal age gap between me and my young sister, Jennie. We were a strangely assorted trio, but our combined concerts, created by me, with just Mummy and Ruth's mother as audience, would have them in hysterics. God knows why. Perhaps it was the disparity of our ages, the other two being bossed around by this skinny, plain rat of a kid, hogging the main part as usual.

But everything I did my mother always thought marvellous. 'Comic' or 'killing' were the words she most often used when describing my antics to others. My mother's gift of admiration more than equalled my father's over-high expectations, which could be fierce.

One school holidays he sent me, aged 10, on my bike to Hastings with a shopping list and appropriate cash. Nervous about returning the correct change, I frequently dismounted to recount the coins against the receipts, reassuring myself all was well.

He insisted I was a florin short. 'You must have spent the money on yourself!' he accused. Rubbish! I didn't even have an ice cream. But I could never win with my father. I might have been more amenable to his instructions if he hadn't been so inflexible. His ideas were, more often than not, well meant for the development of character and intellect, but he always pushed too hard.

Elinor, by comparison, was probably too soft. She cared only that Jennie and I were safe, warm and nourished. I loved being sick, purely for all the delicious meals and protective care she lavished on me. My father, on the other hand, would drop heavy tomes of literature onto my bed, about which I'd later be questioned. I dreaded his interference in my life.

I still meet people who tell me what a much-loved person my mother was. She was a truly wonderful listener, and the telephone kept her in touch with her best friends. 'It's Number Three,' I would shriek, on recognising the female caller, whose regaling of news took the third-longest to relate. Number One could occupy half an hour of my mother's patient listening. Her friends always sent for my mother when tragedy struck and a shoulder was needed to cry on. She asked so little for herself.

And life wasn't easy with Campbell as a husband. They were both fine people, but so totally different. My father was scarred from a loveless childhood, and therefore extraordinarily insensitive to other people's feelings.

Oddly, I always had a little money, and I used it to insulate myself as well as I could from parental tension. There were orchards nearby where I could pick raspberries for three pence a punnet. The aim was to earn enough money for 'the pictures'. Escape! I was always up trees and building huts. In bad weather I'd hide in the top shelf of the linen cupboard – it was a miracle I didn't suffocate when someone inevitably shut the door.

Father's idea of fun was a fact-packed lecture, thinly disguised as a long walk, in all kinds of weather. We would be shown insects under rocks, told the names of plants and regaled with Maori history. But because he lectured us so demandingly, my response was too often sullen.

In school holidays there would be tramps of a week or more, accompanying my father's Rover Scout troop of 18- to 24-year-olds, to which Father gave sterling efforts, eventually becoming New Zealand's Chief Commissioner. Jennie and I would be hard-pressed to keep up with these young men on the horrendously strenuous tramps, but it was impossible to decline Father's plans.

For backpacks my sister and I had canvas sacks, with a stone in each bottom corner, around which were tied thin leather straps to hoist on our tender shoulders. Our sleeping bags were the synthetic Woolworths variety, in which we froze in the mountains. Father, of course, had quality equipment. There was usually a hut for the night, otherwise we slept outside. Our food consisted of bread, cheese, raisins and oatmeal porridge. Chocolate? Scroggin? Forget it. We would be up at 3 a.m. to climb some peak before slogging on with each day's route, bush-bashing as we went.

I once took a hot-water bottle, only to have it confiscated by Father. 'We don't need such things,' he said. And nor was I allowed to wear sandshoes, instead of the heavy hobnailed boots my father provided, which meant I'd be kept awake with cramp behind my knees.

Strangely, once the tramp was completed, and we returned to Hastings, often on a transport truck on which we'd hitched a ride, I would feel a glow of satisfaction. Pride in what I'd accomplished. I would walk, head high, along the main street, despite unwashed clothes and tangled hair, feeling somehow superior to the predominantly well-dressed citizens in those prosperous farming times.

Elinor would be waiting anxiously at home to fuss over her 'poor little daughters', with a hot bath and delicious food, with the unspoken message that she thought Jennie and I had been harshly treated by a demanding brute of a man.

Well, I suppose we had been. But perhaps it did us more good than harm. Who knows? What I do know, however, is the negative effect of the stomach-knotted anxiety I always felt at home, alert to the difficult parental atmosphere.

By age 11 my athletic prowess had taken a dip. I had previously always come first in my primary school's running races, and no one could catch me on Sports Day. Now I sat on the sidelines thinking there must be some mistake when the prizes went to others. My schoolwork had also deteriorated. From being near top of the class, I no longer shone.

My mother took me to the family doctor.

'Has anything happened yet?' he asked.

I gather he meant, was I menstruating? I could have told the doctor, if he'd asked me, that my hormones were a mess because of the atmosphere at home.

I grew up lean and awkward, with a massive inferiority complex. I didn't fit. No matter how much I yearned to belong within the Hawke's Bay establishment, my father made this difficult, with his eccentric behaviour and scorn of that milieu.

He sent my sister and me to boarding school for our secondary schooling, but would turn up to visit on a motorbike, despite having a superior car in the garage. Did he do this because he was insensitive to his teenage daughters wanting to fit in, or to squash any snobbish instincts? Or perhaps to deliberately embarrass us because he didn't give a damn? Other fathers typically wore grey flannel trousers and tweed sports coats. Father would turn up in shorts and sandals. 'Why can't my father be like other people's fathers?' was the anguished cry in my teenage heart. At that age I just wanted to conform.

On the positive side, boarding school at age 12 was an escape. I could run like the wind again. The emphasis on sport thrilled me. I would race to the noticeboard at morning break to see the lists for after-school games. I eventually made the top teams for hockey, basketball and cricket, and was twice senior athletic champion.

The school, Woodford House, took 183 pupils in the mid-1940s, the majority of whom were sheep farmers' daughters, predominantly from Hawke's Bay, Wairarapa and Gisborne, with a few from professional homes in Auckland and Wellington. Each pupil had a bedroom of her own, which we had to clean ourselves, and a mattress stuffed with horse hair. They were as hard as bricks.

The staff were all female, with the exception of the art master, and mostly imported from England. Miss H, the headmistress, was a formidable little woman who looked like Queen Victoria. While she was said to be very competent, she was totally lacking in glamour.

There were two academic streams to each class. I began with the bright lot, a year younger than the rest, but was demoted in my second year because of my foul reports. I wasn't the slightest bit interested in French, Latin or maths, preferring to read a book under the desk. In the less academic class I adored the anarchy of the troublemakers, who would have me in fits of laughter.

There was a well-stocked apple orchard, just out of bounds, which suffered from periodic raids. We'd stuff our blouses to capacity, then load the elastic-ended legs of our bloomers. Mind you, we risked expulsion by going out of bounds, which no doubt added to the excitement.

The dominant teaching style was traditional. *We write it on the blackboard, you write it down and learn it.* Academically I switched off, although I loved music, drama, art and sport. And English when there was an essay to write. My term reports would regularly declare *Robin could do better if she tried.* The headmistress would reduce me to tears by reminding me of the financial sacrifices my parents were making, and I would vow to do better the following term. But I never did, at least not in the subjects that bored me.

The fees clearly meant less to other parents than mine. An unprecedented prosperity had rolled over the country. Sheep-farming parents were not just comfortable, they were positively rich. Wool prices one year earned a pound for a pound weight of wool, a dizzying amount of money.

Sheep farmers' offspring went home to school holidays filled with tennis parties, dances and visits to their summer baches in the Marlborough Sounds or Lake Taupo, with hunting and skiing in winter. My school holidays were spent picking raspberries, or stumping up mountains with my father.

I applied myself enough to gain School Certificate, because without it I wouldn't have made the Sixth Form. But having got there, I saw no need to bother about University Entrance. 'I shall concentrate on my music,' I told my parents, and passed Grade Eight in piano that year.

I longed to be a prefect in the Seventh Form, my final year, only to have my wish dashed. I was Head of Music, but only a sub-prefect. I was shattered, but immediately decided to be the best bloody Head of Music the school has ever known.

Of course responsibility was just the remedy a naughty child needed, and I flourished in the role. It involved a weekly visit to the headmistress to hear her choice of chapel hymns for the week; a considerable challenge with the HM being tone-deaf. She expected me to recognise the selection from her weird humming, which I would accompany on the pedalled harmonium. Thankfully she took sabbatical leave for six months, and while she was away I was made a full prefect.

Another responsibility came my way, thanks to the Head of English. I was one of three seniors asked to produce a one-act play for junior pupils. I selected *Mary Rose* by J. M. Barrie, and butchered it into one act.

The props department had a bow-window frame I could use on the stage, but I wanted a live tree behind it. There was a wild peach tree in full blossom on the roadside, outside the school grounds. It was clearly out of bounds, but that didn't deter me.

I borrowed the gardener's bicycle and saw, cycled up the drive past the staff hostel, sawed down the tree, and returned the same way, dragging the tree behind me. None of the staff said a word. They were probably too gobsmacked!

The play was a success, and as a result I was asked to put it on again to welcome the HM's return.

Hah, HM, I mused, *not only did they make me a prefect in your absence, but MY play has been chosen to present to you. So perhaps you will approve of me now? And please remember,* I would have liked to have added, *if you have a pupil who is misbehaving in future, probably because she comes from a dysfunctional home, then give her responsibility. That'll fix her!*

WHAT TO DO ON LEAVING SCHOOL? I wrote to the Women's Royal Naval Service (known as the WRNS) in England, asking to join their ranks. They were happy to have me, if I paid my own fare to get there. That put the kibosh on that.

Instead, in order to put some sea between me and my father, I applied to do nursing training in Christchurch, on the other side of Cook Strait. As the only boarding-school product in my preliminary nursing class, I alone loved the food.

I also loved the order and discipline of the well-run hospital. Like the reputable Middlesex Hospital in London, upon whose training and traditions this hospital was based, we wore grey long-sleeved uniforms with high starched collars and cuffs, black shoes and stockings. And of course, no make-up was allowed.

If a doctor spoke to us we had to stand with our hands behind our back, and never, ever, did we administer a prescription drug without a second person to check it. Medical misadventures were unheard of; nor was there a nursing union. Always, always, always the patients came first.

In my contact with sick people I found a previously untapped empathy, a genuine desire to do my best for them. I relished being needed – and more often than not I would be nicknamed 'Smiler'. On graduation I was appointed a staff nurse in the largest women's surgical ward. Looking back, I am astounded by the confidence I had in this role; in charge of some 40–50 patients when the Sister was off duty, with only three or four other staff to help with the hectic workload.

On checking the theatre list one morning I was astounded to see 'onion in anus' recorded. It applied to a patient from a male ward. Did some poor old chap slip when getting out of his bath, and fall down on an onion on the floor? There was a less innocent answer to this, but nothing I was to understand for several years to come. Well, even now I have difficulty!

My nursing training proved an excellent preparation for getting me through hectic periods in future years. It taught me to prioritise, such as times when shearers needed their meals on the dot, while I coped with three small children, and hordes of visitors were expected.

Chapter 4

The first chance he had, Garry offered to drive Tim and me up the eight kilometres of rough track to see our back country.

'Look out!' I screeched, when George the truck seemed perilously near the edge as it took two turns to get round a bend. The offside wheels spun over a creek banked against a straggle of rusted fence, which offered no protection from the cliffy drop beneath us.

'My God,' I breathed, 'it's an abyss!'

The engine panted as we rose over the crest to the very top of the range, where we owned 800 acres. While the soil here was of a better quality than that of our mountain and front country, it was also chest-high with bracken and gorse.

This land had once been seen as a land of promise with a World War One veteran dumped here, with not even a formed road to reach it. There was a little patch of daffodils to show where the family had lived. Their children, with a few boiled potatoes for lunch, would walk down through the gorge on a short-cut to school.

The surrounding country was rugged, so piercingly steep it made me gasp, the hills rearing up with a kind of savagery. Further inland the mountains turned to marble, where, over aeons, gushing streams had hewn secret caves and tunnels deep underground.

To Garry this part of Rocklands on the skyline was a beautiful, glorious landscape. With its own privacy it was a truly separate world, appealing in its remoteness: the virginal bush, the sparrow hawks, and most importantly the creek, which burst out of the bush to flow plentifully down the gorge, and eventually be piped to provide house and trough water.

But for me, for many years to come, it was a foreign beauty. I felt an outsider, longing as I was for open grasslands, fertile and productive. This land in its tortured state scared me, because of the price I knew it would extract from us.

In the meantime I could only try, deep in my heart, to be grateful that Garry, the lion-heart in our marriage, could see potential in this jungle, and was never, ever going to give up. He was determined to conquer Rocklands, to make his family a farm, somewhere safe to live, no matter what.

From this height the boundaries of the dairy farms far below were more easily seen, a patchwork of smaller paddocks divided by shelter belts or modest house gardens. The dairying land was pristine compared to the soaring rough ranges bordering the valley, part of which was Rocklands.

WHEN THE STINGING SMACK OF A RIFLE is heard in the middle of the night, Garry and I are as alert as the deer for which it is intended. In a still night the voices of male hunters can be heard echoing down from our back country as they call for their dogs. We lie awake, worrying. Too often, one or two of the hunter's dogs will become lost, and sustain themselves for days at a time on our flock. Garry once found 30 dead sheep, killed by dogs that had been left behind.

In the following days the hunters will turn up in our front country, shouting for their lost dogs. Two men cheerfully explain that their dogs have electronic collars, and could therefore be traced. So why is it now four days since they last saw their dogs?

TO PROVIDE A HOUSE COW, GARRY PRODUCED a half-Friesian who had never been near a cow bail or even bucket-reared. The dogs hounded her down from the back country and hustled her into the yard. Alarmed at being thrust into a building, the cow leapt towards the shed window, thrust her forelegs through and got stuck. Garry grabbed a bucket and milked her where she was. From then on that cow walked placidly into the bail each day and gave a full bucket of milk.

We killed our own sheep for mutton, and vegetables were planted but not yet productive. In the meantime there was plenty of puha, a native thistle, growing at the edge of the bush which made excellent spinach, and watercress in the creeks.

Even so, we were longing for something yummy. Then, one sunny morning a quiet little woman appeared on our doorstep, carrying a basket.

She introduced herself shyly as Phyllis Thorpe from Glen Rannoch, the hill farm on our eastern boundary, and wondered if I would like a few scones.

'I'd love some!' I exclaimed, bringing my visitor inside, apologising for the clutter while setting out tea for us both on the packing-case table. I explained I had no idea how to bake in a wood stove.

'I wish I'd known before,' said my visitor. Right there and then a day was arranged to give me my first baking lesson.

This was my first meeting with Phyllis Thorpe, who was to become the kindest of mentors in my early struggles with Rocklands' farm life. I addressed her as Mrs Thorpe and she never suggested otherwise. A generation older than myself, she came from a background of ultra-correct behaviour and manners. Poor she may have been, but she was undoubtedly a lady.

From this kindest of neighbours I learnt how to preserve fruit and make jam. She was, I think, a little shocked at my ignorance, but always excused it to herself and me by saying, 'But you have had such a different life. You wouldn't have had time to learn cooking when you worked as a nurse.'

Of course I'd already had a year of housekeeping at our job on the North Canterbury farm, so what did we eat then? Only the most basic and unadventurous meals, I confess, and for much of that year I was so morning sick I don't remember much that was appetising. I should have learnt cooking from my mother on holidays from boarding school, but sensing my disinterest in domestic matters, my darling mother didn't encourage me to hang round the stove. In the end I learnt to cook porridge, and that was about it. I'd grown up in ignorance of many things that would have made life much easier now.

Phyllis and her husband Bob had bought their 500-acre farm in 1937, at the tail-end of the Depression. 'We ran a high overdraft,' Phyllis told me, 'which meant regular visits from the bank manager, who came regularly for afternoon tea.' When the debt was finally paid off in 1960, Bob and Phyllis had a small glass of sherry to celebrate.

Glen Rannoch had steep, scrub-covered hills, but also 50 pastured acres at the foot of their valley. Here Bob had planted wood lots, built shingle-roofed sheds and constructed a waterwheel to harness power from the creek. Whatever he did was a labour of love and skill. If Bob put in a gate post it would last 20 years.

On this little farm, milking 24 cows and grazing 600 sheep, two-thirds of them ewes, the Thorpes had managed to fund a college education for all five of their children. 'Rates and insurance levies were a minimum cost in the 1940s and 1950s,' Bob pointed out gratefully.

He was a stalwart of the local church, serving on its vestry, but could be a little Victorian. His treasured wife was expected, and indeed saw this as her duty, to carry morning tea to wherever her husband was working on the farm, and to sit there and enjoy it with him. With their main meal at midday, this left little time for this talented woman to play her piano or paint her watercolours. She didn't drive, so was dependent on her husband for transport in their 1954 Chevrolet, a former Nelson taxi. Fortunately our homes were within walking distance.

The Thorpes' garden, bursting with flowers, creepers, kiwifruit, old-fashioned apples and quinces, led the way to their old-style kitchen, with its huge wood-burning stove, comfy sofa and a wooden table always correctly set for meals, with blue and white china and linen napkins.

Phyllis's bread was a meal in itself, with added pine nuts, molasses, dried grapes and apple skins. No wonder Bob was such a tower of strength. Even in his late seventies there was no rest for him after lunch. He'd be out grubbing thistles or crutching sheep. And while it may have seemed that Bob was very much the master of the household, insisting on sorting the mail before anyone else could open it, the Thorpe children were adamant that it was their delicate mother who ruled the roost, putting her foot down when necessary.

I had told Phyllis we had no telephone, which was making life difficult with farm business to do. 'Oh, you must keep persisting,' she said. And so I did.

THE POST OFFICE WAS FURNISHED with a polished wood counter, on which lay a rusty pen and a dry ink bottle. Mail was placed alphabetically in little slots behind the counter, where it remained until someone called for it, unless you were on rural delivery like ourselves.

At the back of the building there was a cubbyhole where a roster of people coped with telephoned requests to be hooked up with someone else. Several different lines, fanning over the countryside, were connected here.

We had made endless requests for a phone, but perhaps the postal officials didn't expect our stay to be long enough to make an installation worthwhile. Whatever the reason, they had raised every possible objection. We were told that there were already 12 households on our nearest line, which meant it was overloaded.

'But how are we meant to run a farm without communication?' we entreated, only to be told that adding our house to the line would cause an uproar. 'The existing line-holders, predominantly dairy farmers, have to be humoured,' a postal clerk said. The inference was that anyone who bought Rocklands was definitely not in the same business category.

'But,' I pleaded pathetically, on yet another trip to the post office, 'what happens if our baby chokes on a fern root, and we can't phone the doctor?'

This startled the clerk, his face greening at the prospect of digesting fern roots. 'I don't know what category of priority that puts you under. I'd better get the boss.'

'Please do,' I requested politely. It was always best 'to go to the top'.

The post master appeared reluctantly, obviously irritated at being disturbed by a scruffy-looking couple, with a baby in possibly wet nappies perched on his polished wood counter. 'Look here,' he said impatiently, obviously not believing it possible, but as a way of getting rid of us, 'if your neighbours will sign an agreement to let you on the line, you can have a phone.'

'Thank you, thank you,' we said gleefully, and I grabbed the form needing signatures while Garry polished the damp patch on the counter with his sleeve, before dashing out to George to start calling on the 12 line-holders immediately.

We chugged up 12 strange drives to greet 12 surprised neighbours. We admired their houses, their farms, their children and gardens. We talked politics, or rather listened, saying 'Oh, I agree' to whatever was said. Sometimes just nodding was enough, while standing on first one foot and then the other. We listened to the moans about central government, local government, the health board, and, in some cases the generation-long rows with neighbours. As we were to learn, this wasn't a district where communication was ever brief, but we put up with all this to get the signatures.

And get them we did!

The form was presented to the post office, and we were promised an early installation. Three days later two linesmen arrive, just as Garry was chainsawing a hole in the wall, to create a doorway between the kitchen and the soggy bench area.

'Where do you want the phone?' a startled linesman shouted through a haze of smoke and borer dust.

'There, please,' I yelled, pointing at a spot on the wall still trembling from the chainsaw attack. The phone was a crank-up model, with a handle at the side, to ring the appropriate codes. One long ring was a request for the operator, with each householder on the line having a separate sequence of rings. Our call was to be three short and one long.

I sat and looked at the phone, and waited for it to ring.

It rang all right. It started and seldom stopped, with our immediate farming neighbours beseeching us to rebuild the boundary fences between our land and theirs 'at your very earliest convenience'.

Naturally, they would share expenses and labour.

So, not only were we now united over the busy phone line, but in the following 12 months Garry was to spend endless weeks on boundary fences, cementing the friendships that began with the phone.

Of course, as is inevitable with party lines, there was always someone who listened in to other peoples' conversations. The phone volume would reduce seconds after we answered a call. This usually didn't bother us – we had no secrets. But when a guest had to phone his office in Christchurch, the connection was particularly bad, due to the eavesdropper's breathing noises. 'I don't mind you listening, whoever you are,' our guest requested politely, 'but please stop wheezing.'

'I can't help wheezing,' the outraged eavesdropper retorted. 'I've got a cold!'

For several weeks that first blistering summer, Garry, with Gerry Vavasour and his son Bernard from Rock Glen, the mountain property to the south of us, worked together on a shared boundary fence, where much of the terrain was sheer rock. Post holes had to be drilled. All three men shed more than six kilos of body weight while working on that sun-baked oven.

To reach the site they had to travel up the back road, which climbed 800 metres in eight kilometres. The two Vavasours would arrive at 7 a.m. to park their car, an old Willys, in our yard, then transfer onto their tractor, with Garry also on board.

The two younger men sat on the mudguards with Gerry driving. To while away the hour or more of the journey, good-tempered debates took place, with the three men shouting to each other above the rattle of the tractor on the pot-holed road.

At times their arguments became so engrossing that Gerry, forgetting he was driving on a perilous road, would turn around to emphasise a point. 'Look out!' would come a yell, as the tractor veered towards the bank.

A lifetime spent on hard country had bred in Rock Glen's owner a deep knowledge of farm survival, with opinions both firmly held and stubbornly expressed. There were no grey areas in his declarations. Only Gerry was right. He was convinced that pieces of coloured wool entwined on wire strung between a cross-frame of two wooden battens and nailed to a gate would eliminate foot rot within the radius of the wool's powers. There was no point in arguing the fallacy of this, or asking for proof.

One particular day, having run out of bread, I sent Garry up to the fence line with Weet-Bix spread with marmalade for his lunch.

'What's that mess?' Gerry asked, as Garry unwrapped his crumbling package.

Garry explained his wife had run out of bread.

'Bernard, look at *this*!' Gerry snorted, rubbing in his disapproval over such inadequate food for a working man.

'Good God!' said Bernard. 'That's a bit rough.'

'Well,' said my poor husband, smarting at the implied criticism, 'what are you having?'

'Rhubarb pie,' boasted Gerry.

Poor Garry drooled. 'Bet you haven't got cream with it,' he responded.

'Of course we have cream,' replied Gerry. Silence, while father and son helped themselves to generous slices of the pie, with Garry's eyes popping with envy. Only after the Vavasour men had sat back with their plates full, smirking, did Gerry say to my poor husband, 'Want some? Help yourself.'

The Weet-Bix was thrown to the dogs.

But it was to be years before the Vavasours let me forget.

WHEN WE FIRST MET THIS FAMILY, we had been a little startled at their blunt outspokenness. But we soon learnt that their teasing was tempered by enormous good humour and continued generosity towards us as newcomers, who shared similar nightmare land.

We would be invited each Christmas Day for afternoon tea in their glorious hillside garden. It was something to look forward to after our own sausages-for-a-treat Christmas lunch. The Vavasours would have been to church that morning. Staunch Roman Catholics, they never missed a Sunday. Once, when their old Willys broke down, Gerry transported his wife and five children the 16 kilometres to church on the tractor and trailer.

Their mountain, heaving skywards beside our own, ran 200 wethers on its bluffs. On one precipitous muster wild goats set off a rock slide, with Bernard and his dog directly in its path. Both froze as a truck-sized boulder shot down between them with barely a centimetre to spare. Bernard laughed wryly when describing this. 'There has never been a more knowing look than what followed at that moment between a man and his dog.

Aren't we lucky bastards, we both obviously thought!'

Rock Glen also had some easier country, on which to run hoggets and 13 dairy cows. On Bernard's return home from Lincoln College with his agricultural diploma, his father offered him a partnership. Bernard was to receive a pound a year in pocket money as he bought himself into shared ownership. 'Which means,' said the younger Vavasour, 'I can't afford to socialise with girls or get drunk, so I miss out on youthful fun.'

'Doesn't do you any harm,' his father replied. 'Plenty of hard work and no money, and you're all the better for it.'

Bernard, newly graduated, had alarmed his mother by reducing their dairy herd from 13 cows to 12. The cream cheque was her housekeeping money. But Bernard knew what he was doing. With one less cow the others had more to eat, and the cream cheque improved.

FOR THE BOUNDARY FENCE WITH GLEN RANNOCH, Garry worked with John Thorpe, Bob and Phyllis's 18-year-old son, who was still at home. One of John's charming assets was his tactful acknowledgements of all Garry's ideas for the fence, while the rosy plans Garry detailed for the rapid advancement of Rocklands had the younger man positively gobsmacked in admiration. John, of course, having grown up on this tough range, knew the heartbreaking efforts that would be needed in former beech forest country to halt its regeneration.

One day, when resting their backs after carrying 45-kilogram loads of Waratah standards from the truck, the two men gazed down a steep gulley, the site of a fence line which needed to be built. Neither relished the idea of taking pointed shafts of steel down this treacherous slope. One slip of their feet and the murderous load and its bearer would catapult headfirst to the rocky bottom of the gorge.

After some deliberation, Garry suggested they tie bundles of stakes together, then drag them down the scree with a strap, placing each stake in position as they went. As usual, John acquiesced, confident that the older man knew best.

Garry started off with the first load, pulling the bundle of standards behind him. Frequently the heavy load wedged under a rock, which meant climbing back up to dislodge it. Finally Garry decided that if he ran down the slope the load would go faster, and bounce off intervening obstacles. Better progress would be made. So off he set, rushing down the almost perpendicular scree with the load following with a glissading clatter. Hitting a rock, it would pitch on its end, and then leap off, airborne. Garry had to run faster and faster to prevent the load catching up with him

His feet barely touched the ground – the gorge was so steep he appeared to be almost flat on his back in his flight. As he plunged down, the bundle of stakes set off an avalanche of rocks and stones, which hit him and added to his pace. Eventually, with the bundle about to catch up with him, Garry reluctantly surrendered the strap and leapt sideways into a gorse bush, to watch the stakes rush mercilessly onwards, halting in the creek far below. There was a silence, apart from Garry's heavy breathing, as he leaned over a tree, totally winded.

Relieved laughter echoed down from above, once John realised that Garry was not seriously hurt. Skidding haphazardly down the slope, with nothing threatening behind him, John was screaming with laughter. 'I've never seen anything so funny,' he roared.

Garry stared mirthlessly, assuming a pained expression as he rubbed his bruised ankles and shins, with an egg-shaped lump developing on his skull. 'Damned crazy district,' he muttered to himself.

John halted his laughter, and made a profound remark for one so young. 'If you didn't laugh when things go wrong developing this country, Garry, it would be too easy to cry.'

How right he was. Poverty and hardship bred a desperate sort of courage on the hard hills of Golden Bay. The old pattern of struggling, self-sufficient marginal land farming was changing even as we came to Rocklands, but there was enough of it left for us to appreciate the ancient naturalness of such a life.

In the late 1950s there were still 40 or 50 dry-stock farmers like ourselves on the ranges which bordered the Golden Bay valleys who were struggling to make ends meet. Most of the farms were perilously steep; the hillsides having a brutal, unforgiving look about them, with perhaps 10–20 acres each of comparatively good land on which to milk a few dairy cows. The farmers and their families were eking out an existence. Their forefathers, who felled the bush and sowed grass seed in the ash of the log burns, did well enough, but bit by bit and more and more each year, the bracken grew, followed by manuka and other natives typical of Nature's regeneration back to bush. The work of three or four generations of farmers was being swallowed up by the wilderness.

But it was better than being on the dole – there was a house to live in and it was possible to live to a great extent off the land. Above all there was a measure of independence, a feeling of doing something constructive, and a healthy, outdoor life. Children bred on these hills had grown up watching the hardship endured by their parents, their toil against the environment, the battle against fern and the stock losses, but from this landscape a rugged breed of farmer had been forged, one with a bloody-minded constitution and a deep respect for the terms of Nature.

Jimmy, who was then 78, with 1200 steep acres on the East Takaka road, was such a one. Wearing a sou'wester hat and an old army coat on the day we met him, despite the fine weather, he admitted there was no money to be made from his mountain-bred sheep. 'I don't look to get rich – I keep my sheep for pleasure,' he said.

Ben, aged 82, whose scarred bluffs towered over him further up the road, was pouring fuel into a chainsaw in preparation for sawing up firewood. 'As long as you keep active you're still alive,' he chortled.

A sense of the past clung to the hill farms, indeed to the whole district. Most of the people lived where they had been born, and where their families had lived for generations.

Clive, now 97, was naturally very fit from the amount of time he had spent working in the hills. One of the activities routinely carried out was burning off scrub to allow grass to become established. Once, after he'd put in a very big day burning on the hill, he'd found the walk home that evening hard work.

'I drank a bottle of homebrew while I had a bath and found I was completely cast,' he laughed. 'My family had to prise me out of the bath and help me to bed. Smoke inhalation, I suppose.'

Joe, also of a ripe old age, had been one of seven siblings. As children they'd walked three miles to school where they wrote on slates. The family had been poor, and sometimes hungry, but their mother would tolerate nothing but exemplary behaviour: when Joe found a nest of duck eggs and brought them triumphantly home, she scolded him. The duck was not nesting on their land so those were not their eggs. Joe must take them back.

These were kindly, hardworking people. As with the Thorpes and Vavasours, a close bond soon developed between the district's hard hill farmers and ourselves. With whom else would we have had so much in common? It was a lifestyle our old friends, far away, were unable to envisage.

'Robby, Garry, when are you coming down to see us?' their letters asked. 'Are there lots of parties up there? Do you live in a lovely house, and is it fun?' They were sweet and kind, but how could they understand our life?

People who live and work in isolated regions, isolated even more by their daily slog to survive, imprisoned to a large extent on their endlessly demanding land behind the farm gate, are distanced from the rest of the population, and not just in the economic sense. Our lives were distinctly different from the majority who dwelt in the more materially blessed urban areas. There, one was largely protected from the extremities of Nature. But in the hard hills of Golden Bay there was nowhere to hide.

CHAPTER 5

When we first came to Golden Bay, it was just a sleepy little place in the north-west corner of the South Island, home to a few thousand farmers, two small townships, Takaka and Collingwood, a cement company and flocks of migratory birds.

Takaka, our nearest township, had two dairies, three grocery shops, a butcher, three hotels, a chemist, and two clothes shops. The historic bastion of Takaka was Kirk's grocery store-cum-drapery, with a coal-burning stove in its centre, around which customers gathered on cold days, sharing the gossip. And what a sterling chap Dick Kirk proved to be. Like his father before him, he carried struggling farm families like ourselves for 12-month stretches, until the wool or some other produce was sold.

Of course we weren't worth much as customers. I'd buy raw sugar, rolled oats, Garry's pipe tobacco, matches, yeast and the occasional sack of flour. In those days of business trust, everyone had accounts. There was very little Dick Kirk didn't know about local families – service was incredibly slow, with enquiries made of every customer to learn how they were, and what news they had.

The main street was usually lined with parked cars, yet there always seemed to be more people chatting than shopping, but always with smiles and laughter. It was a cheerful place. No one was in a hurry.

Mr Winter was one of the few saddlers left in New Zealand. On Friday nights there were always men leaning on his bench watching him mend boots and shoes. Several shopkeepers kept a cow to milk, and often a pet sheep to mow their lawn, and perhaps a goat to chew the roadside verge.

One day a big hare ran clean down the main street from Birdsalls' garage to the Odd Fellows Hall, unscathed, with only one youngish chap yelling, 'Shoot it!'

The pubs had their regular patrons with their own stools

at the bar, and look out any newcomers who sat down, in all innocence, on some regular's chair. Inevitably there were a few heavy drinkers. One old farmer would drink his fill on a Friday night, and then somehow make it home over 20 kilometres of tortuous road. On one occasion he set off from the pub with a strange car hooked to his truck's back bumper. And the car had been left in first gear!

Another chap, a war veteran, was invited to meet Peter Townsend at a RSA function. He got boozed up beforehand to overcome shyness, and drove into the creek by the dairy factory. The factory manager, a taller and broader man, lent the bedraggled driver a suit, and the sobered-up chap continued on to meet Princess Margaret's former lover, with his trousers and sleeves rolled.

Also notorious was a local Lothario, who would hire a hall for his birthdays. It would be filled with kids, and when he invited all those who called him Dad to come outside to play, the hall would empty!

These particular incidents, and there were a million others, became part of the folklore of the Bay. It wasn't a sophisticated community, but it didn't matter a stuff what type of car you had or what clothes you wore. People cared for each other.

There was the day George, an elderly resident, died. George was a school bus driver who loved his bowls. When he died during a match at the Takaka Bowling Club, his fellow members laid him gently aside and finished the game, positive that this is what George would have wanted.

The district also had a few black sheep, who had been banished to this end of the empire from some of New Zealand's best-known landed families. In the eyes of their relatives, they'd married beneath them; the maid of the ancestral homestead in one case, the rabbiter's daughter in another. One such scorned wife was particularly kind to us, turning up regularly with a cream sponge and a collection of objects she felt we might need. Coat hooks for the back door, a frying pan, clothes pegs, even a chest of drawers! We were the only people in the Bay, apparently, who were unaware she was a kleptomaniac, and her presents were probably bits and pieces she had filched from others to pass on.

In the 1950s and 1960s very few women drove over the Takaka Hill. For most local children Takaka was the only town they knew.

IN THE EARLY DAYS OF GOLDEN BAY – even up to the war years – the sea was the main route for transport. Many settlements had wharves, and small boats would bring people and freight from Nelson as regularly as the weather permitted. Isolated farmers who had no wharf would have to row out at night to receive supplies and offload produce. Capsizes were not uncommon.

'It wasn't much fun if you were seasick,' a farmer was reported as saying. 'For the first half-hour you were sure you would die, and after that you were afraid that you wouldn't.'

Until about 1913, there was no road between Takaka and Collingwood. Many in both towns opposed the road, claiming it would let in undesirables. If you lived in Collingwood these were Takaka people, and Takaka people were just as suspicious.

The early settlers had been attracted to Golden Bay's lush valleys by the promise of valuable resources such as coal and abundant timber, with boat-building becoming a major industry at the mouth of the Aorere. Once the timber was felled, dairy farms were developed. Tracks became roads and huts became houses.

There is a story about a bushman called Charlie Frater, who was working alone in the forest and was crushed by a falling tree. He cut off his smashed leg with his axe to free himself, used his belt as a tourniquet, and somehow crawled to the nearest settlement where the one-armed Dr Fisher attended to him, and dispatched him to Nelson Hospital by ship. On the journey, Charlie was said to have kept the crew entertained with the poems he roared out, perhaps helped by medicinal whiskey.

In 1860 it was also medicinal whiskey that enabled an earlier doctor, Dr Satchell, to survive the first recorded katipo bite in New Zealand. He'd been bitten while on the wrong side of the Aorere River. Unable to cross until the river ebbed, he'd sipped half-hourly on a bottle of whiskey and survived.

Many people drowned when attempting to cross the Aorere, as more than one tombstone in the old Collingwood cemetery relates. But it was the rivers that ensured the future prosperity of Golden Bay. They clawed at the mineral-rich mountains during floods to build up fertile valley floors, and the glorious wide beaches that encircle the coast.

In 1856 gold was found near the Aorere Valley, where Ned James and John Ellis had been out mustering cattle. After some time, G. W. Lightband, who'd had goldmining experience in Australia, was able to verify the find. The resulting gold rush brought as many as 4000 men from every walk of life pouring into the district. They came by boat, or walked around the coast or over the Takaka Hill.

The new town of Collingwood – originally called Gibbstown after an early settler – developed quickly to cater for the growth in population, with seven hotels, several shops and two banks. A census taken in Collingwood on Christmas Eve in 1858 recoded 700 white inhabitants and 200 Maori. During the boom time the town made merry at Christmas, with the miners coming in from the outlying diggings, dressing up for the balls, horse-racing on the beach, and attending canoe races and concerts.

By 1859 the township was at its peak. The much earlier name Massacre Bay had been changed to Golden Bay. Plans were being drawn up in England for a substantial town to be sited on the lower hills east of the present settlement, but the gold fever didn't last, and the prospectors moved on.

At this time the farming community of Golden Bay had grown to 2000, and dairying continues today, on a very large scale. It's the main industry in the Bay, with milk going out in tankers.

Today Collingwood is a quiet but beautiful place. There are limitless sands on one side, an estuary on the other, and further back wild tangled hills border the lush, green valleys. Old photographs in the tiny museum show that the short main street once had numerous two-storey buildings. Only one of them survives today, the old post office. But the little town has most other essential services: a school, pub, garage with 24/7 fuel, church, library, fire brigade, cemetery and war memorial. What Collingwood has lost, to loud objection, is a doctor's surgery – since the Bay's new Integrated Health Centre was built at Takaka to incorporate the whole district's medical, geriatric and emergency needs.

Heading west past Collingwood, past hills of native forest and narrow paddocks beside the sea, one comes to Puponga. It's as far north as a tar-sealed road goes in the South Island. The tiny settlement nestles against hills which shelter it from westerly winds sweeping off the Tasman Sea.

Trevor Climo, who loves the place, is one of the few permanent residents. He's a builder and gets jobs where he can. 'That's the only problem,' he says. 'My son would love to live here, but apart from a few jobs on dairy farms and at the Farewell Spit café on the hill, there's no work to keep young people here. They love coming back for holidays, but they can't stay.'

Climos have lived at Puponga for generations. When Trevor's uncle, Oscar, left to go to sea in 1938 about 150 people lived at Puponga. There was a two-roomed school, two general stores, a billiard room, and a butcher's shop. Caught in Britain by the war – in which he was torpedoed five times – Oscar would tell Betty, the Londoner he met and married, all about Puponga, this wonderful place to which they would one day return.

But when they got here after the war there was nothing! 'It wasn't that Oscar wasn't telling the truth,' said Trevor, 'but during the war the coal mine had closed, and with it the town. In the early days Betty would have left if she could. She came from a flat part of England, and the hills here oppressed her. But she came to love them.'

Bill Climo, Oscar's son, now a school bus driver and the manager of the Collingwood camping ground, describes his idyllic childhood at Puponga. 'There was endless fishing, we'd make flax boats to sail on the estuary, and in those days there were deer to hunt on Farewell Spit.'

We were made aware that Muriel Bartlett from Bella Vista was a woman of standing. Fifty-ish, red-haired and feisty, she would ride her horse, her back ramrod straight, up our back road. At first she appeared somewhat brusque, a woman who would stand no nonsense. But she became a very good friend, with delicious gingerbread to offer with tea, when I pushed Tim's pram down the road to see her.

She ran the pony club, organised gymkhanas, hosted tennis parties and put on garden parties for charity. As a leading light in the Women's Division of Federated Farmers, she attended meetings throughout the South Island. Stopped once for speeding, she was outraged, telling the traffic officer she had been driving a car since before he was born. The officer quickly retreated.

The Bartletts were better off than most local dairy farmers. Uno, Muriel's husband, had a disability pension from World War One, and had inherited a 30-cow farm which was managed by a nephew. He'd met Muriel, who was a nurse, while he was in hospital recovering from yellow fever. She was the eldest daughter in a family of 11 children, fathered by Francis Ashton-Warner, who, Muriel told me, had English titles in his background. The youngest of the children was the internationally famous author and educationalist, Sylvia Ashton-Warner.

The mother of this brood, Mama, as we all came to call her on her visits to Bella Vista, was a stocky, spirited lady who always wore black, with a chain round her neck on which hung various medals and a tiny ebony pocket knife. Now in her eighties, widowed and having also buried several of her children, she loved travelling in an aeroplane and watching TV, particularly the programme *I Love Lucy*.

'Mama never had a youth,' said Muriel. 'She's still trying to find it.'

With a husband crippled with arthritis and often bedridden, Mama had been the sole breadwinner as a teacher, usually in remote country schools, having to ride many kilometres to work, with two or three of the younger children sharing her horse. Sylvia, as a two-year-old, would be left at home with her father, with bread and milk on a chair by his bed.

'Mama seemed regretful about it,' said Muriel, 'but what else could she do?'

Sylvia once stayed with the Bartletts, during her 10-week summer holiday from Auckland Teachers College. She took a job at a mental hospital that used to be in Takaka, and it was here that she witnessed different forms of breakdown. In Muriel's opinion, 'Sylvia learnt more about the mind at this time than any book could teach her.'

WITH BILL WATSON'S ARRIVAL OUR UNSOPHISTICATED district took a jolt. On retirement from a shipping company in India, he had searched the world's weather maps for an area with an equable climate.

As an officer in the British Army he'd spent three years as a Japanese prisoner of war in Rangoon (now Yangon). There were to be no more monsoons for him.

Nor did he wish to return to England, the land of his birth. 'People who retire to Britain from the tropics die within a year,' he'd explain. 'Their blood is too thin to withstand a British winter.'

And so it was that Bill, like a breath of exotic air, took up a small farm on the corner of our south-western boundary. There was a colonial-era house and 30 flat acres on which he planned to graze dry stock. Twenty heifers were installed. Bill refused to own a dog, but had his own way of moving stock. He would lie on his back in the paddock he wished the cattle to move into, and bicycle his legs in the air. Always curious, the cattle would collide with each other in their efforts to view this spectacle. Bill had only to leap up to shut the gate behind them.

If I was sent round in George to collect sheep that had pushed into Bill's place, I'd be installed in a Victorian chair, a tapestried footstool pushed under my shabby shoes, and served tea from a silver pot. The chintz curtains and chair covers in Bill's sitting room were changed each spring and autumn. His garden became a showcase. His father had been curator of Kew Gardens in London, and Bill had obviously inherited a genius with plants.

Tea was safe, but if Garry and I were invited for dinner, we could be overwhelmed with the unaccustomed wine. After one such dinner we were halfway home before remembering we had left Tim in his carrycot on Bill's bed, below the gold Hindu figures swinging from the ceiling. And while Bill loved his cows, he had no time for children.

In those days, when it was mandatory for mothers to remain in hospital for 10 days after a birth, visitors were a consolation. When Bill was expected for a visit, I asked the nurse to take Sally, my newborn daughter, to the nursery, before he was due to arrive. 'Mr Watson can't stand babies,' I explained.

The nurse could not believe this. While Bill and I were talking the door opened and in came the nurse carrying our daughter. 'Isn't she lovely?' the nurse enthused, uncovering Sally's head under his nose.

'What long hair,' he said nervously, doing his best.

'Oh,' said the nurse, 'that'll come off.'

Bill gave a faint shriek. 'Is it a wig?'

He was infinitely more simpatico with elderly people. Many of his neighbours were third- or fourth-generation dairy-farm families. Some of the 80–90-year-olds had never been over the Takaka Hill. They had been born in the Bay and would die here. Even so, Bill, in his kindness, persuaded several elderlies to ride in his red sports car to Nelson, to lunch at the best hotel. Each of these passengers took the trip only once, but they would talk about that day out for the rest of their lives.

Bill would say that these old people were the district's aristocrats with their fine, gentle ways. 'The blood had thinned with succeeding generations,' he would add. 'Too much intermarriage.'

Foolishly, I was shy about what we could offer Bill with return invitations, with humdrum food on a packing-case table. I knew nothing about gourmet cooking, and nor could we afford alcohol that would appeal to his refined palette. Pregnant again, with Mike, and soon to have three children under four years of age, we saw Bill less and less.

So Garry and I were unaware of the gossip. Only after Bill had left the district, to return to England, the destination he had vowed never to see again, did we learn that some local citizens had decided Bill was a homosexual, and therefore to be scorned.

The same people, when Bill first came to the district, had brought him presents of flowers, eggs and cakes, and would sit for hours in his blue and white kitchen, filling him in on the more salacious details of village gossip. But now, the thought that Bill was gay was something the rednecks among them couldn't accept. Even the woman he paid to do his mending wouldn't touch his clothes any more. A sensitive man, Bill took the message and sold up.

Of course his return to the cold English climate was fatal. He had been offered a cottage on an estate in return for caring for its garden, but come the first British winter Bill contracted pneumonia and died.

Neglecting Bill in his loneliness, and being unaware of the isolation into which others had put him, is one of the regrets about which I feel most guilty. Too late, I realised he would have rather have been offered scrambled eggs on a packing-case table than not be asked at all.

Chapter 6

For me, the valley lifestyle took a bit of getting used to – life wasn't hurried, people weren't constantly busy. For sure everyone had plenty to do, but it didn't have to be done immediately. There was always time for a chat. I could find this rather infuriating, with a newborn baby and so much to do at home. Although, strangely, no one ever asked us about our lives prior to our arrival into the Bay – it was as if it had never happened.

Gradually, however, I came to realise that the shut-awayness I treasured was denying me one of the best and richest things about living here: the neighbourliness of it.

Ernie Jones, a dairy farmer, a champion axe-man and a lovely man, cut and raked hay for us in the one paddock we had that was less topographically perilous for a wheeled tractor. Even so, a big man, he needed to stand as he drove, to force down the rearing front wheels.

'How much do we owe you?' we asked.

'I'll put it on the bill,' Ernie replied.

The bill proved to be mythical. Payment was never asked for by this generous and heroic man.

These were the neighbours we were coming to know and rely on. They'd visit to tell us what to do, how to do it, and what we had done wrong so far. There was a form of polite hesitancy in the advice these local people gave. They didn't want to tread on toes, but what they said always came in a slightly teasing way.

'You know, Robby and Garry, it's very nice you've come to live here,' one neighbour said.

'Oh,' said Garry, 'and why is that?'

'Because it looks like you've got so much to learn!'

I'D SPRINT UP THE HILLS when there was a newly grassed paddock to inspect. But then came the spring, and the first sinister tips of bracken fern protruded through the grass. On went a large mob of sheep to gorge on the grass and nibble the fern shoots, before they could develop into tough, two-metre bracken. Hurry! Hurry! But the sheep couldn't be everywhere at once, and there were other new paddocks which the fern was also determined to control.

It was hard to use our sheep so harshly, to see them worked so hard, tearing their fleeces on the scrub – but this was the only way to develop this land. Cattle couldn't be used to control the new fern, because fern tips poison them. We learnt about that the hard way.

It was bad luck that the first time we took a day off we came back to find a cattle beast stretched out throwing a fit. On rushing up the hill, attracted by the bellowing, we saw its legs thrashing about. It turned out to be a nice little heifer, who got to her feet looking stupid, and then fell over. Dead.

While we were away she'd been filling her belly with the juicy spring shoots of new fern growth. We couldn't have stopped the poor creature eating it, even if we'd been home – there were hills of new fronds – but she would pick an afternoon when we'd come home happy after a day at the beach.

We lost many cattle through toxic poisoning. There were two ways of stopping it: one was to keep cattle out of paddocks of fern until the fronds had hardened and were no longer edible. The other way was to give the animals enough to eat so they wouldn't have to fill themselves up with things that were bad for them. New fern fronds don't seem to hurt cattle if there's sufficient grass to fill them up.

A LOT OF PEOPLE ASKED WHAT MADE us come to Golden Bay – and when the wool was falling off the sheep's back and prices were low, or when it rained for 10 days at a stretch, I wondered too. We had bought optimistically, and at the wrong moment, for immediately after our arrival there began three decades of falling prices for wool, beef and lamb.

There were frequent phone calls from the mortgagors, who seemed to take it for granted that they would get the place back, as they had from the three previous failed owners. The old man, or his wife, would phone to ask why we were putting a fence in a particular place, or altering a shed, as if they still owned the place. The general expectation that we would go bust was enormously stressful, and for many gruelling years we strained every nerve to find the mortgage interest.

My little purse would be anxiously inspected when it was time to pay at a shop. I will never forget the day when I didn't have enough to cover what I'd bought, the sudden panic, then with my head bowed in shame, putting the items back, to the sullen contempt of the shop girl.

We had people openly say to us, 'You're on your way out, aren't you?' And that was difficult. We just didn't need it. We stayed, because this place, for all its failings, represented all we had between us. To have given up on Rocklands before we had even engaged with the struggle to make something out of it, would have brought on a shrivelling of the spirit from which neither Garry nor I would have ever recovered. Rocklands was what we had become. If we'd walked off we wouldn't have had a penny for any other semblance of a home. We were stuck with Rocklands. We had no choice.

It was a happy day indeed when we had proved ourselves sufficiently to re-finance the mortgage elsewhere, at a lower interest rate.

I SUPPOSE WE WERE A CURIOUS PAIR, Garry and I. He was stubborn and determined, a born optimist, ever seeking challenges, only feeling alive when faced with his own mortality. And me, who on earth was I, and what was I doing embarking on this desperate struggle?

There were times when I was totally dismayed by the remoteness and our primitive living conditions. I would hope that this phase in our lives would end and we would return to an easier life, to a house with indoor plumbing, clean water and a roof that didn't leak.

Had I stepped out of life? Become a fugitive from society? These thoughts crowded in on the black days, the days when the struggle seemed too great, the odds loaded against us. The stubbornness of the bracken and other weeds shocked me. 'Bloody land,' I would say to myself. 'Takes everything and gives nothing back.' Our battle, I came to realise, was with Nature itself. I would think our lives were being wasted on Rocklands. I would feel that the property was a great big hole into which we were slowly sinking.

'Why oh why,' I'd ask our unforgiving hills, 'are you so reluctant to give anything back? Are you going to give our children a future?'

Yet here I was, in this isolated corner of the South Island, standing still, thieving time that should be spent on daily tasks, gazing north, away from our harsh land, towards the cherishing sea.

And when the weather turned, and wild daffodils appeared, the universe shrank to the manageable.

Reading a copy of one of my letters to my mother, I realise

how inadequately I had described Golden Bay. *It is governed,* I wrote, *by the tide and the wind and the moon, and everything else becomes increasingly unreal. The place is more beautiful than one can possibly imagine — gentle and agricultural in the valleys, soaring and magnificent in the ranges.*

It was always important to present a cheerful outlook to our far-distant families. I would hoard up every amusing incident, and fill my letters with them.

The view was clearly enough to fulfil my romantic longings, but I never forgot the harshness of the hills behind me on which our lives depended. Garry, by his nature, was far better prepared than me. His drive and focus were so strong that they rather eclipsed mine. I just worried about him taking on so much. I could provide so little physical help, with a new baby to care for at the beginning, and two more within the next three years.

IF I HAD KNOWN WHAT WE WERE TO FACE, would I have wanted us to have bought Rocklands, no matter how tempting it was after we had searched other parts of New Zealand for something, anything, we could afford?

Yes, strangely, I would. It was our only chance of farm ownership. Independence was vitally important to both of us. I guess, looking back more than five decades later, the real story is that we managed to survive without bankruptcy. The coming years were to show that I could adapt to just about anything.

THERE WERE TWO DOCTORS IN THE PRACTICE when we came, but one was often out at sea, bird watching.

While breastfeeding Sally, I noticed a lump in my breast.

'It had better come out,' said Dr Bydder, whose surgery was in his house on the main street of Takaka.

'Well, I can't go to hospital,' I said. 'There's no one to mind the children, and I'm breastfeeding. Can you cut it out here?'

So the doctor, having emerged from his garden, gave his hands a desultory wash and injected some local anaesthetic, which gushed straight out with the milk now pouring down my chest. The scalpel felt like a rusty saw, but the lump was removed and I was stitched up.

It was only a blocked milk duct, but best to be sure.

It was said that Dr Bydder was a brilliant man, who could have made his mark anywhere as a surgeon; but here he was, in an isolated practice, having to take a horse or a boat when called to a mountain or remote coastal settlement. He'd been in Golden Bay 30 years.

With each of my pregnancies, typical of a nurse, I'd worried about birth complications, particularly now I was two hours from the nearest city hospital. There were no helicopters in those days. And whatever complication I feared – a stuck placenta with Sally, and tubes round his neck delaying Michael's arrival – this is exactly what eventuated! But Dr Bydder knew how to cope.

Whatever the complication, each of our infants arrived full of life, perhaps due to the raw sheep's liver I'd eat each pregnancy, to ensure the foetus had plenty of iron.

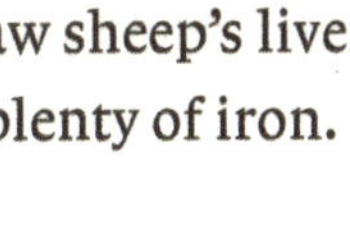

'SUCH-AND-SUCH IS A GOOD LURK' was an expression often used at the time, meaning a good opportunity to make some money – for example, producing pit props for the West Coast coal mines. 'That's a good idea,' said Garry, 'we'll make a fortune!'

He undertook to supply the demand, and set off on the first day with a well-sharpened axe to a large stand of beech saplings at the back of the farm. There were strict measures to comply with. In those days before metrics, the props had to be either 8 or 10 feet long, and no less than 6 inches in diameter. Some of our trees were 8 or 10 inches thick, too small to be split in two, but acceptable as especially strong pit supports. But while handling the minimum size was bad enough, the larger props made a huge load for Garry to cart out on his back to the road. But he slogged away, suffused in a rosy dream of being able to afford fertiliser for the farm. Then he realised that a chainsaw would speed up operations. That was the first large expense.

A contractor who delivered coal from the West Coast to the local cement works was to back-load with our props, requiring a drive up the eight hairy kilometres to collect them. To shorten the distance and time involved, with Garry having to lump the props to the contractor's truck, a bulldozer was employed to extend the road. More expense.

Nevertheless, my brave husband persevered. Until the day, when driving home, exhausted, he missed a corner and shot down the bank. The contractor, following behind, tried to get past George's protruding deck, and also slid off the road. A breakdown truck was summoned, at double the usual rates as it was a Sunday.

Garry gave up the pit-prop business.

Come the spring, with early potatoes earning exorbitant prices due to a national shortage, we planted some for the following season. A frost-free patch of land at the foot of the mountain was cleared of gorse and scrub. It was an excellent crop. We excitably anticipated what we would earn – only to discover that almost every farmer in the province had planted early potatoes that year. Spuds had never been cheaper!

Next we aimed at the possum-skin market. Newspaper headlines told of fortunes being made – people were throwing in jobs, installing wives and children in mountain huts, to emerge after a season of trapping to buy their first house. Skins were averaging 25 shillings each, topping at £3 – which in those days was a lot of money. One of our neighbours was employing three men to possum-trap full-time. Other bush-country farmers, not interested in trapping themselves, were allowing others a claim on their property, for a percentage of the profits. Garry finally decided to join in when he learnt that someone else was laying a trail of poison around the edge of our bush up the back. He let the trespasser keep his possums in return for teaching him the business.

Cyanide was used, laid out in lines 20 metres apart. Cyanide kills immediately, so a possum wasn't going to get more than a metre away from where it ingested the poison. Garry could expect to kill over 60 possums on each line, double that number if the strike was really good. A licence was needed to use cyanide, with a bait made from flour and aniseed.

'Got your antidote?' I'd scream, as Garry rushed off daily at dawn to attend to the possum lines.

'What? Can't hear you?' he would bellow back, impatient at the delay.

'Got your antidote?' I would scream louder.

Garry would smack his chest pocket, with an exaggerated movement for my benefit, with the risk of smashing the amyl nitrate capsules if they had been in his pocket.

The barn filled with luxurious, soft skins, just right for the world's fashion coats. Then we heard that 300,000 skins had already arrived in London, thousands more than expected, with the inevitable crash in prices.

We got out of the possum business.

SOME MONEY HAS TO BE RAISED, so we decide to take a few old ewes to the Takaka stock sale. We sort through the flock, picking out the ones past their best who will only be trouble if we keep them. The 50 to go are marked with green raddle on the backs of their necks. The day before the sale Garry dags the sheep for sale, and generally tidies them up. They're put in the woolshed for the night, with the transport truck ordered for 7 a.m.

The day of the sale is terrible, dark with grey curtains of rain. The sheep yards are a quagmire, with the old ewes slipping and floundering, their fleeces soon black with wet mud. We have visions of dud sales and of having to pay freight for a return journey.

The sale yards have been operating in Takaka for over 80 years, the land leased from a farmer by the local council. But now weeds are filling the pens, and rust on the rails is slowly spreading. The men who are there are among the last from the bracken-covered hills who still farm dry stock.

The auctioneers and spotters creep slowly to our pen. Time drags. It is like pulling teeth to get bids out of cagey farmers. But at last the auctioneer and his spotters are at the pen next to ours, which is offering fat hoggets fit for the butchers, and a Nelson butcher buys them at 56 shillings a head.

Now it's our turn. 'These sheep have come off hard country, so they'll shift well to easy flats,' the auctioneer tells the buyers. 'Anybody got 60 bob? No . . . well . . . 55?' The countdown is on, but how far can he count down?

'Anyone got 15 bob?'

'Yes!' a spotter yells.

It's been a pig of a day.

At the stall run by the Women's Division of Federated Farmers, selling tea and scones, I listen to farmers talking about the sale, and how they've survived another season.

As for the sale yards themselves, no one denies that one of the main problems is that there are fewer and fewer farmers to make it viable.

'Did you see the newspaper this week?' someone asks. 'Plans for the Takaka sale yards. What plans? The only plan they've got is to close them.'

Someone swears. 'Look at the bloody council – not a country person on it these days, not one.'

MICHAEL WAS BORN 13 MONTHS AFTER SALLY. When I brought him home from the hospital in early June 1960, it suddenly felt overwhelming with three pre-schoolers, and Garry away for long hours each day.

I had already decided, for my health's sake, that I couldn't breastfeed this new baby, as I was already skeletally thin from coping with two other pre-schoolers. So I asked the doctor to dry me off. He reluctantly did so, and Mike was put on the bottle.

A sweet and undemanding child, he literally brought himself up. He spent the day on the fenced-off veranda, weather permitting, where I would prop him up on a pillow and hand him a bottle. There was a tattered old leather chair on which Mike would climb to sleep. I think that chair became his mother. As a teenager he painstakingly patched that chair, transforming his nurturing mate.

Mike, as an adult, still teases me. 'You didn't breastfeed me!' I hope he forgives me.

WE OBTAINED A GARDEN TRACTOR, one of those wheelbarrow-type machines. Talk about a boy on a man's errand, with 1500 acres to work. But that little tractor did a stalwart, although slow, job for many years to come. A mower was attached to the front for cutting fern. Stones and rocks would blunt the blades, but Garry cleared many acres in this puttering fashion.

With a small pump and metres of hose fitted on for spraying gorse in summer, the garden tractor could be manoeuvred into precarious positions a large tractor could never have reached. A minute plough attachment did duty in the vegetable garden, fence posts could be carried on a frame, and hay bales carted to tempt cattle into rough blocks, which would benefit from their trampling.

The best example of the little machine's adaptability was demonstrated at docking time. Michael, the baby, was placed in his pram on the front frame, with a view of where he was going. Sally, aged two, rode in the car-seat hanging over the bar between the steering handles, with Garry to drive the equipage.

There also was me, running anxiously beside the procession, saying 'don't go so fast' to Garry, 'don't bump' to Garry again, 'don't touch that' to Sally, fingering the gear levers and 'look out Tim, you'll get run over', to the four-year-old scampering ahead. Up the steep track we would climb, to the paddocks beneath the mountain, where ewes had lambed and docking operations would take place.

One particular day we had just reached the set-up yards, when Garry, impatient to start work, halted the tractor with a jerk. Out flew Mike from the pram, to fall face-down onto a cow pat! The air was blue, but my horrified abuse was unheard as

Garry bolted to muster in ewes and lambs, leaving me to console the screaming baby, mopping him up using a puddle of water.

Worse was to come. Just as docking was about to start, with Tim and I holding the lambs while Garry operated the docking knife and ear-marker, a storm cloud appeared out of nowhere and poured buckets of rain on top of us. Throwing the younger children back onto the tractor, we bolted for home, leaving the docking gear to the elements, to await another family day of work.

While Garry continued with the gruelling physical grind, I learnt to be surprisingly practical. I made most of our clothes with my little hand-worked Singer sewing machine, using flour bags to make underpants, shirts and tea towels, taking out the brand mark with washing soda and soap, then boiling them up. The colour came out and they would be as white as anything. As Garry's work clothes wore out I made the boys shorts out of what was left. I even learnt how to spin wool from our sheep, after carding out the grit, and knitted our jerseys.

I made bars of revolting yellow soap using saved mutton fat, caustic soda, resin, borax, ammonia and cold water, which I laid out in bars on the concrete path to dry in the sun. 'What is *that*?' asked a travelling salesman who arrived at the back door holding his nose.

None of us visited the hairdresser. Sally had plaits, and I cut everyone else's hair. If I got sick of my own, I'd grab some scissors and hack some off, and look like a schoolgirl of 12. It was a real basin job!

Food was always a problem, but I was determined to make sure the family had nutritious meals. Our meals lacked variety, but the family never complained. It was rolled oats for breakfast, and lunches were healthy sandwiches. For dinners it was mutton all the time, with spuds, carrots and silverbeet, all produced on the farm.

We relied heavily on eggs. When one of our hens went broody I did all I could to get her off the nest and back into production. I was advised to douse the broody hen in the creek. I did, but perhaps I overdid the dousing? There was only one thing to do – eat her.

There was the Universal Family Benefit to look forward to, receiving £3 a month for each child. It was an automatic payment, regardless of income, to every New Zealand family. It wouldn't go anywhere nowadays, but at that time it was useful. Never, at any time, did we consider applying for any other welfare payments.

I decided we needed a piano, so I could teach music and the children would learn. I bought a second-hand baby grand. When it was delivered on a transport truck Garry exploded and we had a row in front of the driver. The baby grand, I told him, was actually cheaper than a second-hand upright I'd considered. (Well, it was also a nice piece of furniture which upped our style a bit – although it took up half our sitting-room space.)

Then I advertised to teach music, and was soon fully booked. One chap, a cement worker who could only come for lessons late at night, particularly liked *The Wigwam Dance* from Book One. 'Let's burl it again,' he kept saying, again and again, with Garry fuming through the wall trying to sleep!

We economised in every way we could. 'Shut all doors and turn off the lights,' Garry will instruct to this day. Frugality has become a lifelong habit. I'm not to run the hot tap without putting the plug in the sink. Leftover tea in the pot is not to be wasted. I read complaints in the newspaper about people unable to pay their power bills, after running bar heaters all winter. We've never possessed an electric heater. I still do the washing up with a hot-water bottle between my knees, and it sits on my lap when I work at the computer.

GARRY DOESN'T WEAR SOCKS, which for some curious reason had people at formal occasions getting under the table to check out. He resists spending money on new clothes, and sometimes, I am ashamed to say, the seam in the seat of his trousers has split.

My appearance could be just as shameful. In Takaka one day I saw my reflection in a shop window. It was a moment of self-revelation. An unbrushed woman lacking lipstick, in a tattered jersey, wearing muddy gumboots. In the front of the truck was a scruffy child, with two others wrestling each other dangerously, with loud, tortured yells on the deck.

When my mother arrived for her first visit, I was aware of the shock she experienced at the sight of our ragged clothes, and the desolate appearance of our property. She hadn't expected to find such harsh land. Of course, being Elinor, not a word of concern was ever expressed, only praise for the way we were coping.

I had a large roast sizzling in the oven, but as I stooped to lift it out of the stove, disaster struck. The patch on the seat of my trousers gave way, and in my flurry my hand slipped and the roasting dish fell on the hearth, spilling the roast and hot fat on the floor. Garry hurriedly came to the rescue, quickly replacing the meat, and no one was any the wiser.

Elinor occupied the second cottage, which she just loved, having space to herself. She would get her own breakfast and arrive at our dwelling mid-morning, to slave away for the rest of the day. A superb cook, she took over all meals. All my unselfish mother ever asked of us was a daily swim at the beach.

How I wish I could turn the clock back and give her all that she deserved.

WE TOOK THE CHILDREN TO NELSON just twice when they were small. First to see the film *Mary Poppins*, remembered for the toffee apples they tangled in their hair, the sticky glue they spread onto the theatre seats, and the migraine I suffered on the way home. The second visit was to see the Royal New Zealand Ballet, where the children were too tired by the 8 p.m. start to enjoy it, and one of them threw up on my coat.

One day, however, when the 'get-away-or-bust' feeling hit me, I had an idea. I rummaged in the sheds until I found a grey, mouldering rag that hadn't seen the light of day since we had used it to pack around our china when we moved here. The rag was a 30-year-old tent. Once I had patched the worst holes with old tea towels, it didn't look so bad.

Garry came home to find me throwing articles into trunks and cases. Old clothes, books, potatoes, chops, soap, frying pan and billies.

'Going somewhere?' he asked.

'*We* are going camping.'

'We are?'

'We are!'

Deciding it was wise to humour me, Garry complied with good grace and began loading the trailer.

When all was packed, I prised the five-year-old from the top of a tree, the three-year-old from paddling in a trough, and the two-year-old from under the woolshed.

They weren't pleased to hear they were going camping. They wanted to stay home and hear *Children's Hour* on the wireless.

The great trek started. We drove half a kilometre to the next-door farm. The Thorpes had been approached on the phone, and were waiting to direct us to their prize camping site.

Each summer our beloved neighbours had friends and relations pitching their tents around their picturesque farm. We knew there were a variety of popular spots, but we weren't prepared for the perfection of what we found.

We drove through a gateway and over a bridge into the most heavenly haven ever imagined. It was called The Glade, and it was the most glade-ish glade that ever a fairy danced on. A flat piece of land, tennis-court size, ringed all around with tall Canadian redwoods. A rock fireplace was set into a bank, and wire hooks hung from a nearby tree ready for the meat bag. A cool, twinkling stream could be used as a milk cooler.

It was completely secluded, with not a breath of wind to shake a leaf. The tent was erected and the trailer unpacked. Within half an hour the children had explored the nearby bush, unpacked every box and suitcase to look for yummy surprises, and were sick of the camping novelty.

'Are we going home now?'

'Who is going to sleep in my bed at home?'

'Pussy won't know where I am.'

Loud wails.

Garry and I tried to look jolly in the best Scout and Girl Guide fashion. Covered in smuts and with eyes streaming from smoke we produced some well-charred chops.

When it was dark we all went to bed as we had no night lights, and settled down uncomfortably. The children had mattresses on the canvas floor. I had the only camp stretcher but no mattress, with just a thin piece of sacking between me and the cold. Garry, the tough guy, had a sleeping bag on the ground.

Throughout the night we attended to children hourly. They kept getting up and walking across their siblings' faces. Mosquitoes buzzed angrily.

With the weary dawn I was paralytic with cold and everyone

else was grumpy. It was 5 a.m. and we huddled round the fire and boiled the billy for tea.

Garry went home to work and I settled down for our 'holiday'. The boys fought and asked to go home. Sally, making an effort, busied herself washing dishes, all the dirty clothes, and then the clean clothes. She hung them to dry on the tent's guy lines, which the boys kept tripping over, knocking the washing into the dust. Sally wailed.

Garry returned in time for tea, with a mattress for me and a large bottle of insect repellent. And then our hero announced he was going home to sleep, 'as I have an early start in the morning'. Earlier than 5 a.m. when everyone gets up on this holiday?

'Oh well,' I said bravely, 'the rest of us will stay a week, at least. Once we have settled down things will be a lot easier.'

The children were tucked in and Garry set up a candle by my bed.

'Hope you have a better night,' he said as he left to walk home, leaving us the truck in case we wanted to evacuate.

The children were smothered in insect repellent and I settled happily to my book.

What was that under my bed?

Something emerged and knocked over my bedside box, snuffing the candle. It was the two-year-old looking for his library book. I put him back to bed, with his blankets tucked in so tight he would strangle if he moved.

But the disturbance had woken the three-year-old, who declared she was scared, and wanted to share my camp stretcher.

Come the second, even more weary dawn and I struggled to light the fire on my own, feeling pathetic. The camping holiday was a dismal failure, but I knew a few hours of good sleep would make me feel better.

But I was going to have that sleep in my own bed at home, with cups of tea made from an electric kettle, and with the children not seen or heard for 12 hours of nightly oblivion.

The only time the trio sparked up with enthusiasm was when I asked them to help load the truck. Home we went, the children shouting with excitement as they saw familiar territory. It was as though we had been away for six months.

I slunk home like a defeated general.

'Never mind,' said Garry.

Chapter 7

In 1967 the price of wool fell sharply. Synthetic fibres had made inroads into the textile industry, initiating a 40 per cent drop in the global price of wool. Few sheep farms anywhere in the country were making money. The changes that were beginning to come to Golden Bay's tough hill farms gradually gained momentum in the following decades. As the financial struggle became crippling, a desire developed among the younger generation for an easier life, with jobs off-farm being sought. The high wages at the cement works were a drawcard.

Gordy, up at Kotinga, stiff and in pain from arthritis, was still active on his hills with two sticks, but he didn't expect his sons to follow in his footsteps. 'Make a living on the farm if you can, I tell them, and if you can't, pack it up. These sour hill farms are a thing of the past. All that's keeping them going are old lads like me. A young lad doesn't want to know about it.'

The Wilson farm was sold. Stan Wilson had reached retiring age and his children had no wish to take it on. The 600 steep acres, even with a dozen milking cows on the flatter land, could scarcely support a viable business. Closure was the most rational outcome. The crowds at the sale picked over the remnants of an existence whose time was up. Hay knives, brass scales, horse harrows – implements few could now recognise how to use.

One day, I heard Garry declaiming to a neighbour, 'They can't turn us out. We'll live under an umbrella before they move us from our land.' I worried about the ominous 'they'. Who would turn us out? I came across a pile of unpaid bills with peremptory demands for payment and I felt desperately worried.

If we had to sell Rocklands, what would we get for it, and with such a pittance where would we go? I might moan and groan about our struggling existence, but here we had a roof of sorts over our head. And some dignity. Let's face it, being a landowner of even the most appalling property was much better,

I felt, than working for someone else. Above all, in Golden Bay a lack of money didn't matter. No one had much.

I have always been quite good at talking to myself. Making an effort to be sensible. Sorting out things in my mind.

Rocklands was progressing. Not as fast as we would wish, but large areas in the lower hills had been grassed. The fern was retreating and stock numbers rising, although it was far from being an economic unit.

Fertiliser was essential, and we put on what we could afford. On the steep country, fertiliser had to be carried by packhorse, and spread by hand from heavy bags slung round Garry's neck. The worst part was having to lift 86-kilogram bags onto the hook of the pack saddle – work far too hard for a man who already had a bad back.

More than once Garry slipped a disc in his back. We were fortunate in having an old van at that time, so he could lie flat on its floor as I drove him to a chiropractor in Nelson. On one visit the chiropractor bent one of Garry's legs at the knee, pressed it hard against his chest, then leant heavily against it himself. The patient, unable to withstand the pressure, let fly with his leg like a spring, sending the chiropractor flying, to splat against the opposite wall.

That was our last visit to the chiropractor. A visiting president of Federated Farmers taught Garry an exercise that strengthened his back muscles, which we decided the chiropractic treatment had been tearing apart. Garry no longer slips a disc, but his back always aches.

THE MAJOR CONTRIBUTION TOWARDS doubling the carrying capacity on Rocklands was internal subdivision. Fourteen kilometres of fencing was erected, making 23 separate paddocks. Garry had done this completely alone, apart from some assistance from various members of the family.

Sally, as a three-and-a-half-year-old, would always be a starter, watching over the wire jenny like a clucky hen, to make sure the wires didn't tangle. She also kept an eye on where her father put his hammer, pliers and tobacco, knowing he would be looking for them a hundred times a day.

Mike, in his turn – even younger, at two-and-a-half – thought nothing of climbing the mountain to give a hand, but wasn't as conscientious as his sister, preferring to play roly-poly down steep slopes, scattering staples. That is, until the day came, with his parent temporarily out of sight, when the little boy panicked and headed for home. I could hear him bawling from a very far distance.

Days off, even on a Sunday, were rarely taken. There was always something urgent to be done.

Above all, the children were not to ask for things that cost money. It was a sort of tough-love upbringing for our offspring. I was to wonder, in later years, if the stoical stance our three children have always displayed, seldom telling their parents of any real worries or concerns, has perhaps shut us out from what is really going on in their lives.

OVER THE YEARS WE HAD A SUCCESSION of second-hand cars, with not one of them having the reliability of George, our ex-army truck, which continued to do valiant work. If I needed the car it was important to ask Garry, before he took off in the morning, to get the car out of the garage, to crank it if necessary, and park it facing down the sloping drive. Then, if the battery was flat, I could start the engine in gear by letting it roll downhill.

I never did learn to change a tyre. On one trip to Takaka I became aware I had a flat tyre, but kept going, eventually driving on the metal rim, with the flattened tyre and tube going *bang, bang, bang* on the road. Astonished bystanders were laughing their heads off as I made for a garage.

Somehow we managed to scrape along and pay our bills, although once a cheque I wrote for £7 was refused by a shop. When I returned home in tears, my gallant husband tore into Takaka to confront the bank manager.

'How dare you humiliate my wife for such a paltry sum!' Garry roared at the cowering little man, who was shrinking back into his chair. 'As a result, I'll remove our business from your bank,' he added. To the relief of the bank manager, no doubt!

Garry had then to 'don his best waistcoat', as he facetiously described it, and hasten to Nelson to find someone else to cover our loans. This he found in Peter Hansen, manager of Levin & Co. Years later, Peter gave us the store's old black-and-white TV. 'Because you need it more than us.' There were stock firms then, before the days of massive amalgamation, who took a paternal interest in their clients. Peter, more than once, did us a favour behind the scenes.

IT WAS UP TO ME TO FIND some extra income. How was I to do it? I embarked on several sidelines, not always with success.

The first year I was occupied with painting the cottage, inside and out. We couldn't afford turpentine as well as paint, so both Tim and I became spotted with various colours. He was a windy baby, and I'd have to constantly descend the ladder, with paint on my hands, to settle him.

The second year I grew tomatoes to sell, but blights, bugs and wasps ruined the crop. I bottled what I could salvage. Then it was banana passionfruit I was after, which grew wild in the bush, with a market in Christchurch when other fruit was scarce. Tree tomatoes, easily grown from cuttings, were another successful crop.

I did up our second cottage and made it available for tourists. As fast as their deposits came in I bought the furniture. In the end, it was a satisfactory sort of compliment when a neighbour said, 'Robin could make a living where a rat couldn't.'

But one fine day Garry found me sitting in the middle of the yard, with a pile of washing on the ground, in floods of tears. I had washed one load, hung it on the line, and returned with a second load, only to find the line, strung between two rotting wooden poles, had come down, dumping the washing in the mud. Garry rehung the line and I went back to rewash the first load. Emerging outside once more, I found the line had collapsed again, dumping the second load. By now I'd run out of hot water.

At full speed I drove into Takaka, and for the first time in my married life bought something on tick, charging it to Garry. I came home with a carton of steel bits and pieces, but then had to wait until my husband had time to erect the manufactured clothesline, which required a cement base. He might have told me to take the clothesline back, but he didn't. This was a rare instance of me making domestic demands in full voice!

A specialist agricultural journalist, in the Bay to do some research, told me all the wives of the marginal-land hill farmers he'd met had eyes that blazed with inner rage. He added, kindly, that I was the only wife he'd met, so far, without that distinctive look. Well, he hadn't seen me on a bad day. 'Life's a bastard,' I'd tell Garry forcefully. 'Everything's such a bastard!'

Poor Garry. He never complained, was always optimistic. He wanted to make Rocklands work. But to me, at times, it was as if there was a curse on it. 'I'll be gone with the truck when you get back,' I'd yell, as Garry went off on the horse to the back of the place, packing wire and grass seed. 'I'll be gone!' But I was always there when my husband came home.

Is it conceivable he never really understood how important I felt it was to be investing our lives in something worthwhile? Something that responded! Or perhaps, knowing that he had to make a farm out of nothing, that we had no other choice, was all he had strength for? My carrying on was a stupid distraction.

Once or twice, in my lowest and most unjust moments, I'd tell Garry that none of his previous girlfriends – a string of high-society Canterbury girls – would have put up with our way of life. What cheek I had! Those particular young women had well-off parents who could have installed Garry as a son-in-law onto a decent farm. I hadn't contributed a bean as a dowry!

But I was tired of the farm earning so little. 'I could have guests for B and B,' I'd suggest defiantly, knowing Garry would hate having paying guests in the house.

Garry wasn't listening, though. He thought we could achieve some security by milking a small herd of cows. With this suggestion I realised the situation must be pretty desperate, for like most sheep men he had a deep-rooted dislike of dairy cows, although he had always been good about the house cow. I decided I must help. Most farmer's wives can milk, surely I could learn?

ONE NIGHT, WHEN GARRY WAS HOME much later than usual, while worrying he might have had an accident, I also realised the cow had to be milked. So I brought Floppy the cow in, and set to work. Only then did I realise, in a humiliating moment, that I am nervous of cows. I, who have never been afraid of the beef cattle, and who always gave a hand in the cattle yards. But to be shut in a small confined space, with a cow watching me malignantly from the corner of her eye, is an entirely different matter. However, it had to be done, and having leg-roped the cow, I put the bucket underneath her udder and set to work. A meagre trickle rewarded me, then the cow kicked the bucket, with extreme accuracy, into my lap.

Something was wrong.

I had roped the wrong leg.

It took me an hour to milk Floppy, but I had done it, and I meant to go on. We bought three more cows, who were shortly due to calve, and registered with the dairy company to whom we would sell our cream. We would use the skim milk to raise some pigs.

To extract the cream from the milk we bought an old hand-operated separator. Morning and evening I emerged from the house with a bucket of warm water to wash the cows' teats, and with the separator parts to be assembled in our improvised cow bail, a corner of the vehicle shed. Each morning our little cream can would be left at the front gate to be collected by the cream truck, and the four cows earned us £100 a year. But I was never relaxed with the cows. I hated their sudden movements, the attempts at sly kicks, and especially when a tail, dripping with mud and dung, flipped out to hit my face.

The dairy inspector made frequent visits to leave little notes, insisting that manure had to be cleaned off the wall and the yard, or else we could no longer sell cream to the factory. I scrubbed and scoured, but with a cobblestone yard, on which the cows dropped bucketloads of hot liquid poo to splatter up onto the walls of the shed, it was a never-ending job.

As an alternative to milking by hand we obtained a half-horsepower motor, which was expected to drive a large vacuum pump, well hung about with pulleys. I'd crank the pulley wheel, and if I was lucky, the machine would burst into life after a multitude of attempts.

Sometimes there was a harsh grating sound, accompanied

by a galaxy of sparks, and the switch would be turned off immediately. Only when there was a regular *chuff, chuff* from the engine were the cows and I in business. The first time I was to cope alone with the vacuum pump I asked Garry to demonstrate how to use it, but the machinery did nothing but shriek. After a fuming half-hour turning the switch on and off, and wrenching the pulleys, Garry took off, threatening to shoot the bloody cows. Left to myself, I filled some hot-water bottles, tucked them round the motor, and went to collect the cows. On my return to the shed the warmed motor shot into action.

Whenever possible I enticed the children into collecting the cows. Mike was the most willing. He'd bolt round the paddock, waving a stick, shouting fiercely, 'Go on, you buddy cows!'

Sally would oblige, which was brave, as shrill screams could be heard each time a cow took a lunge at her, but as long as she could keep the cows moving she could cope. Of course Sally had good reason to be wary of cows. As a two-year-old she once slipped into a paddock with some large yearling calves. One started licking her hands, then her skirt started disappearing into its mouth. Finally our daughter was glued firmly to the calf's nose. Luckily I heard her screams before the calf galloped off with Sally attached.

I had my hair-raising moments. One cow pulled several boards off the shed wall after being milked, as I had forgotten to untie her leg rope. Another cow backed into the central pillar of the shed, in a 'let me get out of here' charge, and nearly brought the roof down. A third cow drank a bucket of detergent and I thought her last days had come, but she survived, apart from blowing bubbles.

In time, however, I came to relish the early morning milking. Noises in the distance were more audible first thing. A tui singing, our stupid hens clucking, the hollow knocking of sledgehammer on a fence post elsewhere, the spatter of something falling on the leaf floor below the trees.

I would squelch off in my gumboots, through the muddy patches on the path, often wearing one of Gary's old jackets, too big but very warm, with fantails flitting along with me, catching insects disturbed by the cows' hooves.

With the day beginning and ending with the soothing hum of the separator, I felt that here was one branch of farming in which I was becoming proficient.

Meanwhile, Garry patrolled the sheep, spread fertiliser from sacks attached to the horse, resurrected fences, endlessly climbing the steep hills. He was away from dawn to dark, returning tired and aching for bed. Did he lie awake, perhaps in the dead hours, riddled with the fear that we had made a mistake? I'm not sure about that. If Garry ever worried, he never let on to me. And now, so many decades later, I realise how lucky I was, that whatever doubts he may have had, he never, ever burdened me with them.

THE WIRELESS, WITH ITS NATIONAL PROGRAMME, was my main source of stimulus, with its news of the world and fascinating interviews. I often wonder if the programmers in Wellington appreciate how very important, and so avidly listened to, National Radio is in back-country areas.

As a pre-schooler Tim loved the *Listen with Mother* programme, run by Kate Harcourt on National Radio. Together we'd bunny-hop round our small kitchen. Why on earth did they stop that programme?

We couldn't receive the Concert Programme, but I had a little turntable and a collection of vinyl records. Sometimes at night, when the moon struck a pattern of beaten silver across the dark ripples of the Bay, I would listen to Mozart, the sound filling my veins with liquid gold.

If the New Zealand Ballet was to be televised, I'd take the children to see it at Rosie's, an elderly widow who was glad of the company. Also watching the programme, more often than not, would be her pet rooster. He'd be rolled up in a towel, so he didn't mess the carpet, and sat in front of the TV.

Until the late 1960s we had no television ourselves. We wanted books to be more important than TV, so we waited until Mike was a passionate reader like his siblings. Even then there would be some battles with our youngest. Having been told it was time to go to bed and read, he would slam every door between the TV set and his bed.

To get a signal, the receiver had to be on top of the bluff behind the house, requiring such a long cord that our picture was very weak. Garry would be sent up the bluff, while someone watched the set and bellowed instructions to adjust the receiver to this position or that.

WE WERE AMAZED AT THE NUMBER of visitors who found their way to Rocklands. Friends and people we hardly knew arrived to see us in hordes. Perhaps I had been a little reckless in my casual invitations, and it was startling to find out how many of them were accepted. There was, I fancy, a certain measure of curiosity to see how we were getting on in this new life, which I had described in my letters, probably with exaggeration and brave attempts at humour.

Apart from that, there was genuine friendship, for it was an ordeal to make the journey. None of our guests had been over the Takaka Hill before. Nor had they known people, in the second half of the twentieth century, living in such materially deprived conditions: muddy water in the taps, an outside loo, and a meagre, unreliable income.

One elderly visitor looked about her with an air of outrage as she descended from her car, to ask demandingly, 'How on earth did you find such a place, and why?'

The lack of beds didn't worry anyone. Visitors set up camp stretchers on the shaky veranda, or spread feathers from their sleeping bags on the sitting-room floor. If the cottage was packed, they slept in the barn loft. They were the brave ones, with various vermin for company. Two young men arrived, took their sleeping bags to the loft, telling us stories the next day about rats as big as dogs, who'd attempted to share their sleeping bags and chew their hair.

Another couple, newly engaged and quite besotted, spent most of their time wrapped up together on the sofa, with the door shut between me and them. I was on the side with the sink and the meals to be cooked. 'Excuse me!' I'd mutter as I shot past the couple with a bare child under each arm, after their bath.

'Not at all,' the girl would reply. And then, 'You don't mind if we have a cuddle, do you, Robby?'

'Sure, go ahead,' I'd respond through clenched teeth. Heaven save me from dreamy couples!

One wet day an old boyfriend turned up. The children were scrapping at my feet and I looked like an old tramp in a patched-up coat with my hair all over the place. He didn't stay long. When heading back down the path he met Garry, to whom he happily reported, 'Well, I've got over Robby now.'

But one morning, with the cottage full of smoke from burnt toast, I looked at the children and felt a sudden surge of optimism. There was Tim holding a book upside-down, reading something he had made up to Sally. And she was listening, and laughing.

OUR CHILDREN CONTINUED to provide our entertainment. Mike, when small, was brave with cows but scared of spiders. He'd ask for the 'buzzy bee' to be removed from the long-drop loo each time he saw a cobweb. But he was far more into 'birds and bees' questions than his older siblings. He'd ask people, with genuine interest, whose tummy they'd come out of. He believed that on your fifth birthday you learnt to ride a bike. Not over several days or weeks, but on this day. Garry and I watched, wincing, as our determined little son set off down the sloping drive on the bike, only to keep falling off, yelling abuse at himself and the bike, with blood flowing. But not for one second did he give up, all day, until he had mastered cycling. On his birthday.

'If you want to make an island, do you throw earth on a whale?' Sally once asked.

Another time she was composing a rattling tune on the piano. 'Listen to me!' she called. 'You aren't listening to me compose my tune.'

'I am listening,' I replied from the kitchen.

'No, you aren't listening. You're peeling potatoes.'

'I am listening *and* peeling the potatoes,' I insisted. 'I could have had the wireless on, but I wanted to hear your composition.'

'The wireless wasn't on before. You're making that up!'

You couldn't win with our daughter!

She could be stubbornly confrontational, questioning everything until she was satisfied everything was above-board. When I took the two younger children to the post office to deposit money from their savings boxes, Sally counted out loud as the clerk checked the amounts. He had to do it twice to satisfy her supervision. Mike was more interested in how much interest he would earn, and then shouted us all a milkshake.

I WAS DETERMINED TO BRING UP CHILDREN who would never say they were bored. Sally and Mike, only 13 months apart, did everything together. They had no toys to speak of, but Rocklands offered a wealth of things to do. They slid down hills on nikau palm leaves, caught freshwater crayfish, made mud pies decorated with ferns and daisies, and excavated clay to make model animals.

Tim was more of a loner, and had a vast imagination. On his first birthday, he didn't walk, but ran, as if there were so many enthralling things to be seen, touched and knocked over that he couldn't wait to begin. With two siblings to endure by the time he was four, Tim missed out on a large share of my fuss and attention. It was therefore agreed he could tag along with his father during the working day on the farm, as long as he realised Dad was no nursemaid!

So it was, at four years old, that Tim would take off with his father straight after breakfast. There went the stocky, broad-shouldered man, striding impatiently to get on to the job, perhaps a couple of kilometres away, and beside him a small, tousled-haired boy, running flat out to keep up.

To me our eldest son was still only a baby himself, but he skipped babyhood in a house containing two younger children. With Garry beginning to pant as they climbed the steep hills, the small boy would run ahead, talking all the time in the big, deep voice he assumed especially for conversations with his father as they went about their work.

When at the scene of the day's labour, mostly fencing in those early days, Tim would dip into his lunch bag for an early morning tea. He had a playground of broken, uneven ground, studded with rocks of fantastic shapes, a forest of manuka scrub, a prairie of fern fronds, glades of native trees. What more could a four-year-old want? There was such a glory of entertainment that Tim could never settle long to any particular game, but would run from rock to tree, from sapling-made swing to creek pool, from his houses of rushes to the castle knob at the height of the paddock.

On paddocks that had been disced and broken in from scrub country, knots of twisted gorse roots and burnt-off stumps offered a wealth of ideas. Indulgent father staggered home nightly under a load of timber – all Tim's imagined animals. There would be imaginary pigs to keep in the woodshed. A rhinoceros lived in a patch of wild mint. Giraffes sat up trees, while the bulk of the claimed gorse roots were Tim's sheep and cattle, grazing on a mound of earth he called his farm.

Until he went to school, Tim would happily spend his day in our wild hills, with never a hint of tiredness. He would stump fearlessly through cattle, which trailed behind him inquisitively, as he sang his busy little songs. I could hear his chattering voice as he came up the gulley, upright and grubby on his way home for tea. His nightly chore of filling the yard trough could take at least two hours if he was diverted by a mouse, a thistledown, a shining stone or a rather interesting hoof-print.

I could yell myself hoarse at bedtime, and Tim could be tucked beneath a hydrangea, right behind me, but he wouldn't hear a word. He would be busy talking to a worm.

AGED FIVE, TIM STARTED SCHOOL AT MOTUPIPI, to which he travelled on the school bus, after a kilometre walk to the main road. 'What was the name of the man who was shot?' he asked on returning home one day. It was 22 November 1963.

'President Kennedy?'

'Yes, well, we put a flag up at school, but only halfway up, to show we loved him very much.'

Tim made a taiaha for the school concert, by gumming smelly hens' feathers to a stick of bamboo. I wiped the feathers with soap, which didn't help much. On the night of the concert the audience sat on forms outside the classroom stage. The infants brought the house down, particularly one child, thank God not our own, who was picking his nose and eating the bogeys. Sally kept pushing the rug off her knees so people could see her dress, a cast-off party frock someone had given her. Mike, who'd never been up so late before, was more interested in the stars. 'Look at all those the holes in the sky! Is that where the rain falls out?'

The school's reading system at that time involved sending children home with an isolated word in a tobacco tin. Then the system changed to the Janet and John books. So dull. *See the boat, John. John saw the boat*. Tim was still not interested. He remained uninterested in school reading until he was seven, when he was given a supplementary book about pirates. He'd finished that pirate book by the time he got off the school bus. From then on he was a bookworm, but a lot of confidence had been lost in our son's first two years at school, because of those early reading tools.

In the weekends Tim was always so busy that he would appear at midday for his breakfast, and then immediately have lunch. He was always constructing something: a theodolite, a radio, a telescope. He bought a magnifying glass, and with some broken bits of mirror made a trace-o-scope, to capture the landscape and trace it onto graph paper. Nelson's Cawthron Institute became interested in the cod flies he was finding in a creek, and requested other specimens, which Tim put in jars, carefully typing the labels.

Washing his hair in the bath one day, I commented on my son's big head, suggesting it must be full of brains. 'It's full of dreams and good ideas,' our eldest son replied.

IN NO TIME ALL THREE OF OUR CHILDREN were at school. They walked to the main road, barefoot in summer, to catch the school bus. For lunch they had home-made bread sandwiches with farm-grown fillings, wrapped in re-usable plastic bags.

Everyone else, I was told, had white bread, jam and cake, wrapped in clean pieces of greaseproof paper.

Sally's best friend's mother apparently felt sorry for our daughter with her 'dull lunch' and was sending her cake and sweets. I didn't learn about this until Sally was grown up and confessed. Now I knew why she was the only one of our children who had holes in their teeth.

The majority of the school parents were comparatively affluent, with the fathers earning high wages at the cement works. I dreaded the never-ending fundraising schemes. I'd bake a date loaf for the stalls, and inevitably bring it home. Everyone else would have produced show-off cakes. Cake baking was definitely competitive.

The head teacher wouldn't give written reports; we had to make an appointment for a verbal discussion. Sally had been losing weight, and was very nervy. I'd discovered that the head teacher, whom she adored, had been putting her down at every opportunity. Fired up, I went to the appointment having thought about what I would say.

'Steve,' I addressed the head teacher, 'Sally adores you, but she feels you don't like her.'

'Well,' he said, 'I have to knock her back, as she is too bright.'

Shocked, I suggested that this didn't appear to worry Sally's classmates, considering her many friends. 'It's very important that she feels her teacher likes her,' I said.

Nor did this head teacher ever accept invitations to any parent's home. His motive, it seemed, was to not be seen as favouring anyone. No child must be seen to be brighter than the others, and no home more popular.

This same head teacher had ignored the date of the school's centennial, to bypass potential problems. His successor was more naïve, with astronomical rows erupting between the descendants of the first settlers. Meetings to organise the event were punctuated with explosive 'shut ups' from the exasperated principal. He even threatened to shoot a few people!

The climax occurred when one pupil's father, the district's most decorated war veteran, chopped down the school's flagpole overnight, because the Maori flag – te tino rangatiritanga – had been erected. 'Having fought for this country under the New Zealand flag, I considered that idea outrageous,' he said.

But the highlight of the school year, such fun, was the annual home-made billy-cart competition. Fathers would help make the carts, and push their children, who steered. It would be held in the school paddock on a summer evening when all the dads were off work.

CHAPTER 8

The Takaka Hill is the door that shuts out the rest of the world.

Sometimes I feel like I'm in a little isolated bubble. There's a big wide world out there and somehow I can't reach it. Calling it a hill is an understatement. Only Nelsonian diplomatic blindness refuses to label it a mountain. It's a great divide, shaggy with bush, and bristling with rocky outcrops which precariously span the road out of the Bay.

At 791 metres it's not the highest hill in New Zealand, but it is the longest hill road, 25 kilometres in length, with 365 bends between Riwaka and Upper Takaka. It isn't unusual to meet holidaymakers in Takaka, with the wife shaking and demanding to go back to Nelson by a different route. There is no other way. The Hill is a large psychological barrier between me and the life I once knew.

A woman doctor, new to the practice, said she had seldom seen so much depression, anxiety or marital strife as she met in Golden Bay. 'It isn't only animals that get bush sickness,' she said. 'People get it, too.' To travel to Nelson by bus took three hours, or even four with one particular driver, who would stop to pick up fruit and vegetables en route. It was said he even had a girlfriend along the way on whom to make a call!

On one such journey an American tourist became apoplectic with fury over the delays, and complained. An inspector came, anonymously, to accompany the Takaka to Nelson bus trip. That particular morning a reserved passenger failed to turn up. So what did the driver do? He bussed his other passengers to the woman's home to wake her, with everyone having to wait while the woman grabbed some breakfast and got dressed.

'How can you sack a driver who is so considerate?' the inspector apparently decided.

Most Golden Bay residents love the Hill. They say it keeps people out. Some, who have been born and plan to die here, don't see any need to go over it. Ever.

'I like it here,' said Bruce, an 83-year-old. 'I'm not moving to an old people's home. When the doctor asked me where I'd like to go, I said the local cemetery is my next destination. Some old people go over the Hill to be near a hospital when they're getting on a bit, but they go over there and die. You can't transplant old trees.'

Access to Massacre Bay, later to be known as Golden Bay, was at first confined to boats sailing round the coast from Nelson. In 1844, Charles Heaphy and two companions were the first Europeans known to have walked over the Takaka Hill from Riwaka.

There had been little need for early Maori to venture inland, with the coastline providing ideal conditions for their planting, hunting and fishing, although it's been confirmed that on two occasions, in 1844 and 1853, settlers were escorted across the Hill by way of a Maori track.

When George Spanjer brought the mail from Nelson in the early 1860s, he drove to Motueka in a horse and cart, saddled a carthorse and rode to the foot of the Takaka Hill, crossed the hill on a donkey, and at Upper Takaka changed his mount for a horse again to complete the journey to Collingwood.

It wasn't until 1906 that Newmans and Gibbs motor coaches were bringing passengers across on a somewhat hair-raising journey, with the crossing by buggy taking over five hours.

Clive, 97, remembers his grandparents buying one of the very first cars in Golden Bay – a 1922 or 1923 Oakland for £500 – and the occasional family expedition to Nelson. 'We'd take our lunch and boil the billy on the top of the Hill. Dad didn't want to meet the service car on a bad bit of the road between the top and Kaiuru. It was a bit of a dirt track.'

The Depression of the 1930s saw relief workers widening the road, blasting their way through the marble. The teacher on the Takaka Hill was usually warned of any blasting, and the classroom evacuated. But one day she wasn't warned and a cricket-ball-sized lump of marble hurtled through the classroom window, knocking her unconscious.

None of the men working on the Hill had cars, and when they cycled down they had to tie a branch to the back of their bicycle as a brake. If a teacher wanted a lift down the Hill, she'd get a lift on the back of a workman's bicycle.

Down a side road to Canaan there is a 183-metre-deep abyss known as Harwoods Hole, the second-biggest hole in the country. When the opportunity came to stand on its edge I never went near it again. It felt as though the mountain wanted to suck me into its gigantic throat. At one time a river plunged into this marble plughole, but gradually the water sank down through the cracks in the rock, back towards its source. Now the hole is dark and silent.

Menacing.

As are the signs on the Takaka Hill in winter, warning *Ice/Grit*. Maintaining the road has always been a battle with snow and slips. Heavy rain in August 1990 caused more than 80 slips, washouts and blocked culverts, marooning the Bay for a week.

INTRUSION, I LEARNT, WAS UNKNOWN IN THE DISTRICT. You can't, indeed mustn't, be an island. If you choose to live in Golden Bay then you're part of the family of people who share the isolation. People here don't wait for invitations.

A woman called Nancy once turned up and put a box on the table. 'Hope you can make use of some raspberries?'

'Thank you. How delicious.' I went on to apologise for our shabby dwelling.

'My parents started farm life in a rough shack,' she said. 'Your cottage would have been a mansion to them.' She put an arm on my shoulder. 'Just show the district that the struggle and hard work can't get you down. Spit in its eye,' she said.

Indeed, there were other ramshackle dwellings in the district. Bill, 69, lived in a house his grandfather had built 84 years ago out of corrugated iron. There was a potato plant sprouting from an old boot on the porch. 'If you put my house in Nelson it would startle the natives,' he said.

Bill was a dairy farmer. His 90 acres were his share of the 400 acres his grandfather bought in 1905 for £28 an acre. 'With a smallholding the options are limited, but dairying is where the money is,' he said. 'The income from dry stock can't compare with dairy. But at calving time I sometimes don't get home until midnight. If I didn't have a wife to cook my meal the price would be too high.'

He was the first to acknowledge that, when it came to dairying, it is often the women who keep the dairy farmers afloat. I'd seen the procession of mothers pushing their babies in battered prams across paddocks to the milking sheds. From a pram poked in a corner of the separator room, they graduated to a box nailed to the wall of the shed, until a succession of babysitters is bred.

Emma, a lively 70-year-old, ran her own dairy farm. She hadn't travelled far. 'It's hard to escape with all the animals,' she explained, although she had made a few long journeys to Nelson when her brother became ill.

Emma's farm was a sheltered patch of land which she'd farmed all her life. She lived alone. In her childhood, she explained, there'd been more than a dozen other small farms in the area, 'but they've been bought out by the bigger dairy farmers'.

She gave me some advice. 'You must never get despondent. You have to keep on doing things,' she said.

The truth is there were many distractions. People came. Strangers. They'd come up the drive, park by the shed, and walk across the footbridge. They'd come out of curiosity, boredom, expecting to talk, but sometimes having nothing to say. I'd give them tea and conversation, with me doing most of the talking, getting a fever from the effort.

People would make Rocklands the purpose of their Sunday Drive. I was not the earth-mother type. I was too shy to breastfeed in public. With three small children there was no energy to spare for outsiders. Looking back, a lifetime later, I wonder why I didn't hide at their coming, or make an excuse that I was about to go out. But I didn't, did I?

The pace of life was so different. Used to Canterbury farmers leaping off their tractors to run to open a farm gate, I found the wry, gate-leaning, why-bust-your-guts attitude of local farmers considerably laid-back. Perhaps the shadow of the Takaka Hill, a protective barrier against go-getters, had something to do with Golden Bay minds?

What I had to learn was that in this valley it was impossible to be entirely independent. You were a community, and you were expected to help one another in time of need. Your neighbours stood by you and you by them. That was the unwritten law and was necessary for self-preservation.

But I sometimes wondered if we'd come to cowboy country. One neighbour took another to court, accusing him of stealing his cattle. The suspect was well-known as a ratbag, prone to setting fire to his property to get the insurance money – a boat once, then his woolshed and a barn. And then the alleged cattle rustler got off, because he pointed out that the boundary fence was not on the survey line.

When the Greytown rugby team from the Wairarapa came to the Bay for a match, they let it be known, loud and clear, that they considered they were coming to a one-horse town. So the boys of the Golden Bay Rugby Club held their bus up just out of Takaka and kidnapped one of the more troublesome blokes at gunpoint. He was loaded onto a horse and cart and taken into the town tied up. A mock lynching took place outside the Telegraph Hotel. 'He only got slightly injured, I think,' one of the locals reported.

I WAS DETERMINED I WASN'T GOING TO SUFFER from bush sickness.

One wet day, after we had been on Rocklands for six years, with the children in the woolshed helping Garry make gates, I sat down to write an article about how we came to buy Rocklands. I sent it to the *Auckland Weekly News*, the pink-covered newspaper-sized magazine published by *The New Zealand Herald*, and it was accepted.

So I kept going, producing an article every two weeks, describing our pioneering life, attempting to be humorous. The magazine illustrated the articles with extraordinarily adept cartoons. Later, as I grew more confident, I interviewed other farm families in the Bay, and illustrated the articles with my photographs.

There was no lack of subjects. The pioneer instinct of toughness and ingenuity seemed to have lasted longer in Golden Bay than in other parts of New Zealand.

The two remarkable Richards brothers, Jack and Ned, who owned a large cattle property on the western coast of the Bay, were 85 and 83, respectively, when I met them in 1966. A tough breed, the brothers bought in store cattle from as far distant as the Marlborough Sounds, fattened them on their land, and then drove them out to the butchers in Nelson, a journey on the hoof that took five to six days.

Great mobs were taken, up to a hundred at a time, with the cows and the bulls mixed together. The brothers would take the chains off the bulls and let them run loose. 'They drove better that way,' Jack explained, 'although in the early days, when there were no fences to speak of, the bulls would disappear into the scrub.'

Another problem was keeping cattle out of people's backyards. 'One time,' Jack recalled, 'we got near Riwaka, on the other side of the Hill, and one old bull went off around someone's house. The bathroom window was open, the old sort that slides up and down, and the bull got its shoulder under the window and lifted it clean off! There was no one at home, and the window wasn't broken, so I kept going!'

Years of droving life had taught this old widower a good deal of self-reliance. He made first-class porridge in an ancient iron pot, and grew his own vegetables. He had a little ginger cat that came and went, and Jack reckoned the animal's mother had mated with a wild possum.

Once, a young travelling salesman arrived to sell him a refrigerator. It was a silly thing to do with the power kilometres away, and no prospects of it being laid on for years. But Jack appreciated the effort. 'If he had the guts to come out here, crossing two rivers, I reckoned he deserved a sale,' he said, pointing to the refrigerator where he kept his favourite saddle.

THE HARWOOD FAMILY NEVER GIVES UP EASILY. In 1894 James Septimus Harwood, aged 25, was sent to be assistant lighthouse keeper at Farewell Spit. When requisitioning stores, young Harwood also asked the Marine Department to send some seedling trees to plant near the keeper's huts. The seedlings were carefully planted, but they could not survive the severe winds and briny sand.

James then spent many months gathering in seaweed until he had a great pile. Again the trees were planted, each given a quantity of seaweed. They also died. Most men would have abandoned the endeavour, but not James Harwood.

Over a period of years, when he journeyed the 25 kilometres to Puponga, usually once a week, he made the long walk home carrying a sack of soil on his back. This went on until a great pile of earth had been accumulated. After a third attempt at planting, the trees grew and thrived. Today, that magnificent grove of macrocarpa pines is conspicuous seaward, and almost as valuable as the light itself.

Some years later James bought a farm at Upper Takaka, where he and wife Robina raised a family of nine children, of whom Arthur was the youngest. Older siblings were named Septimus and Octavius. It was as though the parents had run out of names. It was Arthur who was to take over the farm, and he achieved what he did through almost superhuman efforts.

Not for nothing did he become known as 'Night and Day Harwood'. Tall, dark-haired and alert, Arthur carried with him an air of boundless energy. I thought of him as an Ed Hillary type – driven, determined and capable.

On finishing his education at Nelson College he came home to work the family farm with his brother Jack. There were almost 200 acres of light, swampy land covered with logs, rocks and weeds, with a further 1181 acres of steep limestone country running under a thick carpet of fern up the slopes of the Takaka Hill.

The two boys chopped at the scrub, scythed the blackberries and slashed the fern, trying to maintain enough grass to feed their eight cows and 800 sheep. With a four-horse team they dragged out rocks, and struggled up the hills with sacks of burnt lime on their backs for top-dressing.

In the meantime, Lillian, a cultured girl from Christchurch, had arrived in the district to teach at Uruwhenua School in the Takaka Valley. 'I'd looked at a map,' she told me, 'and seen that Uruwhenua was about an inch from Nelson. I didn't know about the Takaka Hill, so the long, windy drive into this isolated valley came as a shock.' So did country life.

In Christchurch Lillian had enjoyed balls at the Winter Gardens and the stimulus of university life. In Uruwhenua, a minute settlement, it was gravel roads, no electricity or public transport and a different social life. There were three rugby teams in the district, and Lillian noticed most of the men had no teeth. 'I thought this might have been for practical reasons. It was a two-day mission to get to Nelson for a filling or an extraction, so it saved money and pain to have the teeth pulled out.'

As a first-year teacher, feeling professionally isolated, she often cycled to the Upper Takaka school, seeking support from the head teacher there. And Arthur, either by accident or design, would happen to be under the gum trees on the corner just as Lillian returned to her boarding place.

In 1932, the couple married. A year later, at the very bottom of the slump, they took over the farm from brother Jack, and faced the hard grind of farm survival on their own.

When the construction of the Cobb hydro dam began in 1937 – the most ambitious civil-engineering project undertaken in the country at that time – Arthur undertook to pack in stores and equipment up the mountains for the workers. It involved a two-day trip on tracks that were narrow, icy and dangerous. He'd let his horses walk in front, knowing they could see the perilous track better than he could, while he trudged along at the rear holding a horse's tail. Or, sometimes, in utter weariness, he slept on the back of a horse.

Lillian would be sitting up watching the clock, and listening in the darkness for the first sound of the returning pack team. Seven, nine, 11 p.m., and then perhaps at 2 a.m. she'd wake the cow-boy and together they would start up the mountains to look for the horses and man. Inevitably the weary packie would shout when they met, 'What on earth are you worrying about?'

Arthur kept six harness horses for farm work, with two

always resting. But there was no rest for him. He'd rise at 4 a.m. to work on the farm, sledging boulders and stumps and ploughing the lower land for crops until 8 p.m. each night. As he could afford it, more and more land was added.

It was the high wool prices at the time of the Korean War, when woollen uniforms were required for the armies, that put the Harwoods on their feet. The good prices allowed massive investment in aerial top-dressing. This was to prove an important standby when the tough times came, preventing the land from reverting.

Arthur died in 1974, and his sons Mac and David, with David's wife Elva, took over and faced the tough years, with prices of wool, lamb and beef steadily declining. But the Harwoods know how to survive. 'There's one thing we've learnt,' David says. 'I'm no cow-cocky, but unless you have a dairy farm, you can't afford to run sheep and cattle.'

Today, two of David and Elva's three sons work the 2000-hectare holding, running not only sheep, cattle and deer, but a 650 dairy-cow farm, with the help of 12 employees. The third son runs a dairying enterprise in Chile, all part of the family company. And the Harwoods are still expanding.

In 1990 David took on a 760-hectare property called Turimawiwi, on Golden Bay's far western coast. Two unbridged rivers have to be crossed before you get onto the property, with three more rivers on Turimawiwi itself. Six thousand sheep are fattened here annually for the export market.

When it's time to get the sheep off the place, to be transported to the freezing works north of Wellington, it involves driving the sheep across the mouth of the Anaweka River at low tide, with a 'coacher' singled out from the flock, tied by a length of rope to a quad bike, and quietly pulled across. Only then will the other sheep follow.

Chapter 9

When my sister invited me to the Auckland Arts Festival, in the winter of 1964, I had no hesitation. Blow the cost! Equally important, Garry said he could cope with the children.

I threw myself into attending several events a day. I'd expected the poet, reading his work in the art gallery, to be long-haired and in corduroys, but he was distinguishably suited. Twice I hurried into full-length mirrors in theatre foyers, and apologised profusely to myself.

Soon I became adept at making little darts towards kind faces to ask directions.

'Here, Sophie, take this lady to the bus stop,' shrieked a small girl to her friend who was going my way.

There were six festival films, including the exhilarating and naughty *Tom Jones*, where I sidled past the policewoman at the door, feeling at least under 16 in my holiday exuberance.

I saw all three productions by the New Zealand Opera Company, with my mind going back to the early days of the company, when they'd visited our little town of Collingwood, to give us a taste of professional artistry. Now I sat in an audience sporting furs, fashions and jewels, hairdos and scents. 'Have a scorched peanut?' asked a stranger at *Cosi Fan Tutte*, as if realising I'd missed a meal.

Invited to call on the *Auckland Weekly News* staff, I nervously climbed four flights of stairs, too scared to use the lift. Neil Robinson, the country editor, took me to morning tea in a café where I left my sandwich crusts, with my sister hooting with disapproval when this was reported to her!

I was asked by the *Weekly* to write a report about my enjoyment of the festival, to be completed by 5 p.m. in two days' time. It made me feel like a real journalist! And the *Weekly* also said they would pay my expenses to go further afield than Golden Bay, to research material for articles.

I asked Neil for some helpful criticism, and he told me I wasn't to worry about learning the dos and don'ts. 'One can either write or not, and you have sparkle . . . and that can't be learnt, so you're lucky.'

Wow!

Once home, Garry asked me if I still felt like champagne after my holiday? I do, I do, I said.

I began to worry less about Rocklands, and think more about the successful properties I was writing about for the *Weekly*. Stock agents fed me suggestions about which farms to visit. Some were in Murchison and others were in Nelson's 88 Valley. My expenses were paid so I could go anywhere.

With the children parked with my mother for a week, I tore round Hawke's Bay collecting interviews, to write up once home. The highlight was my visit to Kopua Abbey, the Cistercian monastery, where the monks were permitted to break their vow of silence to talk to me.

I spent two days at the abbey, while staying at a Norsewood hotel. On the second day, a Sunday, I arrived at the abbey at 3 a.m. to share the monks' five hours of Mass, to be withdrawn, halfway through, to be fed bacon and eggs and steaming milk coffee. I learnt later that the monks had bread and butter with tea twice a day, with vegetable soup at midday.

'What about some protein in their diet?' I asked the Abbot.

'What is protein?' replied the old man, Irish, like all but three of the monks.

While the monks were in their picturesque black-and-white Sunday robes, I persuaded one of them to allow me to photograph him on a hilltop. The monastery land was flat. So there we were, a monk in his Sunday robes and myself, tearing up the road in the farm truck to look for a suitable hill. Drivers, coming the opposite way, were almost careering into ditches at seeing a monk and a young woman heading for the hills.

The photo, with the monk framed between two trees on a green hilltop, with a glorious blue sky behind, made the cover of the magazine, which by now had discarded its pink cover for glorious Technicolor and was called the *New Zealand Weekly*.

Seven years on, after supplying a 1200-word article to the *Weekly* each fortnight, quite a strain with young children, I began writing journals for School Publications of the Education Department (later, the recently defunct Learning Media), and then readers for a commercial publisher, Price Milburn. I photographed our children to illustrate the stories, which followed their farm adventures. These were entitled *The PM Country Readers*, and sold in Australia and Britain as well as New Zealand in the late 1960s and early 1970s. This led on to two series of social-studies books, the *Families of New Zealand* and *People at Work*, both published in the 1970s.

The *Families of New Zealand* books, published by Price Milburn, followed real families, sometimes for a year if it was an agricultural subject, such as a dairy farm or an apple orchard. I'd describe each family's work and recreation, their worries and joys, involvement with the children, always emphasising good values. Local teachers would help me choose suitable models.

I had only one week, between trips of the weekly mail truck along the shifting sand at low tide, to cover the lighthouse family at Farewell Spit. The keeper's children were so shy I had to drop bits of fruit cake through the sand hills to entice them to where I wanted them photographed.

Four-year-old Mike came with me to study a timber-mill family at Mangarakau, on the western coast of the Bay. Together we battled sandflies and trudged through the mud to follow the proud skills of the workers, who downed tools at the end of the working day and immediately headed back into the bush to go hunting. Aunt Bet had come south to mind the rest of the family.

For the country-town family I featured Maori friends.

Ramari, the mother, of noble heritage, was a hairdresser. Andy, her husband, had worked in the Bay since he was 22 – he had a second-hand furniture shop, was a land agent amd an auctioneer, taught a Sunday school class, and was in charge of bread delivery. The couple's four children were involved in countless small-town activities, from ballet to rugby.

All the families studied for my books became close friends.

Sally was invited to stay with the orchard family at Riwaka, on the other side of the Takaka Hill, where she amused her hosts with her description of her father's role in a Civil Emergency, as we knew it then. 'It's Dad's job to ride across the river, because the bridge will be down, and no one else has a horse.' Exactly what Garry had to do after riding across the river Sally didn't know, and we were still waiting to find out.

My *People at Work* series featured local people in various occupations, such as truck drivers, the milk lady, a district nurse, shearers and a teacher. Those portrayed like to remind me, many years later, that they appeared in one of my books. I loved learning about other people's lives, and being able to share this understanding in what I wrote. Social studies is my passion. To this day, I want to know all about the activities of whoever I meet.

In 1968 I set up a Community Arts Group, to bring artists, musicians and academics to Golden Bay. At that time, there were about a hundred local people I could rely on to buy a ticket, which I needed to sell in advance of a performance or lecture, to ensure the flights and fees were covered. Seeing me appear at their door, my best supporters may have felt they had little choice about buying a ticket, so I had to make sure I didn't let them down with the standard of the actual event.

The first talents I brought in were Tim Eliott and Martyn Sanderson from Downstage Theatre in Wellington, to perform Gogol's *Diary of a Madman*. I'd hired the largest hall in the district, having sold 293 tickets. It was a huge success. With two of New Zealand's top actors performing, you could have heard a pin drop.

Bruce Mason came for his solo performance of *The End of the Golden Weather*. He had requested a venue where he could perform in the round, under a spotlight. So where did I put him? In the rugby clubrooms, which had circular seating, and for a spotlight, lacking anything else, a bathroom heater lamp.

There Bruce sat, steaming under the heater lamp in his suede jacket, but as the ultimate professional his performance was superb. Years later, I suggested to Bruce he must have dined out hysterically about his trip to Takaka, which included staying with the Robilliards. 'Not a bit of it,' he said politely. 'It was a unique occasion.' I bet!

Well, we did want visiting talents to enjoy their weekends. They would be introduced to interesting locals over shared meals, taken for walks in glorious scenery, and generally made a fuss of.

Academics came to give talks. Jack Shallcrass's rental car bumped cautiously up the drive. He had come from Wellington, where he was senior lecturer in education at Victoria University. I greeted him with particular gratitude – Jack had reviewed my social studies books on National Radio with praise.

We drank coffee sitting on ramshackle chairs on the veranda. Jack's eyes missed nothing. I had tidied up, of course, but to a man more perceptive than most, whose eyes were quick and scrupulous, the cottage would have appeared primitive and unkempt.

'Awful! Chaotic! A tip!' he laughed, recalling his first visit to Rocklands, when I asked him about it years later. Jack was the most urbane person I'd known. To him, Rocklands was 'a bleak tangled wilderness', completely different from anything he'd previously experienced.

I pushed him. 'And what else? How did it strike you when you first came?'

His expression softened, and he chose his words carefully. 'I had a feeling of freedom, not just physical, but an atmosphere of spiritual freedom I have rarely encountered before.'

Well, Jack knew how to dig into a woman's soul. Women could say things to Jack that they wouldn't say to other men, and he listened. He had a way of squeezing his eyes, narrowing them slightly and nodding when you made some point. It made you feel original.

But it was 10-year-old Sally who interested Jack the most; he found her remarkably composed.

Jack charmed the audience with his talk, and enjoyed those he was taken to meet. But not his visit to a local pub, with its usual ring of men at the bar, perched on their accustomed seats. They viewed the outsider suspiciously.

'Take me out of here,' said Jack. 'I'm frightened.'

Of a different cloth – literally – in his odd and brightly coloured clothes, was Dr John Moffat, a genuine eccentric and lecturer in languages at Canterbury Teachers' College. He arrived in Takaka on a Newmans bus, where Garry met him with our old Chev car.

'What a beautiful car,' raved our guest, patting its bonnet. Here was a scholar steeped in classics, languages and philosophy, who composed and played serious music, painted, knitted and sewed clothes, wrote books, articles and newspaper columns . . . and drove and tinkered with classic cars.

Garry took him for a swim at Pohara Beach, where John dog-paddled happily, before asking Garry to point out our farm from this distance. Our mountain was identified.

'Ha!' said John. 'You must be blood group AB.'

'I am actually,' said Garry. He knew his blood type from his six weeks of compulsory military training at age 18. 'But what's that got to do with anything?'

John explained. He had spent six months translating a French doctor's book on the relevance of blood-typing in the perception of human character, and now blood-typed all his students. 'For example,' he said, 'students with blood type A are particularly sensitive and need more encouragement than others. A pat on the back, even when they haven't done well, can work wonders. Blood group AB people are only happy when things are difficult. They are usually only found in isolated parts of the world. Not for them an easy life.'

Well, I thought, when this was reported to me, *that certainly explains a lot about Rocklands' ever-cheerful farmer!*

John didn't want any social visits, preferring a tramp up a gorge, happily bashing through gorse and scrub, to strip off each time a pool was deep enough to hold him. He was superbly fit through his practice of yoga. He denied being labelled an eccentric, saying people were eccentric if they subjected themselves to conformity and ended up in a rut. We had heard his students adored him, with his message to 'Be yourself'.

His talk in Takaka, chosen from the list of 200 topics offered, was autobiographical. It included his first memory, aged three, observing the incandescent beauty of hen's droppings on the sunlit netting of his parents' chook house. He also described a near-drowning experience, when prior to giving a talk in Timaru he did some relaxing yoga in the hotel bath. Having put himself into a challenging position, with his ankles locked behind his head, he'd tipped over and became stuck.

'Only the prospect of my family reading of their father's death upside-down in a bath forced me, somehow, to right myself.'

Some of John's audience decided to be upset at these two revelations, and didn't come to any more Community Arts Group events.

FURTHER DOWN THE COAST, A COUPLE our age were in a similar situation. Mary and John Crockford had bought 2000 sour acres at the same time we bought Rocklands. The Marginal Lands Department, to whom they went for a development loan, were amazed they had bought land so cheaply. They obviously hadn't seen it. It was a peninsula of gutless granite soil smothered in tauhinu, gorse and bracken. But John was incredibly adaptable for a Londoner who'd previously worked in an office.

On immigrating to New Zealand he'd worked for the Forestry Service, and then as a farm worker in Golden Bay, where he'd met Mary, also English, who was here as a midwife.

With the loan from Marginal Lands, John bought a truckload of netting and Waratah standards to fence the property. Wild pigs got into the fences and rolled up all the netting, making the subdivision useless, but John persevered, always cheerful.

He rebuilt their derelict dwelling and harnessed a creek to provide power, to dramatically announce on the phone one evening, 'There's a hedgehog in m'fluming, and he's boosted m'nozzle!'

John and Garry assist each other's musters, spending the night in each other's home to get an early start. Homebrew beer is produced, with sampling lasting until midnight. With the alarm set for 3 a.m. I sit bolt upright, concerned that the men don't sleep in. Garry stumbles off to make breakfast, crashing around the pot cupboard, dropping cutlery, muttering about where is this or that.

With chops sizzling he goes to wake John, who is lying doggo in his sleeping bag. Shaking and hoarse whispers have no effect. It's necessary to pull the body off the bed.

'Get up!'

Nasty mutterings from John. Some time later I hear him drag one foot after another into the kitchen, stumbling into things, scraping his chair on the floor. Porridge and chops are eaten in morose silence.

I don't relax until I hear the truck's wheezy start. The men's dogs are ordered aboard where they scrap and snarl, provoking responses of 'shut up!'

John Thorpe is collected en route, and he and his dogs add to the crush. Six more kilometres to where our back basin looms vaguely in the darkness, and the men ease their legs on the dew-wet grass.

Garry has mustered the higher slopes the day before, pushing the sheep onto the back of the mountain, ready for the joint effort and the final burst homeward.

The musterers separate towards their usual beats, treading softly towards the sleeping sheep camps, from where the dogs are sent out. By getting an early start they avoid trying to move sheep in the heat. After the sun has sent warm, pink glimmers onto the valley floor, it can take four more hours to reach the mountain face.

I rush to clear away the men's breakfast, feed the children theirs, and prepare smoko for the musterers' arrival. It's 9 a.m. before I approach the cow shed. The cows are sulky with neglect, and although bulging udders are dripping they are reluctant to come into the yard. It's now 16 hours since they were last milked, and they provide twice as much as usual. The bucket plant chugs on and on. I use Sally's doll's pram to cart the heavy cream can to the gate, and the pram sheds a wheel under the load. My daughter is furious.

With the sheep in the yards, the men race towards the teapot.

John Crockford is rubbing his bottom, painful from a slide over rocks on his beat. He threatens to sue us for a new pair of trousers. Garry tells him it's not worth the legal fees unless he breaks a leg.

The men look up at the mountain and see a few stragglers. 'They must be yours,' one man accuses another.

'Bet they're not, I didn't miss one.'

The muster is only a prelude to hot, dusty hours in the yards, drafting the sheep. By lunchtime the sheep are sorted, the dogs' barks have run flat, and the musterers are craving a cold beer.

And then small Mike appears, to proudly announce, disastrously, how helpful he's been. 'Dad, Dad! I've opened the gates and let the sheep out!'

IN THE EARLY YEARS, THE SHEARERS LOOK on Rocklands as a shearing paradise, the sheep being mostly bare bellies and necks, with just a little bit of wool on the rump. They arrive in their large shiny cars at 5 a.m, the sheep having been packed into the woolshed the night before, to ensure the wool is dry.

Mick, in blue singlet and jeans with the knees torn out, is in good control of his sheep, but never stops talking. Even from the house I can hear his continuous high-pitched voice above the whir of the shearing machines.

Rob is quieter, preserving his strength. As he dispatches a shorn sheep and collects another woolly from the pen, he shuffles with a stoop characteristic of a shearer who has been around many a shed, a back more stiff than sore, and not worth straightening.

Garry collects each fleece as it falls free and throws it out onto the slotted table, where he pulls off the greasy bits, bracken sticks, gorse and other embedded objects.

Wool isn't worth much these days, compared to the heyday in the late 1940s when high prices were legendary. That's nothing more than a memory now.

At lunch I ask Mick how he manages to talk and shear at the same time. He shrugs and says, 'I'm having a running argument.'

'About what?'

'Politics, of course.'

'I don't listen to what he's saying,' says Rob. 'But Mick's piping screech is better than the music that he used to bring along!'

We learn that Mick had worked in the freezing works as a lad, where he'd listen to the older men argue politics. We also hear how the freezing workers would pull bits of mutton out of their pockets, to put in their bags to take home.

'Yer see,' says Rob, 'if you learnt your politics from those rats, it's best I don't listen!'

COMPLETING THE SHEARING WAS TRICKY with the district's high rainfall. Often there was a rush to get the mob under cover. If the weather was bad and the shearing delayed, the wool deteriorated quickly as bidi-bidi burrs from a ground plant ripened and clung to the fleeces, matting them beyond repair and making them practically worthless.

Meanwhile, the endless farm work went on: post-splitting, fencing, mowing the steep slopes with the garden tractor, using the little machine's plough attachment to cultivate the vegetable garden.

THERE'S NEVER A DULL MOMENT ON ROCKLANDS. Take a sample of morning requests from my husband.

'Tie the dogs up while I shoot into Takaka for some tobacco, will you?'

'Have a look to see if Thomas – the bull – is still in his paddock.'

There will be a request to 'draft a few sheep'. 'A few' usually means two to three hours in the yards.

I am asked to sweep the board for the shearers while Garry fills the shed with more sheep. 'Put the eye-locks in one place and the crutchings in another,' I am told. That's the wool around the sheep's eyes and around its rear end. 'Don't get them mixed.' And a parting shot: 'Count out, will you? The book and pencil are on the ledge inside the door.'

I'm not good at counting sheep. They keep moving. The only way to get them to remain still is to stand at a high point and shout. They will stop to gaze at me stupidly, until one or two become restless and start to run away. If I let them get away with it, the others will do the same. 'Keep still!' I bellow. 'Yes, I mean you. Idiots!' When I do this they turn and stare at me with a vaguely guilty expression and stop moving. It's a bit difficult to have an interesting conversation while counting, but I try.

Something I'm good at, however, is rounding up animals. Unlike the dogs, I understand and obey commands swiftly, and am eager to please. I can run pretty fast.

'Over there!' Garry shouts, waving his arms at one end of the paddock, and I race round the sheep. 'No! Change direction! They're getting away from you!' the boss bellows, and I gallop.

One day, Gerry Vavasour watches this performance, smiles approvingly, and says, 'There was another couple in the district, just the same, except the wife was in her eighties, and they used proper sheep-dog commands.'

TIM HAD AN INFANT POSSUM WHOSE MOTHER had been caught in a trap. He fed the tiny creature with an eye-dropper, and it slept in the pocket of the old suede jacket, an adult cast-off, which Tim wore at night to keep the possum warm. Tragically it was squashed when Tim rolled over in his sleep. Always stoical, Tim didn't say much, despite being distraught.

But death is something our children were exposed to from an early age. They came to accept that animals are born, live their time and die when life is finished. And when life is finished on a farm it often means it ends up on someone's plate, or in a dog bowl.

'The trees are dead,' said three-year-old Sally one winter, as one might announce that a war had started, or Australia had won the Rugby World Cup.

'Not dead,' I said, 'just resting.'

'Are they sleepy?'

'Yes, I suppose they are.'

'Then why aren't they lying down?'

MURIEL BARTLETT HAD CANCER. This was my first experience of having a neighbour so unwell. The local doctor advised surgery, but Muriel preferred the methods of a woman doctor in Hamilton, who was prescribing alternative methods for other cancer patients in the district.

This meant sacks of carrots, which Uno, Muriel's husband, was juicing by the litre.

It didn't work. Muriel's pain increased. She asked me to phone the Hamilton doctor and seek some reassurance. 'Just keep up the carrot juice,' was the reply.

FROM TOP

Me, my mother Elinor, and sister Jennie. Jennie and I in Woodford House uniforms, 1950. Me, age three. Jennie and I, ready to cycle 5 miles to Queenswood, our primary school in Hastings, 1943. Me, age five, with my father Campbell.

THIS PAGE

Me as a Girl Guide in 1944, starting my nursing career at Christchurch Public Hospital in 1952, and my wedding day in 1956.

TOP
The Aorere River that gnaws at the mountains in floods to spread fertile soil in the valleys.

BOTTOM
Looking down at Upper Takaka from Takaka Hill.

TOP
The mountain on Rocklands.

BOTTOM
The woolshed amongst
Paulownia trees.

TOP

Edwin (Ned) Richards, droving cattle with his brother Jack from their west coast Golden Bay farm to the freezing works in Nelson – a four- to five-day journey – in their eighties.

MIDDLE

The Rocklands sheep yards with our early home at the far left and the barn on the right.

BOTTOM

Garry, Sally and Tim with the garden tractor – the only tractor on the 1500-acre property for many years.

FROM TOP

Tim, Adrian Moleta and David Edmondson – 'The Good Guys Club' – Tim's friends from neighbouring steep hill farms. Mike and Sally fishing for freshwater crayfish. The annual pet show at Motupipi School; Sally is in the middle. Sally, age seven.

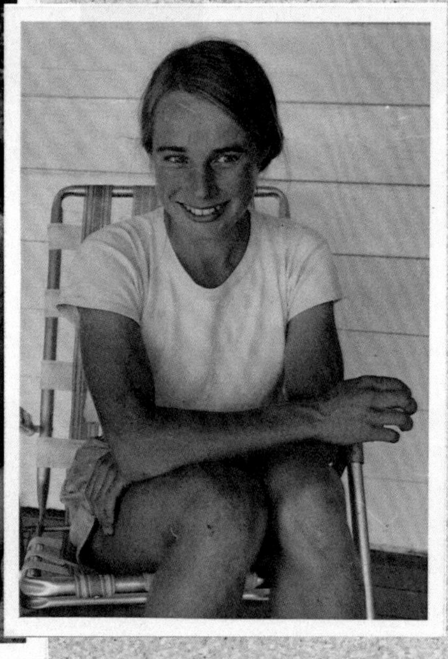

TOP
Jock Stocker, who led the family on annual tramps in the mountains of Golden Bay.

BOTTOM, LEFT
Tim, age 14, in 1971.

BOTTOM, RIGHT
Sally, age 12, in 1971.

TOP
Tata Beach with the golden sand.

MIDDLE
Collingwood, Golden Bay's second small township.

BOTTOM
Takaka township.

LEGENDARY GOLDEN BAY PERSONALITIES, CLOCKWISE FROM TOP LEFT

Paul Kilgour – happiest when tramping alone in New Zealand's remotest areas. Derry Kingston, who runs Heaphy Help. Joyce Wyllie from Kaihoka Station. Frank Soper, who was instrumental in having Kahurangi National Park established.

CLOCKWISE FROM TOP LEFT

Jane Dixon, co-owner with her husband Andrew, of The Mussel Inn. Gerard Hindmarch, author and journalist. Albie Burgess, inventor and computer specialist. Leentje and Richard Thorpe. Sandra and Ken Closs, sitting on their house steps at Te Hapu.

TOP
Milnethorpe Park Scenic Reserve.

MIDDLE
Dick Nicholls, who created Milnethorpe Park Scenic Reserve.

BOTTOM
Dairy cows grazing in Takaka Valley.

TOP

The house Garry built himself over four years, designed by architect Ian Athfield.

BOTTOM

The same house perched on its hill overlooking Golden Bay.

TOP
The 100 acres of flat land bought in later years in front of Rocklands' mountainous country. The current Robilliard home is at the edge of Motupipi Estuary, out of sight on the left.

MIDDLE
Garry at peace on the farm.

BOTTOM
Garry's barn surrounded by Paulownia trees in flower.

BELOW
Me on my daily walk up a hill.

RIGHT
At Bluff on my cycle ride around the South Island, age 69.

BOTTOM
The Wednesday Walkers group on a tramp to an early settler house at Awaroa.

PHOTOS © NUSHKA LANGE

TOP
A hilltop walk near Cape Farewell.

ABOVE
Harwood Hole Track.

TOP
Wainui Bay from the Abel Tasman National Park.

MIDDLE
Separation Point, Abel Tasman National Park.

BOTTOM
Sunset at Patons Rock beach, north of Takaka.

The time came when Muriel's pain was unbearable, and she gave in.

I accompanied her in the ambulance to Nelson Hospital. On the return journey, worried about my friend, I was glad of the distracting conversation of George the ambulance driver.

I'd heard people mention his 'exuberant driving' but I had nothing but praise for his skill. George had coaxed and bullied a succession of ambulances over the twisting mountainous road in all kinds of weather to carry all types of patients. On one occasion the roof of his vehicle had been ripped open, leaving a gaping hole which he'd plugged with towels and sheets. He'd also faced medical emergencies on the road, frequently involving administering oxygen to patients in the front passenger seat.

George told me he'd arrived in this country in 1911, aged five. He'd drifted into teaching, eventually reaching Collingwood's sole-charge secondary school, where he'd taught himself shorthand and typing, keeping a day ahead of his pupils.

'With some kids you might want to wring their necks, but there will always be intelligent children, and you have to recognise them.' George wanted to see changes where children didn't have to stay at school until 15 or 16, and annoy the teachers and class. 'Let them go out into the community and find their own way. Then, when they have reached an age of reason, allow them to return to school.'

At 74 George had shared the district's sadnesses and triumphs, disputes and agreements, for more than four decades. His years at Collingwood had coincided with the Doctors War, the Cream Can War and the High School War – local arguments and debates, with family members who'd participated in one or all of these still not speaking to each other.

Muriel was not to return from the Nelson Hospital.

ONE OF THE FIRST THINGS WE DID on taking on Rocklands was to find a suitable hack for Garry's farm work. Florin was bought, a 14-year-old mare who was the proud offspring of several prize-winning show horses. She was level-headed, most of the time, never flying into fits over flapping tin on wind-battered sheds or earth-shaking dynamite blastings, and docile as a cow when being led while giving children rides.

But once she was out the gate and up on the hills she walked only sideways, and always bolted homeward at the end of a long, hard day. I didn't consider Florin my cup of tea, with each addition to the family making me increasingly nervous of horses.

A woman visitor asked for a ride one day. On being assured she was an experienced rider I saw her canter off, only to return half an hour later in a neighbour's truck. Apparently, Florin had set off and jumped three fences, parting company with her rider on the fourth – the rider having had no intention to jump any of them.

We were given a huge draught horse to be killed for dog tucker, but the animal was so immense and loveable that no one wanted him killed. So Dobbin lived on a few more years, making himself useful carting fence posts, and gently living out his last days until he died quietly by himself where no dogs could find him.

A neighbour gave us Lassie, a brown mare who also had several famous offspring. There was something wrong with her back. Riding her was like driving a truck with one wheel missing, bumpy and lopsided. She was also adept at shying. Once, when Garry let go of the reins to roll a cigarette, Lassie saw something worth a fright and ducked sideways, down and out of Garry's legs, leaving him astride a thistle bush, still rolling his smoke.

We bred a foal from Lassie. Lucky was born one hot February, and after a few months in the front paddocks, where she would create havoc by scattering sheep and cattle, she was banished with her mum to the back country where she grew up strong in the high altitude and sure-footed among the rocks and steep hills.

The fifth horse acquaintance then arrived – a fat chestnut pony named Goldy, with a cream mane and tail. No show pony but a quiet, suitable mount for our young children.

Garry was telling me how much grass a horse eats, and I was telling him how lucky we were to get a reliable pony. My husband also said that children didn't need a pony until they could catch it themselves, but I assured him that would be no trouble at all.

The day Goldy arrived, trotting gaily up the road with her long-legged former owner, I eyed the new pet with interest. I noticed that she swerved when she saw the children's and my eager faces, showing much white of eye and generally looking suspicious.

Taking the former owner aside, I questioned her about Goldy's 'little ways' and learnt that she didn't like men. Bang went my rosy dreams of sending Garry off with a leading rein towing keen little riders as he went about farm work. Nor did Goldy like rushing, yapping farm dogs. I realised Goldy and I were going to see a lot of each other if the children were to learn to ride.

Daily the lessons progressed, but the children weren't yet strong enough to stop the pony plunging her head down for grass, with an outraged rider sailing over her head.

The grooming sessions were more straightforward. It was common to see Sally and Mike with their hairbrush and a fork for a comb, untangling Goldy's mane, with two dairy calves shampooing what was left of the pony's tail with their chewing and slobbering.

WHEN TIM WAS SIX HE WAS INVITED to spend a few days in Nelson, his first stay in a city. I took him to the bus, with a card pinned to his jersey giving his name and destination, and looked for a kind fellow passenger. A dear soul, having observed my anxious look, offered to make sure Tim got back on the bus after the loo stop in Motueka.

I waved goodbye to the pale little face, and a brave smile peered back at me.

Five days later I was late in meeting the returning bus, and expected to find a bereft son in tears. Not a bit of it. There Tim was, puffed up with importance, directing the driver concerning his luggage. He appeared to have adopted the confidence of a world-class traveller. Overflowing with exuberance he described ships loading at the port, the comings and goings at the airport, axe-chopping competitions and, best of all, the fairy-tale delight of Pixie Town. The new confidence our son had gained in less than a week was extraordinary.

He leapt onto Goldy's back one day and suddenly became a rider. Thrusting his feet into the stirrups, he asked for a stick, roared in stentorian tones to 'giddy up' and took off. All arms and legs, Tim and pony shot down a steep bank, disappeared behind the hen house, swooped under low tree branches, and tore back to the woolshed at a canter.

'Well done!' I yelled, as Tim tore past. 'Hang on!' I shrieked as he tipped precariously over one side of the saddle.

It was a six-foot six-year-old I tucked in his bed that night.

'Did you see me ride fast?' Tim piped. 'Did you see me?'

'I saw you, little man,' I replied. 'I saw you grow up fast.'

AFTER SOME YEARS WE COULD AFFORD a real tractor. The day the small crawler arrived I refused to watch it unloaded, worried about the risks Garry would take with it. Sure enough, it was off and away up the hills to be tried out before I even knew what colour it was.

Dragging one foot after another as he returned from the school bus, Tim saw the track marks and shot off after them.

Three times – that I know of – in coming months, Garry rolled the tractor, each time, thank God, landing on his feet beside it.

It was often well after dark when he returned to the house. I would worry that he might have had an accident, but once he went out the gate in the morning I would have no idea where he was. He might tell me where he intended to go, but that wasn't always where he ended up.

Once, however, he came home from the back country to inform me that one of the dogs had fallen down a tomo. 'I thought I'd better tell someone before I go down the hole to rescue it.' But if Garry didn't reappear, how was I to know which hole? The land was riddled with tomo. Fortunately, both man and dog made it home safely.

A PADDOCK HAS BEEN PLOUGHED AND HAND-SOWN with turnips and grass seed. I become involved when Garry constructs an apparatus to blow lime onto the hillside. It is a huge blowing machine, run by a petrol engine, which eats up sacks of lime before blowing it out a side funnel. The apparatus is bolted to the tractor-drawn trailer.

It's my job to stand on the tilting, rocking trailer and tip sacks of lime into the blower. But soon I'm hanging upside-down from the moving trailer, with Garry yelling from the tractor, 'Drop off! Drop off!' I'd do just that if a hefty bag of lime were not clamped across my feet. A sudden jolt has made me lose my balance and upset the stack of bags at the same time.

We decide to swap jobs. I am to drive the crawler. It has five different knobs with which to work it. There is so much noise, with the petrol motor chugging and the blower whining, that directions to tell me how to drive have to be bellowed.

'As long as I know how to stop the thing,' I yell back. I scream at the children to stay well away. I get the tractor going while Garry balances himself on the trailer, with the lime spreading clouds of dust across my path. Visibility is nil.

'Look out! Keep left! Turn! Rock ahead!' Garry shouts.

It's a nightmare. I'm terrified. I ask for my old job back on the trailer. This means keeping my balance while I lift heavy bags to pour lime into the blower. And then, with the last sack emptied, the lightened trailer tips and catapults me down the hillside. I keep myself rolling, faster and faster, imagining the blower and its motor chasing after me, to suck me into its system. Not until I reach a creek at the bottom of the gully do I look back, to see the trailer still attached to the tractor, and Garry roaring with laughter.

'That's it! I'm fed up!' I stamp off home. To hell with this lime-spreading job.

Next day I calm down, and offer to be tractor driver again. But I'm so nervous that I'm constantly jamming on the brakes while I examine the rocks ahead. After a day of this slow progress, Garry takes on both jobs. He sets the crawler moving, jumps onto the trailer to feed the blower with lime, and leaps back onto the tractor when it needs to change direction. Highly dangerous work.

I'm a useless sook. I know it!

Chapter 10

Having had a week away myself in the depths of a damp and drippy winter, when I fled like a drab moth towards bright city lights, I was determined that Garry should have his turn.

Day after day he had toiled on the tractor, reducing a gorse-ridden hilltop to smooth soil. When at last the seeds were sown and top-dressed, I sped the reluctant farmer on his way to the airport.

'Have a good time,' I insisted, hoping there would be enough excitement once Garry was with family and friends to prevent him worrying about rain needed for the crop and my ability to cope alone, and not be regretting a 'wasted week of social frittering' as he called it, when there was so much work to be done at home.

I envisaged a peaceful time, with meals at regular hours. Ha!

I had been boss for barely half an hour when a young heifer got out of the calf paddock and met up with her milking mother, whom she hadn't seen for eight months, and proceeded to suck her dry. A carton of six pullets was delivered, which Mike opened, allowing the pullets to find seclusion under the house. Then another heifer got into trouble. She had been grazing beside the woolshed and put her head under the outside steps and got stuck. A vet came to tranquillise her while we cut away the steps, at great expense.

The local librarian phoned to say she was sending me two visitors, one being a radio personality from Wellington. But there was a stinking dead sheep where the visitors would park their car. I struggled to get the rotten corpse onto the back of the truck. I got the front of the sheep on, but when I heaved up the back quarters the front fell off. By the time I succeeded the smelly corpse had disintegrated further. I took a shower but still smelt of dead sheep!

No sooner had the bemused visitors departed, when I noticed

that sheep were streaming away up the mountain, having broken down a rough gate of netting and barbed wire, which cut into my hands as I tried to close it. A gale roared in from the coast. 'Other people have proper gates and posts to hang them on,' I screamed into the wind. 'Why can't we?'

'All down, all down!' shrieked the wind. And down went the flimsy gate, time after time, as I tried to resurrect it. A mob of happy sheep surged past, tumbling me about on their backs. The last ewe hooked one foot inside my boot, adding my prostrate form to that of the gate.

FOR TASKS NEARER HOME, I had a tourist family in the second cottage to help. The father, called Jack, was happy to carry pig buckets, mend Tim's bike puncture and generally be on hand. Little did I know, at the beginning of their holiday week, what great efforts I was going to need of him!

While milking one evening I was visited by three errant pigs who had escaped from their sty. They were grubbing their way around yards and bush with excited snorts. Calling my willing bucket-carrier we sped up the gulley, laying a trail of food scraps to entice the pigs back to the sty. But a fourth pig was nowhere in sight. Calling failed to produce a sight of him.

The holiday-makers had planned to go fishing. I insisted they went, leaving me to trail the bush line, calling the pig, who, with his mates, was due to go to the abattoir and therefore worth a lot of money.

Hearing a scuffle where roosting hens had flown squawking, I pelted up the rocks towards the disturbance. Only to find, once up there, that the snuffling now came from ground level. The land is riddled with tomo. Back down I went, spilling bits of potato peel and burnt custard all over my rushing tracks.

Once down I again heard the snuffle up above, and one more climb found me face-to-face with my missing porker. Face-to-face but separated dramatically by a metre-wide chasm, at least 18 metres in depth. There stood my pig, on a small islet of rock, trembling at the brink of the crevasse.

'Stay there, nice piggy,' I urged, terrified he would move and disappear into the tomo. I retreated into the bush to have a little think. I couldn't imagine how the pig had got there. But more importantly, how to get him out?

I fetched a rope from the shed and some skim milk. When I returned the pig had disappeared from view and was scrambling and snorting in a smaller hole, right at my feet.

I edged down a ridge until I could lean out and drop a lasso into the hole. I trickled drops of milk down the rock to entice the pig forward, and tried time after time to hook the rope around his neck. Several times I succeeded, but one wild pull and the slippery pig backed out. Just as well. If I'd managed to lasso the pig's neck, I could have strangled him, and him not even bacon! I went home to put the children to bed. There was no sign of the tourist family.

Returning to the scene of the drama I found the pig had scrambled up to an isolated rock pinnacle. I climbed into the hole below him to set up a rope trap, so that when food enticed him back into the hole I would have him snared. He leapt into the hole in a great hurry. I shot up the opposite bank even faster, and neglected to take time to pull in the noose. By now it was dark. I reluctantly went home to bed.

Crack of dawn found me heading up the well-worn track, trailed now by Jack, with his wife and small son, and piping along in the rear, with lots of advice, our daughter.

The pig had come back to the top storey. We needed to construct a bridge for the pig to walk across. Jack axed down some bush and I collected some wooden railings. These, covered in sacks, made a shaky, but passable bridge to terra firma.

Jack climbed into the hole behind the pig, while I crept across the bridge on all fours to meet the pig with a bowl of porridge. Slowly I edged back, enticing the pig onwards with soggy piles of food and endless sweet nothings. At long last we had him on firm ground.

I wasted no time in ordering the pig truck.

AS AN ECONOMIC MEASURE, Garry does the crutching himself, when only the wool off the face and the poo-matted wool around the rear end of the sheep are shorn, to limit fly infestation in hot weather.

My heart bleeds for my man as he labours day after day. It's backbreaking work for someone who doesn't do enough of it to become hardened. When he comes in at night he stretches out on the kitchen floor to straighten his aching back.

And then there is dipping, to rid each sheep of lice. Not to dip your sheep is unlawful. Garry wakes me at 5 a.m. with a cup of tea. 'Want some bread?'

But he's gone before I can answer. He's already been up for two hours mustering in the sheep. Now I must join him in the yards.

I have a long hooked stick with which to push each sheep under the foul-smelling mixture in the deep trench, laced as it is with rank-smelling pesticides, to make sure they've each been adequately submerged.

Knowing what confronts them, the sheep dash this way and that in the yards, kicking up dust, exasperating the boss. But the sheep have just got to put up with it, like the docking, the ear-marking, the shearing and all the rest of it. The oldest sheep are the worst. They keep turning back. They remember earlier dippings, and inevitably have to be persuaded, wheelbarrow fashion, with Garry holding up their back legs to propel them forward. Faced with the dip, they make a leap, with Garry hanging on until the last second, forcing them to dive in head-first, rather than soar over the dip. The odd one makes a belly flop and doesn't get its head wet. It's my job to force it under with my crook.

The annual dipping provides the opportunity for me to check sheep numbers. How many have we lost this year?

Garry prefers not to know.

IN GOOD WEATHER LAMBING IS A FAIRLY SIMPLE AFFAIR. The older ewes are sensible mothers, best left to themselves to get on with giving birth and bringing up their offspring. It's the younger sheep, the two-tooths, who can be scatty. Sometimes there is a young ewe without much milk who tends to keep forgetting about her baby, until the lamb falls prey to a hawk.

There will be cases of mispresentation which need help. The lamb's head and two front legs should be the first to show, but sometimes one leg is tucked back. It's then necessary to gently press the head back into the uterus, lock a finger behind the knee of the backward-lying leg and carefully pull the limb forward to the position for correct presentation.

Bad weather brings the real trouble. A spell of cold rain can lead to disastrous results, and half the newborn lambs can be lost. Heavy rain will so chill a weak lamb that it never rises to its feet after birth, and flooded streams will drown others. Garry heads out into a flooded dawn, to return with his shirt bulging with its load of limp newborn lambs. We dunk them in tubs of warm water, and place them on sacks before a heater lamp, until, hopefully, the first feeble mewing is heard, and they start to stand and look for supplementary feeding.

Suitably revived, most are returned to their mothers, with the ewe tied to a fence, or placed in a small pen to make sure she allows the lamb to drink, and thus accepts it. It doesn't always work, and the lamb returns to the house as a pet.

Little lamb Charlie had been born to a bossy mother, who surprised Garry by producing a lamb at his feet when she already had a week-old lamb at her side, which, he surmised, she'd kidnapped from another ewe. When her own plopped out, she sniffed scornfully and walked away with her stolen offspring, without a backward glance.

Charlie thrived at the house and grew sturdy and bouncy. At meal times he was sometimes approached by all three children, each with a bottle of warm milk. Accepting this doting homage, Charlie would drink till fit to burst. He won prizes at the school's Pet Show, but not for the lead competition, when he set off at a gallop, dragging Sally, spreadeagled on the grass, behind him.

Lucy Lamb thought she was human, and insisted on coming inside the house, scattering pellets everywhere. Once, unknown to me, she urinated on my iron, which exploded in a mass of stinking flame when I switched it on.

The day we put pet lambs into the garden they only wanted to eat flowers and vegetables. 'That's the silverbeet gone,' said Garry when he'd come into lunch. As he went out he observed there weren't any carrot tops either. A gang of lambs would follow me when I hung up the washing and would wipe their faces on the sheets.

Another event at the Pet Show was the sand saucer and sand tray competition. 'Come on, get up,' I'd yell to the children on the day of this event. Not only were the pet lambs to be washed, dried and pushed into the car, but sand trays and sand saucers had to have last-minute touches, with fresh flowers and greenery added.

With the children fighting for space on the back seat among the lambs, I'd tear down the road to the school. One time, arriving late, I slammed on the brake as the school bell tolled, causing the decorated exhibits to crash off the front seat. Ruined! Yells of outrage. I slunk home to be calmed by my cows.

BIG STRETCHES OF FENCES WERE IN CONSTANT need of repair. Sheep-yard gates were rotting, shed roof iron was leaking. And yet every moment seemed to be filled with routine and seasonal farm work; there was no spare time for improvements or repairs.

But the lack of these made routine work take longer. Sheep escaped through gaps in the fences and had to be retrieved; gates sagged on their hinges. Some of the repairs would have taken only a few minutes, but there never seemed to be minutes to spare.

Garry's multipurpose tool for gate latches, fixing fences, holding up trousers and leashing dogs was binder twine. When accompanying him in pouring rain in the truck, I cursed the broken, tied-up contraptions that pass for gates. They were a fiddle at any time, but in the rain the string was wet and my fingers cold. How did Garry drive through these gates every day and not go insane? When we were finally done, it came out of me. 'How do you live with these gates?' I asked.

His reply was explosive. 'When can I fix them? The only spare time I've got is between 10 p.m. at night and 5 a.m. in the morning, and then I'm sleeping!'

There was work on this place for six men, and Garry was only one.

'If money was no object, do you think we should carry on battling Rocklands?' I once asked.

Money *was* the object, but Garry tried to answer my question anyway. 'I see no reason to leave,' he said. 'It's a privilege to have had this opportunity.'

Then the fresh smell of spring would make up for my doubts about battling this land and making our future here. With wild daffodils appearing, and quail families with 10 or 12 babies each, and fat pigeons flying *thwack, thwack* overhead like overloaded freight planes, I realised, tough life or not, there were definitely compensations.

Again, lecturing myself, justifying things, I had absolutely no doubt at all that were we to sell Rocklands when the prices were bad, with the house just a shack, and, most importantly, without giving the children a country childhood, it would have brought on a cowardly sense of failure. I could not have forgiven myself.

THE CHILDREN ARE EXPECTED TO PITCH IN with farm work, and every penny available goes back into the hungry land. Even as four-year-olds they were helping with musters, climbing the hills like mountain goats. Hauled out of bed they stumbled into coats of sorts, to dodge ruts and stones, often barefoot. Their usual task was to reach Coppells Spur, a branch off the mountain, which had a fence of sorts running from bluff to bluff – and wait there, to make sure the sheep didn't double back.

Docking became easier once the children were older. In the early years we would have an infant in a carrycot parked in shady rushes, or in a sacking bag suspended from a tree or a gate, with holes for their little legs to stick out. The lambs were docked in September. That's getting rid of the tails, and the purse on the male lambs. If the tail is left on, poo will stick to it and attract flies, then the sheep become flyblown with maggots. The whole family helps with docking. Garry goes off ahead to muster in a paddock of ewes and lambs, with the children and I to follow to help set up the temporary yards.

'Hammer, Mike,' the boss calls, and our youngest staggers

up with a sledgehammer bigger then himself.

'Stakes, Sally,' and she brings an armful of manuka stakes.

Tim's task, if not at school, is to count the tails at the end of a morning's work. The children catch the lambs and pass them to me, to hold on the docking frame. Garry uses a hot iron to burn off the purse and tail. This way there is little bleeding or chance of infection. Each lamb is ear-marked with a clipper, either left or right ear, according to its sex.

Mike, knowing his father is cheered by a majority of females to increase flock numbers, will be crouched down in the mob, looking at each lamb's genitals. 'Here's a girl,' he will shout, but is eventually knocked over by a stampede of sheep. Only a bellow tells us where he is in the smother, to plunge an arm down to pull him out. His task having palled, our youngest sits on a rock, dangling a piece of a lamb's anatomy from a stick over a puddle, in the imagined hope of catching a fish.

The lambs are weaned in late November. We do a sex draft, when I work the gate, with Garry further down the race to observe from the ear marks the sex of each sheep. He yells me gate instructions. 'Left. Right. Right. Left. Right. Right.' But I can't always remember six instructions ahead. Swearing, Garry has to catch the lamb I've misdirected and heave it into the right pen.

WE WOULD TELL EVERYONE we had a multitude of house sites on the hills in front of the mountain – we were just putting up with the cottage in the meantime. But the putting-up part began to look like lasting many, many years. No sooner had we arrived in 1957 – buying our sheep at golden-fleece prices – than wool prices started a decline which lasted for over three to four decades, before we could even get the first wool off their backs. One by one, the old envelopes sporting a variety of house plans were discarded. And while it's all very well to say one can live in a log cabin as long as it's one's own, this palls after several years' acquaintance when in reality it's a shabby, damp dwelling.

A family of mice lived behind the bulges of the ripped scrim of our bedroom. They were forever squeaking and scrabbling. This could make reading in bed quite difficult. 'Will you please be quiet?' I'd demand, staring vexedly at the sagging wallpaper. About once a year I'd do a prima donna act, and declare with passion, 'I can't stand this mess any longer.' This was particularly effective when Garry had just put his foot through a rotten floorboard.

So a rash promise was made to spend some precious 'not-increasing-sheep-numbers time' on renovations. We started at one end of the dwelling, and over the ensuing years worked our way ever so slowly through it.

Almost everything in our building construction had once belonged to someone else. We bought a lean-to from a derelict cottage in a nearby paddock for £20. Garry collapsed whole walls with his chainsaw, and delivered them on George, prefabricated fashion, to our doorstep. He'd carefully marked numbers on doors and windows he'd removed, to simplify putting it back together, but somehow that didn't work out, and the windows had a drunken slant.

An unsuspecting friend arrived for Easter, and was roped in to hold up whole walls while they were nailed into place. The veranda was renewed from timber felled on the place, and milled locally. But the timber was green and buckled, leaving gaps through which our children, when small, pushed cutlery, plates, knitting needles, or meals they didn't want to eat.

There were months between building activity, when

sawdust, old planks of wood holding rusty nails and untidy heaps of corrugated iron lay everywhere. For six years we lived in a timberyard, surrounded by pieces of board salvaged from someone else's demolition. The children lost tools, played perilously under gaps in the floor, spilt nails and covered themselves in wood shavings which they spread through the house. Treading on rusty nails was a daily hazard, and we all took long-lasting anti-tetanus injections.

We haunted house sites where new homes were being built on the site of old dwellings, and found a pair of French doors which had been lying under a hedge. We obtained old matchboard lining to make window seats and cupboards. Nobody but us wanted the old-fashioned lift-and-heave sash windows – they were usually given away. Nelson City Council advertised three large square windows with small panes, from a demolished building, with only the freight to be paid. These suited our old-fashioned cottage.

'How sweet!' visitors exclaimed when observing alterations in progress, having also observed our original squalor. The sight of whole walls collapsing, or being held up by a weary wife, while an irritable, thumb-hitting husband bashed at second-hand bent nails, moved onlookers to admiration.

Our best bargain was obtained when a mine in the Cobb Mountains was closed and its buildings were auctioned. Each building purchased had to be removed within 48 hours. Garry set off with chainsaw, food, billy and a sleeping bag to sleep overnight in the cab of the truck in freezing conditions, and was besieged by mosquitoes. He bought the bagging shed for £7 and chainsawed down the corners to pile the walls onto a transport truck. This purchase provided two more bedrooms and a bathroom, where at last we could install a flush loo.

The kitchen was the last renovation. A dividing wall was to come down between the kitchen and scullery, with large windows added to bring in the sun. With a forecast for rain, Garry agreed to start work. An electrician and a Post and Telegraph technician were needed to move the electric stove and the telephone, which were attached to the wall we wanted to take down. Garry had the outside wall down quickly, thanks to his chainsaw, and now the weather pelted in. The technicians arrived and gaped as he carved out great hunks of wall, saying to anyone interested, 'That's a doorway, and the window can go here.'

With the noise of the chainsaw, and the fumes of its smoke, the atmosphere was intense! Shrugging his shoulders, the electrician got out his power drill and added its whine to the commotion. The Post and Telegraph technician, having asked where I wanted the phone re-installed with signals, looked nervously at the chainsaw attacks.

And then the bees arrived. Finding a hole in the wall, where the sink pipes had been withdrawn, and furious at being disturbed, they flew at everyone. 'I'll fix them,' said Garry, tearing around the swarm with his chainsaw. 'This'll scare them away.'

Not a bit of it. Above the din I heard Garry's yelps of pain as the bees retaliated.

I remembered something I'd read. 'Don't be scared of the bees,' I yelled. 'They know when you're scared, and they sting scared people.'

'How can I not be scared?' Garry shouted. 'I'm terrified of bees. But somebody's got to get the buggers out of here!'

A shiny car arrived at the house, and a commercial traveller emerged. What would he think? A small, shabby house, open to the elements, a wild-looking woman swatting bees with a rolled-up newspaper, and an even wilder male chasing them with a chainsaw. The technicians were out of sight, hiding in their vans.

I explained about the bees, and Garry's efforts to frighten

them away, to which the traveller explained, bellowing above the din, that beekeepers rattle a tin to call in their bees. With the roaring chainsaw we must have called in every bee in the valley!

'But hey,' the man said, 'I have just what you need.' He pulled out a tin of insecticide from his bag, which he sprayed around until every bee had fled. Or was dead.

'Hurray!' I thanked the salesman.

'Do you like our altered kitchen?' Garry asked him cheerfully.

'Is that what it is?' the man looked at the gaping abyss exposing us to the elements, the borer-ridden boards, dislocated pipes, and the telephone wires trailing from a half-demolished wall.

'Man,' he said, 'I am so sorry!' And he gestured away payment for the insecticide.

WHEN THE VAVASOURS' ANCESTRAL PROPERTY on the east coast came up for sale, Gerry had the right to take up a block at less than market value. 'If we don't buy it we'll lose capital, because the land is undeveloped,' Bernard told his father.

Gerry was uncertain. Having, in his relatives' opinion, married beneath him, he knew there'd be no easy acceptance by Marlborough's squatocracy. He also considered he'd thrived, been happy, on his difficult farm. 'My life has been tough, very tough,' he said, 'but I don't farm for money, but because I like the life.' He knew, however, that for his children's sake they should take up this opportunity and move to decent land.

Would they be able to sell Rock Glen, Garry and I wondered. It wasn't everyone's cup of tea.

'It will sell,' said Gerry with his usual faith. And indeed it did.

Our new neighbours on Rock Glen were Jan and Salvy Moleta. I met Jan when I was becoming exasperated by my attempt to retrieve a mob of sheep that had got onto the road. There were a multitude of little tracks up through the scrub lining the road, and the sheep found them all. I had chased them exasperatedly for about an hour when this attractive young woman stopped her car, and expertly blocked the sheep in their attempts to escape.

This was the beginning of my friendship with an exceptional woman, who combined a trained teacher's wisdom with determination and endurance. Someone my age, with young children, who also faced the battle of survival on a mountainous landscape.

We didn't meet often, but talked almost daily on the phone, sharing our frustrations and jokes. Such as the time Jan forgot to put her latest baby in the car when delivering her other five children to school. Five minutes after she left Salvy discovered the baby on the kitchen table, screaming blue murder, with his only food source in the world heading down the road at 80 kilometres per hour!

Jan went at life at full steam. She would be up half the night preparing nature projects for her children. Collections of native flora to be pressed and named, native birds studied. The Moleta children always won first prize in the annual Forest and Bird competition.

The eldest son, Adrian, with David from another steep farm, were Tim's best friends. They formed the Good Guys Club, with a disused pig sty on Rocklands for their club house. They'd bike to visit each other in weekends, and were, by and large, left to fend for themselves.

We mothers agreed that our insistence on fresh air, stinginess with pocket money and intolerance for anything with a plug or a battery served them well. Of course the boys were going to do dangerous things, but they'd been taught to think for themselves, so no serious harm resulted. Perhaps most importantly, they had a great deal of fun.

But the story of Jan is an incomplete one. The struggle on tough land she could cope with, but of more concern was her children's education. One day, when the four daughters were between eight and 12, they and their mother disappeared. They'd moved to Auckland to live in a basement, with Jan working at three jobs, in order to afford top city schools for her daughters.

Salvy, bewildered, was left with the two sons, with Leon only two. There was a custody battle. Social Welfare said Salvy could keep both boys if he had a woman to help.

There were three spinster aunts, Salvy's sisters, elegant, charming women, living in Wellington. One of them, Lena, came to live at Rock Glen, with Aunts Muffy and Maria visiting at Christmas.

On Salvy's death Adrian took over Rock Glen, to drop dead, tragically, aged 40, on a muster. His widow, to survive, sold off the place in blocks. Leon, after working for 17 years as a shearer, and then with better wages at the dairy factory, has managed to buy back most of Rock Glen – with just 11 hectares still to purchase. He uses days off to spray gorse and barberry, and look after his 150 sheep. The flatter land is leased to a dairy farmer to pay the interest on two mortgages.

Leon and Garry were talking recently about the Moletas' back country, the sheer, rocky, piecing land I had viewed from our back boundary. Awesome, vicious land I'd observed, where Garry and the Vavasours had erected a boundary fence in the late 1950s.

'It's terrible land,' I pointed out.

'Nonsense. I love it,' said Leon. Just as Garry has loved every inch of our own hard country.

AS THE YEARS WENT ON, WE FOUND other friends we treasured – unique, extraordinary people, such as are attracted to isolated regions, from whom we learnt so much.

One of the most influential was undoubtedly Jock Stocker, who lived with his wife Eve and three children in a little house up among the limestone outcrops on the outskirts of Takaka. It had been built cheaply during the war, with fibrous board walls and a Malthoid roof, but no other dwelling in the 1960s attracted such intellectual debate and discussion. Each Friday evening it was the venue for a Workers' Educational Association (WEA) discussion group. In later years, when WEA was no longer government-funded, Garry continued his Friday-night visits. There he would talk with Jock over endless cups of tea, sometimes until 3 a.m., and then be too stimulated to sleep.

Jock was an ideas man, a good listener and a gentleman, who never spoke ill of anyone. Totally unambitious and unpretentious, for most of his adult life he was a shift-worker at the local cement works. I never saw him in anything but shorts and hobnailed boots. His parents had lost their North Canterbury farm during the 1930s Depression. Ten years old at the time, the eldest of three brothers, he told how his family walked off the land with just £13 in a golden-syrup tin. 'We used the tin as a football when we picnicked en route to Christchurch, to live with our grandparents.'

Having left school at 15 to work as a drover and shearer, Jock educated himself from books. With several clergymen in his ancestry, he was religious until his late teens. He could still quote the *Prayer Book* from memory, but, after studying science and philosophy, he replaced religion with atheism. The cement-works job paid well, but was soul-destroying in its boredom. Jock was far happier in later years with lower wages from the Catchment Board, and the chance to learn botany.

A friend introduced Jock to tramping, and from then on he

never left Golden Bay for a holiday. Each January he'd lead a party, which came to include Garry and our children, for 10-day tramps into the mountains.

Everything you see in Golden Bay leads up to the mountains. Much of it obstinate and unforgiving, spawning names such as Kill Devil Creek, Dragon's Teeth, Devil's Dip, Rheumatic Creek, The Drunken Sailors and Break-Me-Up Creek. But no child or adult who wanted to come on Jock's tramps was ever refused. He believed that providing alpine access to people who wouldn't normally consider themselves capable could change people's lives.

Jock's trips were never on marked tracks. Climbing in the Anatoki region into Slate River Peak, when our children were five, seven and nine, took three days, with Jock and Garry cutting the route as they went. And there were no light saws in those days – or cell phones, radios or safety beacons. Our children wore basketball boots and carried their own school-bag packs. Garry and Jock could be carrying 20 kilograms each. Jock's makeshift pack consisted of a large canvas duffle bag secured with leather throngs to a timber-framed back rest. It didn't always protect him from a sharp object inside the bag, which once caused an open wound on his back.

'A bit tender,' was all he said.

Fantastic stews would be cooked, using bacon, salami, dried vegetables and rice. Chocolate and barley sugar were distributed at morning and afternoon teas. The young were expected to pull their weight with the chores; to scrub out the porridge pot and do the dishes.

Worldly, urbanised people from other parts of New Zealand came on Jock's tramps, to declare it a momentous experience. One regular family included three dysfunctional sons. The father was far from athletic, and a somewhat proper Englishman, but to his credit, his efforts to accompany his boys on these rigorous tramps led them towards successful adulthoods.

For our children these expeditions were the highlight of their year. They'd arrive home elated after a period of sustained and rugged effort, and above all by their growing knowledge of the environment. An albino kiwi had been seen at Green Saddle above Boulder Lake, lots of rock wrens, and once a rare sighting of a blue duck or whio. There were always huge kea, who would try to rip the tents. And sometimes the gurgle of a kaka could be heard.

A local botanist on one of the trips, to Jock and Garry's excitement, showed them a recently identified *Pittosporum dallii* at an elevation of around 1100 metres between Boulder Lake and Cobb Ridge. It's a curious spreading shrub or tree that grows up to six metres high, and is found nowhere else in the world.

Of course there were risks to these alpine adventures. There were forces of Nature to contend with, and you had to know what you were doing. But to Jock, facing the challenges that mountains threw up was one of the things that drove him. 'It's funny what then becomes important,' he said. 'You discover so much of the crap in your life is just crap, and really not important at all.'

The annual tramps continued until the late 1970s, when arthritis brought an end to Jock's leadership. But our children, as students, forged their own expeditions, and continue to do so with their children. And now our older grandchildren visit the Bay for tramping holidays.

UNDER THE WIDE OPEN GOLDEN BAY SKY, free from social pressures, eccentricities flourish. The Bay is a natural haven for characters who are perhaps only to be found in out-of-the-way places. By the late 1960s, people of retirement age came to live in the Bay who talked about ideas and experiences, concerns and reflections, who made gentle jokes and had reasoned discussions.

The house of Bet Wishart, a friend in her seventies, began life as three army huts bought at a local auction. The huts were moved to sit proprietarily on the sea's edge at Ligar Bay, on land she couldn't claim as hers. It was Road Reserve, hence there were constant rows with the local council, who wanted to move Bet and the six other squatters. But our elderly friend remained steadfast on her perch, one of the most scenic in Golden Bay, with the sheltering arms of the Abel Tasman memorial cliff to the south, and Tata Hill to the north.

There were, of course, countless physical tasks with which Bet needed help from her younger friends, such as shoring up her seaside garden against the tide, the challenge of her illegally constructed plumbing, and countless carpentry jobs – such as building a tall wooden fence on the roadside, 'so the neighbours can't see what I'm up to'.

Bet liked to feel she could depend on Garry and me for moral support in her never-ending crises, without which, we used to think, her pulse would stop beating.

There would be endless tales of her dust-ups with bureaucracy, lawyers, accountants and every tradesman she employed. And heaven help any medical professionals when she fell into their hands!

Her periods in Nelson Hospital were notable for the chaos she caused. 'I can't sleep, nurse,' she'd complain, 'surrounded by all this snuffling, hacking and snoring.' When Beth had made herself unpopular with everyone else in the ward by ringing her bell every five minutes, the staff would inevitably shift her to a single room, leaving our wicked friend smug with satisfaction.

She once sent urgently for Garry when we were in the middle of lambing, to mend a puncture in the second-hand bicycle she had bought. He exploded. 'You got me here in the middle of lambing for this?'

'Well of course,' Bet replied blithely. 'I'm not going to pay the oil-shock price of petrol to fuel my car. I'm taking to the bicycle.' We never saw her ride it!

But to be invited to Bet's house for Sunday supper was a very special treat. Sometimes I'd set off ahead, to walk the five kilometres down the coast, with the waves splashing across the road if a westerly was blowing, leaving Garry and the children to follow by car.

I would sit on the window seat, retrieved from the dump like most of Bet's joinery, beneath portraits she'd painted at the Canterbury Art School. The conversation was always scintillating and the food delicious.

Bet's downfall, when she became boring, was when she took a negative approach to so many situations. Her frequent trips to Nelson, invariably to extract some bargain from a timorous shopkeeper, would be bound to involve the complaint that someone had diddled her, a shop girl had been obstructive, or a parking official hadn't made allowances for her age. Too often she wanted more of a bargain, more from people than was fair.

Had she ever contemplated marriage? 'No. I couldn't imagine putting up with a man in my house,' she'd reply when asked. 'Although I've been chased round my sitting room plenty of times, by people who should know better.'

Bet preferred animals to people. She would stop her car to belabour a farmer for what she considered ill-treatment of his stock. 'I'll run you in, you brute,' she'd say. And sometimes she did.

She once accosted a man who was dragging his dog along Takaka's pavement. 'Your dog wants to do poos,' she shouted at him, 'and if you don't let him, I hope some day you will want to do poos and somebody will prevent you!'

Bet loved Sam, her cat, and would hang him upside-down to be brushed with the hearth brush, which he relished. Sam was 18 years old, with a sawn-off tail and a wobbly walk. 'He's an ecological cat,' Bet informed us. 'I've told him not to eat birds.'

Weka were our elderly friend's pet enemies, for their attempts to destroy her garden. She once put a weka under a wooden box for several hours to teach it a lesson. She'd hoped other weka would take notice and learn. Another time she took an invading weka to the local rubbish dump. 'He stood still in shock, his eyes protruding, and I swear he turned pale.'

But Bet hadn't the heart to leave the weka there, and brought it home.

I FIRST SAW JUNE WASHBOURN WHEN she flew down from Wellington for the auction of Bill Watson's antique furniture and rugs. Her husband, Rear Admiral Richard Washbourn, was Chief of Staff of the New Zealand Navy at the time, a position he had taken up on retirement from the Royal Navy.

When June swept into the hall in Takaka to inspect the goods, people subconsciously backed away to leave space around her, as if she were royalty. She bid on most offerings, to the chagrin of the dealers from Nelson, who had hoped for bargains.

As it happened, Richard didn't complete his time in the New Zealand Navy, as symptoms of Alzheimer's disease had appeared. 'The first indication was a complete blackout one day,' June would explain. 'He couldn't remember one thing about a meeting he'd just attended. Doctors suggested he should retire as early as possible, and then, with the strain of the position removed, he would probably be all right.'

So June and Richard left Wellington and came to Onekaka, across the Bay from ourselves, six months earlier than planned. The 30-acre property had been left to Richard by an uncle, and they'd had a lifelong dream to retire there.

They built a small house, with a long, windowed sitting room overlooking the beach from its cliff-top position. A tangle of wild roses and hydrangeas lined the path to the sand below.

Richard continued to enjoy his classical music records, his embroidery, painting and workshop. He could drive, but June said he wasn't really as capable as he appeared to be. 'And what is very interesting is that neither he nor I had any inkling of this at all. In fact it was some years before I realised how bad he really was.'

She had been talking about good friends of theirs in England, when Richard said he didn't know who she was talking about. 'What rubbish,' June had scoffed. 'You'll be saying you don't know who I am next.'

And Richard replied, 'I don't. Who are you?' He wasn't joking. By then June and Richard had been married for 25 years, and it became very clear to her there was something wrong with his brain.

June took him back to his specialists to ask what was going on. They said he had Alzheimer's disease, and there was absolutely nothing she could do about it. There was no cure. The problem for June was that nobody could help her. She kept asking people, 'What should I do?' And the doctors would say, 'You seem to be doing very well, your guess is as good as ours.'

Eventually well-meaning family members and friends began to suggest it wasn't right to keep Richard at home – that he should be in hospital, where he could be properly looked after. June, however, was convinced that Richard would be happier at home, and she was a real fighter for anything she believed in. She mounted an amazing campaign to look after Richard herself.

Things were far from easy, but this courageous woman persevered and found time and energy to fight for a better deal, not only for herself, but for others caring for people at home. She pressured health authorities for assistance and equipment, lobbied medical manufacturers to suggest improvements to their goods, wrote articles about Alzheimer's disease, and was interviewed on National Radio.

She would eventually say she knew more about Alzheimer's disease than doctors who had studied the subject, because she had been involved with this condition, day and night, for 20 years. 'So I can say things with authority, particularly from the point of view of the relatives who have to cope with this situation. If someone wants to cope with a patient at home, they should be given everything they need to help them.'

June got things because she demanded them, and if she didn't get them one way she got them in another. For example, one day a naval ship arrived in the Bay, with sailors rowing ashore to erect a helicopter harness from a hook in the bedroom ceiling, so June could hoist Richard in and out of bed. 'The hospital board wasn't keen to do things like that,' she said. 'I had to fight for myself, and thus been able to manage.'

Nor was June someone to sit at home and mope. Situated halfway between Takaka and Collingwood, she encouraged groups to which she belonged to meet at her house. A dozen or more of us would bring our lunch and gather around her table for a monthly women's discussion group. At our feet three spaniels were tied to the table legs, to prevent them running after the cats. Two donkeys grazed outside, as did two Jersey cows June milked daily. There was a poster above the door declaring: *God is a woman and she's black.*

National Radio's *Nine to Noon* weekday programme, to which we were all avid listeners, supplied endless topics for discussion. Someone would introduce a subject. 'What do you make of Watergate? President Nixon?' Later there were questions over Iraq. 'What a mess! What's the answer?'

Indeed, one of our group, Betty Duffield, an 82-year-old Quaker, set off in December 1990 to join an international peace camp on the Iraq border, in an attempt to stop the First Iraq War. Her participation at this age made headlines throughout the world. 'Everyone wants peace except the governments,' she reported to the media on her return.

If one of us brought a VIP visitor to sit in on one of our discussion groups – perhaps from the sphere of politics, education or the arts – they would inevitably admit they didn't have the time we had to follow world affairs so avidly, and would invariably say they envied us.

June believed everything that happened to us had a purpose – that we got what we deserved in our lives. 'I've had to come to terms with the fact I wasn't good at dealing with sickness or dirty nappies. Our children had a nanny to cope with all that. But now, with Richard's illness, I have accomplished something I had been putting off in previous lives.'

She saw it as part of her evolution. 'I was given a husband I love, and a situation which had deteriorated physically, and I had to come to terms with it. And now I can do it more easily.'

In 1991 Richard died, and on 26 March 1993 June followed him. She was driving her Jeep across a causeway near her home, probably in a hurry, after spending the morning helping her daughter Liza finish her entry for the Wearable Arts competition.

June had recently developed diabetes. Did she skid on the gravel road, swerve to avoid a pukeko, or have a blackout? No one knows. A roadman found the little Jeep upside down on the incoming tide. June, a very young 70, was dead when emergency services arrived. Barely two years had passed since her beloved Richard's death, after which she had been free to visit city galleries and concerts, and travel overseas.

It's not fair, thought her friends. June's children, Liza and Joe, thought differently. It was their parents' wedding anniversary the day June died. She had gone to join her beloved husband.

By the late 1960s Golden Bay had been truly discovered by the summer hordes. There were three kinds of tourists, broadly speaking, who poured into the Bay for summer holidays, tripling the population.

There were the wealthy professionals, who left the cities to hobnob for 'gins at five' with others of their kind. The fact that locals like ourselves were invited was probably to provide some exaggerated stories, back home, about the eccentric characters they'd met.

Garry and I were asked for a drink at the holiday home of a doctor and his wife. There were other medicos present, all with second homes in the Bay. One leant over to tell me how fit he was. 'I see 50 patients a day,' he boasted. 'I could see 20 more, but I would earn the same income.'

Another doctor chipped in. 'Ignorant Maoris earn more than I do.'

A third medical man expressed regret that his two sons had agricultural degrees, but could only earn mediocre salaries as bureaucrats. 'They'll never have the capital to buy a farm,' he said.

Garry suggested they could work as sharemilkers, and gradually build up equity.

'Oh,' said the doctor, horrified. 'God forbid I would see my sons milking cows!'

'Or you could sell your beach house,' I suggested.

The doctor raised his eyebrows and moved off.

Then there are the Holly Pollys, as Bet Wishart liked to describe the type of tourist others might call the 'hoi polloi'.

'Little boy, little boy, drop that at once!' she would shriek as she leapt the bank protecting her house from the waves, and an errant son of a Holly Polly dropped his armful of Bet's firewood and took off.

'And what do you think you are doing?' Bet demanded of a Holly Polly man, who, to amuse himself, had diverted the course of the creek running through her garden, which was now likely to erode her vegetable plantings. 'Please put that creek back how you found it. At once!' she commanded imperiously.

'You can't be too careful at this time of year,' Bet would say. 'Not with Holly Pollys around.'

The third type of tourist saved all year for their holiday in Golden Bay. These were the more rugged types, often with old cars which barely made it over the Hill. They camped in a leaky tent, or rented a small bach if they were lucky. Not for them gins at five. They were too busy tramping, botanising, looking for fossils or exploring rock pools. Garry and I were like two thirsty plants as we drank up the lives of this kind of visitor, whose values we admired and shared with our children.

One of the best examples of these was Alwyn Owen's family, who rented our second cottage for several summers, involving our children in all their adventures. Alwyn, better known as Hop, was the presenter of National Radio's *Spectrum* programme.

For the Owen children, Mary, Dillon and Whena, who were being raised in a Hutt Valley suburb, Rocklands was more than a holiday destination. 'It was an adventure,' according to Dillon. 'We'd swing high and wide on supplejack vines, swim and catch eels in dark green pools, with the scattering of bones in a cave, where a wild dog had once lived, providing a layer of mystery.'

Dillon developed a passion for geology, with his pockets full of stones to identify. To a boy from a landscape of ubiquitous greywacke, Rocklands was metamorphic bliss. In Dillon's view, 'Rocklands rocked!'

Whena, recalling her impressions some 40 years later, described their trips to Rocklands as classic Kiwi holidays, now largely only found in literature. 'It was Outward Bound, in another time and generation,' she said. Our children were described as 'hard-out country kids, generous with their time and knowledge. I looked up to Sally,' she added.

Hop's affectionate memories included 'a huge electrical storm that shattered our sleep one night, ripe tree tomatoes, the noise of weka calling at dusk and the hiss of opossums'.

One winter holidays we did a child swap, with Dillon coming to us and Sally spending a week with the Owens. Taken to a café for a treat where Devonshire teas were served, our daughter announced forthrightly that this wasn't proper cream. 'Because it doesn't have cow's hairs in it!'

Sometimes famous people turned up on our doorstep, who I doubt would have crossed our path if we had lived elsewhere. Olivia Spencer Bower, the Canterbury artist, arrived unannounced late one night. The 70-year-old was on her way to camp at Totaranui, the headquarters of the Abel Tasman National Park. We suggested she stay the night, rather than tackle 20 more kilometres in the dark. Two days later she appeared again, this time drenched. We ran a bath to thaw her out. Despite warnings from the national park staff that Cyclone Rosie was imminent, she said she had 'mucked around', and didn't start packing until it was pouring. 'Some men,' she said with some annoyance, 'had hammered my tent pegs in too hard and I couldn't get them out.'

She insisted on leaving for Christchurch the next morning, despite the creek between the house and the drive being a torrent. Her VW coughed a few times then surged off – to our horror not across the ford, but following the flooded creek. Garry ran after her, yelling directions, and eventually, after wild plunges and splashing, that amazing little car reached the bank on the other side.

Frank Alack, the mountain guide, was happy to sleep in his car with its fold-down seats and preferred to eat his own raw food, but joined us for coffee.

We apologised for our outside loo, with its hanging sack for a door, but Frank extolled its virtues. He'd recently stayed in a diplomat's house in Wellington, a house of three storeys, where people had been invited to meet him. He'd used the upstairs loo before the guests arrived and the door had jammed. 'I didn't like to holler, so I looked out the window and saw water pipes descending. So down I slid, hand over hand, right past the window of the reception area.'

'Burglar!' screamed the guests. Someone fainted.

Frank explained he was practising for a difficult climb the following week.

A letter came from a publishing firm, asking us to host their founder, A. H. Reed, for a weekend. The elderly gentleman was famous for undertaking long-distance walks throughout New Zealand. His cheerful wave on the road, always dressed in a suit, was a familiar sight on TV.

We were soon disconcerted, however, to learn that our guest was extremely deaf, and could only hear when we yelled. Even worse, having had no children of his own, he ignored our three, so they played up. Tim cracked his mouth on the edge of the table at dinner, putting a tooth through his lip, with blood spouting onto my apple pie. Exhausted from all the yelling and the children's behaviour, I put him to bed, saying firmly, 'Now stay there!'

I took our visitor to the local dog trials, to discover he had very poor sight. Not only did he reject a hearing aid, but he didn't own spectacles either. Screaming a commentary about the dogs and their owners, I attracted startled looks from the trialists, to whom our guest gave his familiar wave.

On the morning of our guest's departure, I had him, at his request, at the bus depot half an hour early, arriving at 7 a.m. on a cold, frosty morning. I continued my efforts to entertain him.

'Would you like to see the aviary?' I shouted. 'It has some monkeys.' Shutter windows from the bedrooms above the shops flew open, to see who was shouting at this hour.

The old man did his famous wave. 'No, thank you,' he said. 'I don't approve of animals in captivity.'

I tried harder. 'The monkeys have had a baby!' I scream. Again the shutter windows flew open, with the occupants now looking belligerent.

Our guest did his wave. 'No, thank you,' he said.

Thankfully the bus came. I put the great walker aboard.

Then I got the famous wave!

WHEN BOB AND PHYLLIS THORPE RETIRED to live in Nelson, their eldest son Richard, with wife Leentje, took over Glen Rannoch. Bob must have missed his sheep, but he settled down cheerfully enough, with the local church glad of his loyal support. We were so sorry to see them go.

Phyllis was such a darling and, as an acquaintance said, 'You don't meet a Bob Thorpe round every corner.' This was so true. He was a symbol of the old gentlemanly farming life, which was changing before our eyes.

But in Leentje I was to discover someone utterly special, even inspirational. She was almost of another age, in another world, with her acceptance of a way of life that was unacceptable by modern standards.

She worked so hard she seldom had time to sit and talk, but one afternoon we sat on her veranda and I heard about her dreams to live on a farm, when she was a child in Amsterdam.

'As a schoolchild during the war,' she began, 'I would ride my pretend horse along the pavements between the high buildings, with no trees, no grass, with everything dull and grey. But I only saw lovely mountains with snow, beautiful trees and streams, grass paddocks, sheep and cows – things I had never seen in real life.

'I would bring home lost kittens, and once a pigeon with a broken leg. It was sitting in the middle of a busy street with crowds of people walking past, cowering down. I took it home and nursed it, and later it flew away and lived on the rooftop. When I came outside the pigeon would fly down and sit on my shoulder.'

With no opportunity to farm, the best way Leentje could think of to become close to Nature was to study biology. By the age of 17 she had her degree.

'Then I read a book about a man in England who farmed organically, with beautiful animals, and the farm was such a success. So I wrote and asked to visit this farm. He tried to put me off, because the farm was not nearly as beautiful as it was in the book, but I was not put off.'

Leentje crossed the English Channel with her bicycle, and rode all the way to the farm.

'I stayed with a post mistress who had one or two rooms to rent. On my bed was a little chook, with another in front of the TV. But also staying in this cottage was Richard, my future husband, who came from a farm in Golden Bay, so of course we had much to talk about.'

But while Richard came from a farm, he didn't own it at the time – his parents did. And with only 500 acres, much of it scrub- and fern-covered, and only 50 acres of good pasture, it couldn't support two families. It was to be several years before Leentje and Richard could live there. In the meantime, after their marriage, they went to a missionary settlement on Groote Eylandt, in the Gulf of Carpentaria, to help Aboriginal people.

'It was very primitive. We had no electricity, but I loved it there. Aboriginal people are very natural and love a joke. But after two of our children were born, we had the opportunity, when Richard's parents retired, to take over the farm, where four more children were born.'

In later years, when a market developed for reared calves, Leentje began milking 12 cows. The calves, when weaned, were in demand for the export market, so successfully did she rear them. Richard looked after Glen Rannoch's sheep and beef cattle.

Leentje's day was long, but she thrives on it. 'I love every inch of this place. It has been the farm I dreamed of – somewhere for my husband and I to work together – and above all it's been a magical place for our children to grow up.'

THE VAVASOURS RETURN FOR A LOCAL WEDDING, and to tell us how marvellous their Marlborough farm has turned out to be. We hear about their multiple bales of wool, the thousands of fat lambs produced, the successful crops. Above all, how satisfying it was to be on good, fertile land.

But the parents part with tears in their eyes and say they'll soon be back. 'This is where our friends are,' Gerry says, clasping my hands in both his own.

WITH TIME WE BEGAN TO HAVE MORE OF A SOCIAL LIFE with newcomers to the Bay who had children the same age.

At the time of the Cuban missile crisis in 1962, the Climpson family from England – Alan, Sheila and three children – emigrated to New Zealand. Having decided to tour the country before choosing a place to settle, they got no further than Golden Bay.

Initially Alan was a scallop fisherman and then farmed mussels on the coast, with Sheila a potter and a self-taught bassoonist.

Later they bought land near our own, to farm Sussex cattle and produce organic salami, which sold all over New Zealand.

Whatever Alan took on he usually did it better than anyone else. This irritated some people, especially if he had suggested a better way of doing something against everyone else's opinion, and was inevitably proved to be right. He had this incredible talent for thinking outside the box.

He used old-fashioned methods that worked. For example, instead of cleaning the gungy old troughs, from which his calves were fed, he put yoghurt into the mixture, and none of the calves got the skitters.

Alan had grown up quickly during the war. Evacuated as a seven-year-old in order to avoid Germany's bombing route across Kent, he did not enjoy the experience, and soon took himself home by train. No one was going to tell this little lad where he should live.

At his grammar school, finding the dormitories cold, he 'had the common sense', as a fellow pupil described it, to break into a storeroom to chop up several antique wooden desks for firewood.

With a war job delivering telegrams, he'd used a railway phone to report bomb damage to his village, and was reprimanded for giving the message to Headquarters in the wrong order. From then on Alan had a lifelong distrust of bureaucracy.

We couldn't have had a more helpful neighbour. He seemed to sense when Garry could do with a hand, and there he'd be, beside the yards, or blocking a road when sheep were being moved, before we'd even thought of requesting his help.

There were countless examples of Alan solving a friend's agricultural, veterinary or engineering problem that in many cases had fazed so-called experts. He was a genius in ways that would never have been recognised in an orthodox academic system.

With four or five families we would picnic at one of the beaches, essentially where there was a creek to dam, which would occupy the boys for hours. The girls would be building houses in clumps of manuka scrub, with floors of deep moss, or huts made of driftwood and branches.

The adults would collect firewood for Garry to boil the billy for tea, and, once embers remained, chops and sausages would be cooked. A favourite picnic spot was Doctor's Beach, where the Burrells, a former Wellington family, had a private track through the bush to reach a rough cabin, where an early doctor had once spent his days off.

Beaches with Maori names ring the Bay – such as Pakawau, Puponga, Pohara, Paturau – most with safe swimming and some with golden sand. The Tata peninsula, in our early years, was smothered in gorse and lupins. Today it's a suburb of million-dollar holiday homes.

There would be an annual trip to Wharariki, on the Bay's west coast fronting the Tasman Sea. It's the most dramatic bit of coast you'll find anywhere, with wild and thunderous waves too dangerous for family swimming, but with great hills of sand that are marvellous for children to leap off.

'Look, a hermit!' shouted a stranger. They'd seen Tim in his favourite garment, a cast-off adult suede jacket, which reached his knees, and a battered sou'wester hat. He was tickled pink. He had already informed us, as a seven-year-old, that he was going to live in our back country when grown-up, 'without any wives or newspapers and things'.

Tim and I are directed to grub heather on the mountain.

The 11-year-old climbs steeply, straight up with long strides, with me taking an easier zigzag route. We leave our swags in a cleft in a rock and I try not to look down. The height makes me dizzy, so I clutch some grass and sit down. Tim, unperturbed, with his back to the sheer drop behind him, grubs on, filling multiple sacks with heather.

'Go home, Mum,' he says. So I leave him, to slide down much of the way on my bottom. I look back from time to time, to see Tim, now a little black spot, his parka flapping in the wind, as he swings the grubber. He works up there all day on his own.

Tim once stoically ignored a poisoned thumb until we noticed, while Mike was always concerned with every prickle. But he was such a charming, bright, bouncy little boy, so confident with his sporting successes, a natural at any sport he tried.

On the day of the junior tennis championships, Mike, now eight, is up long before anyone else, to wash the dishes from the night before and set the table, to make sure we get away early. 'Where are my clean grundies?' he asks, making wild swipes with his racquet.

There are 22 entrants in the championship. Mike loses the final, 6–5, against a 15-year-old. 'But I did some good shots, Mum,' he said.

One of the best investments we make is to install a ping-pong table in the woolshed. Marvellous for entertaining children and adults. Mike leans forward to do a killer shot, and bashes his stomach on the table's edge. 'Hell! My guts!' he says. Then he bashes his head against a pillar, when rushing back to reach a ball. Tears, then a determined 'I'm all right!'

Garry, walking past, catches the ball as it slides off the table, from a shot sent by Sally. 'Dad,' says Mike, 'next time you do that you'll go over the net yourself.'

'You wouldn't have reached that ball,' says his father.

'I would have had a good try,' Mike insists.

He would have, too. Whatever sport he took up, he could beat any of us.

One terrible day, we nearly lost four children on Rocklands. Sally had been dropped off at the foot of the drive after spending a day with friends, and took a shortcut to the house. It had been a windy day and a power-board technician had been to restore lost power. He'd put a fuse back on a power pole, without observing high-voltage power lines lying on a fence. Sally went to climb through and got stuck, with high-voltage power shooting through her. Tim heard the screams and went to see what was wrong, to be caught in the same electrified fence, which released Sally. Fortunately Tim was wearing gumboots, and was able to throw himself off. Mike and a friend, close behind Tim, had also been running towards the screams.

A doctor came to see Sally, whose muscles were quivering in seizure. There were no lasting effects, but it was a salutary lesson for the power-board technician, who came back to apologise the next day.

In the early 1970s there was a total renaissance of Golden Bay society. This isolated region had become part of the back-to-Nature exodus from the cities, with the new settlers, who were mostly under 30 and often well educated, attracted to the inexpensive land and a favourable climate.

The locals were horrified by the sight of long-haired men with shaggy beards, and long-skirted women who didn't hesitate to breastfeed their babies in public. Nor was it easy for these new arrivals to take up an alternative life, with most of them from middle-class backgrounds.

BJ was one of the first to arrive, to set up a commune on top of the Pikikirunga Range. As a 19-year-old from Wellington, married with a baby, he was seeking a different life. 'It was really, really hard,' he recalls. 'Nappies had to be washed in the creek. If you wanted to go, you had to dig a hole. We'd come here with ideals, such as getting a cow and having a bountiful organic garden, but the possums ate everything we grew, and we could never find the eggs from our free-range hens.'

'It had sounded so easy,' a young woman said, 'but it was a nightmare of work. The literature hadn't prepared us for that. We felt betrayed.'

The instigator of a commune at Onekaka, a former radical activist from Lincoln University, was swamped with arrivals. How to feed them? 'Every divorcée from New Zealand and Australia seemed to have arrived, planning to just lie around sunbathing with a daisy tucked behind each ear,' he reported.

Growing cannabis was a success, however. I'd gape at the loaded trolleys in the supermarket that the 'alternatives' could apparently afford. But it was risky. The district's sole policeman had his hands full pulling up plants and arresting the growers.

And there were large welfare funds to tap into, not just the dole and PEP schemes, plus sickness and domestic benefits, but also add-ons for house extensions, allowing the hippies to erect creatively quirky dwellings.

But then district councillors became fed up with the flood of applications for house permits and made a new rule. Subdivision into less than 50 hectares in any rural zone was disallowed, and no building permits would be granted to anyone who already owned such a block. The alternative community united to form The Rural Resettlement Association to oppose the local councillors.

They produced an A4 stapled newspaper called the *Golden Bay Community News*, with talented newcomers writing satirical reports of council meetings, with every insular and prejudiced argument described as though it was some great farce. It kept the district highly amused but really got the councillors' goat.

Gerard Hindmarsh in his book *Swamp Fever* has described how Chip Williams and his wife Hess, with 109 hectares of idyllic native bush at the head of the Pupu Valley, applied for a building permit, and the councillors tried to change the rules again. This was because Chip had been one of the funniest reporters who really got under the councillors' skin.

Now there was a council ruling prohibiting building on any piece of land, whatever the size, if it was not an economic unit. Only large-scale farming scenarios were going to be allowed. Never mind that Hess was a secondary teacher at Golden Bay High School and Chip had talented joinery skills. Indeed, amongst the 'alternatives' many thriving industries now existed, producing everything from pottery to organic vegetables, honey to patchwork quilts, jewellery to baking, but that did not count with the council.

The council were oblivious to the fury being stirred up among the increasing number of rebellious residents. At the next county elections, Philip Woollaston, one of the alternatives, was voted onto the district council. He lived on a 10-acre block at Parapara, first in a railway carriage he had moved there, and then in an adobe-block house he and his wife had built. Philip was highly articulate, as the rest of New Zealand would find out when he went on to become an MP, a government minister, and later mayor of Nelson.

He was appointed chairman of the shell-shocked council, to announce not only that Golden Bay was nuclear-free, but also that farmers were now allowed to sell off small blocks of wasteland.

IN THE LATE 1970S IT WAS STILL POSSIBLE with little money to take up land in Golden Bay to farm conventionally – if you had guts, determination and were prepared to live frugally.

Sandra Closs, born in London, with a dance-teacher mother and a theatre-producer father, had, like Leentje and myself, dreamt as a child of owning a farm. In her case she'd just wanted a pig, some chooks, and to make bread in a self-sufficient lifestyle. However, she married Ken, a New Zealander, and her new husband had a different idea . . . and it wasn't that.

After a year of travel the pair arrived in New Zealand with $50 between them. They bought an old Vauxhall car and worked in shearing gangs, up and down the South Island.

It was well-paid work, with Ken a wool presser and Sandra a rouseabout, and they began to save money. 'We would buy stamps,' said Sandra, 'and that was about it. We didn't buy clothes. When the shearers threw away their trousers I'd grab them and patch them. When a job was finished I'd collect the old half-finished tubes of toothpaste. We were miserly.'

By 1976 they had saved enough money to buy 800 acres of steep, gorse-covered land on the Pikikirunga Ridge near our back-country boundary. There was a two- by two-metre mustering hut to live in, with a fire that smoked at one end.

'We had to sit with our heads down in order to breathe, or leave the door open,' Sandra said. Ken would have been happy to live like that forever, but the couple wanted to adopt a baby, and Social Welfare said they had to have a proper house. So they put up a prefab garage costing $3,000, lined with packing cases.

To make ends meet Ken worked as a shearer, and it was while working at Te Hapu, on the far western coast of the Bay, that he had the feeling they were going to live there one day. There is a two kilometre-wide strip of sweet limestone country, running from Farewell Spit to Kahurangi lighthouse, with some of the province's best sheep and beef farms.

Two years later, when Te Hapu came onto the market, Ken and Sandra went to the Rural Bank for a loan, and were laughed at. Later, when the property was split in two, and on the market again, the Rural Bank agreed to look at it, if the Closses found a buyer for the other half. They did so in 1980, and moved to Te Hapu.

The farm's green hills roll steeply down to the Tasman Sea from a back boundary of towering bluffs. There are rock pools on the coast with paua and crayfish, and kiwifruit, tamarillos and banana palms grow in their frost-free garden.

Te Hapu means 'fertile wind', and there is a story behind that. In 1836 Te Puoho, a Ngati Tama chief, assembled a taua of about 70 warriors and set off down the coast to the Heaphy River, marauding Maori settlements as they went. The last inland stages over Southland saw them short of food and weakened, and they were defeated and slaughtered by Ngai Tahu forces.

News of the defeat was brought back by Te Puoho's slave, Ngawhakawa. Finding a thriving Maori settlement, which he thought had been wiped out, where the Closses live today, he named the area Te Hapu.

And maybe there is something in the name, because after eight years of not conceiving Sandra became pregnant, having already adopted two children, both of whom she'd breastfed. 'It's a La Leche thing they do in America,' she explained. 'You tie a plastic bag holding milk round your neck, drained by a tiny, soft tube which goes to your nipple. The baby sucks through the tube, and you get the feeling of bonding.'

Thirty years ago, when the coalmines and timber mills filled up the Mangarakau School classroom with kids, the Closs children had only five kilometres to travel to get to school. But the school is history and so is the Correspondence School unit that succeeded it, despite the efforts of parents. It fell victim to the benefit–cost mentality of the education authorities.

Despite the falling population, the remaining people of Paturau and Mangarakau are determined to maintain the district's sense of community. 'In a smaller area you have to make more of an effort to have a social life,' said Ken. 'You can't simply pop in the car and drive a short distance to the pub or a film. Collingwood is an hour away. We organise children's games evenings, shared teas, when everyone chips in. A lot of entertaining takes place in private homes. Everyone dresses up.'

But Ken is cautious about the future. 'It's good farming country, among the strongest hill country in the Nelson region, but transportation costs are high. The country is dependent on fertiliser – and that's expensive to get out here and apply. In Nelson you buy it for $120 a tonne. But it takes another $40 a tonne to get it here, and another $20 or $30 to apply it, depending on whose airstrip you use.'

By far the biggest threat to these coastal properties is if their sheep and beef farms become unsustainable due to rising costs. Ken says compliance costs from new regulations might force the owners to look at changes in land use – for example tourism, forestry or power generation. The best way to protect the land in its current use is to support the farmers to continue doing what they are doing and doing well. Any extra rules and regulations, to take cultural and heritage areas out of production, could lead to more foreign and corporate ownership of such land.

'Somehow,' says Ken, 'the layers of bureaucracy need to be peeled back, and not added to.'

Te Hapu is a far cry from where Sandra grew up in London, but she loves the place – although she feels guilty about owning so much land. When single she'd worked in India for three years, organising well-digging and road-building on a Food for Work project. 'When I write to Indian friends I don't say how many sheep or cattle we have, or talk about my washing machine or automatic this and that, because I know it would boggle their minds. Instead I talk about things they can relate to – the house cow, our dogs and the vegetable garden.'

CHAPTER 12

Our children had been free to develop naturally, but a childhood spent in isolation from the mainstream can be a handicap in adult life. They needed to know about opportunities on the other side of The Hill. Boarding school had to be faced.

With school fees to find, I sought a job with wages. I applied for an advertised job at the cement-works office, saying I was willing to be a welfare officer, social worker, or typist (with two fingers?) and could take dictation at speed (well, I'd been able to scrawl long-hand speedily enough when interviewing as a journalist).

I heard nothing, so I followed this up with a telephone call to a woman neighbour, who provided board for the work's deputy manager. 'Don't bother to apply,' she told me. 'They only employ men in the office.'

Undeterred, I phoned the office manager, to ask if I could see the works manager himself. 'Just write an application form and post it,' the office manager said. I gathered references to send with my application, and delivered them in person to the office. The office manager read my application, stapled the papers together, and said he would pass it to the works manager.

I hear next day I have the job, starting at 8 a.m. in two days' time. I am to be an invoice clerk – and while I have no idea what this means, I am determined to prove indispensable.

The deputy manager's landlady phones to advise me to be 'quiet and subdued' in my new position. She says the staff had been against me taking the position, 'because your references said you had lots of vitality – but then they decided you might also be efficient'. She also tells me her boarder is terrified I will ask for a lift to the office in his company car. As if I would! I will travel in the company bus with the other humble workers.

I take the car the first morning and arrive at the office at 7.45 a.m. – way too early – and the door is locked. When Lois the cleaning lady turns up, she shows me the washroom, along with the notice she pasted up, telling the office men to put the lavatory seat down.

Ian the pay clerk arrives. Then comes Mr T, an elderly clerk, who reminds me he helped me once when our car ran out of oil, and I had reached his house as the engine seized. 'Perhaps you will write about me?' he asks hopefully.

'Oh, I'm not writing about anybody anymore,' I say. 'That's why I'm here.'

Mr T shows me what to do. I have to check that invoiced goods have been received, and by what department. The office manager then writes out the cheques. Morning tea is at 10 a.m. and everyone has their place at the table, with the women at the bottom, then the male clerks, with the executives at the top. Bill, who I am to replace, returns from holiday. I stand up and offer him the chair. He doesn't want it. He and Ian, the pay clerk, spend much of the day outside, smoking.

I go with Ian in the works van to collect the workers' pay from the bank. The cash is carried in an old doctor's bag with a broken catch, and holds a pistol. No one has taught us how to use it. Is it loaded? I guess we just point it at anyone who attempts to snatch the money. Ian is reluctant to return to work immediately, and suggests we muck around in town for a while. I'm nervous about this, especially on my first day, and say I'd prefer to go back. We hand out the pay from a downstairs room which opens onto the road. That would be handy for a thief!

I come home exhausted.

At morning tea on my second day, Doug, head of the laboratory, speaks to me about the tennis team for which we both play. The quarry boss tells me about his daughter's prowess at sewing. Lois, the cleaning lady, gives me disapproving looks for conversing with executives. The deputy manager grunts hallo now and then. The office manager passes where I eat my lunch at the wharf. He looks approvingly at my brown-bread sandwiches, and tells me his wife drinks lemon juice each morning.

Mr T tells me I can make the toast and tea when I work overtime with him on Saturday mornings. I return home from this overtime session to face a week's housework, but go to bed for two hours instead.

I stick with this job for three-and-a-half years and become thinner and thinner. Boredom can kill, it seems. I have never, in the whole of my life, known time to go so slowly as it did during the hours I spent as an invoice clerk.

In efforts to regain my health I take long walks on Sundays. One day I walk to the top of our property. When I stop there is absolute silence, then I become aware of an encompassing fog. Suddenly I can't see a metre in front me. Which way is the track home? Terrified, I don't even know in which direction to look. Nobody knows I have walked up here today.

'Please God, help me,' I pray. And then, out the corner of one eye, almost behind me, the fog lifts for barely a second, to reveal the Tarakohe Harbour. Now I know where the coast is – in a kind of panic I rush in that direction, ignoring the curls and twists of the road, plunging straight down through gorse, tangled fences, over rocks, crashing time after time, until I am out of the fog and close to home. It's an experience I have never forgotten.

I BOUGHT SECOND-HAND UNIFORMS FOR THE CHILDREN. Poor Tim, the first to go to boarding school, had a jacket hemmed up so high that the pocket linings reached waist level, and his trousers were hemmed up 25 centimetres to allow for growth. His first letter was full of humour, bad spelling and awful handwriting. He praised his English teacher, 'who didn't spend time teaching us manners like Mum'. He had been into the city to get new socks, 'but there were none my size, so I bought a book on *How to survive in mountain, bush and sea*'.

'Tim is the sort of boy,' wrote the headmaster in his first report, 'who when asked to do a job, will do it willingly and efficiently, thanks to his good sense and his secure family background.' He was also described as 'a keen games player, a devastating tackler, delightful, quiet, unassuming, always cheerful and thoroughly honest and reliable'.

Mike's first letter from boarding school – neat and articulate – was heart-wrenchingly brave. 'I don't get bored,' he wrote, 'because I am allowed to hit a ball against the wall.' He liked his Latin teacher. 'Please look after Puff [the cat], Mum,' he asked, which had me blinking back tears.

We visited the children once a term. Mike, excelling at his athletic sports, won the high jump and long jump and by lunchtime had cleaned up the 400 metres. He led the field on all four circuits of the handicapped marathon, half the size of the senior cadets. Growing up on Rocklands had made him fit.

Planning to watch Tim play rugby, Garry and I had left home at 6 a.m. to start the seven-hour drive to Christchurch. Then, at the top of the Takaka Hill, the old Land Rover began to labour. I could see wisps of steam whirling away from the bonnet.

'Blast! The radiator's boiling.'

Something was wrong. Garry had filled up before we set out. The trouble was, our creek water was never exactly pure. An accumulation of sand and grit had been collecting in the radiator.

When the engine had cooled a little we coasted downhill to the garage at its base, a journey that took an hour – already we would be late for Tim's match. Now there was an overpowering smell of diesel. The fuel pipe had fractured.

'It would happen today!'

The garage was only recently acquired and not yet equipped for repairs, so we filled up with water and hoped we would manage to get to the next garage at Riwaka. All this took time.

Eventually the repairs were done and the journey continued, with me, to occupy my mind, timing each urban landmark to check if, as usual, it took an exact hour between each. One hour to the Kohatu pub, an hour to Murchison, another to Springs Junction, and an hour to the turn-off to Hamner. We passed Culverden, but broke down again at the Hurunui Hotel. At 9 p.m. we rang for a breakdown truck and asked for sandwiches.

At the bar was a glamorous young woman in evening dress, escorted by two dashing males in white tie and tails. They were on their way to the winter ball at Hamner.

Another world. Another way of life.

There were no treats for our children on boarding-school visits. We'd bring a cold leg of mutton and a cabbage for salad to feed ourselves. It was a subsistence diet. But they'd got used to anything – even mould on the bread which I would scrape off!

But always I believed that if you put your heart and soul, effort and hard work into anything worthwhile, everything would come right. 'When chances come, my darlings, you must seize them with both hands. Grab everything!' I'd tell our children.

THE WEATHER WAS GOOD FOR THE SUMMER holidays of 1972, and the children and their friends had a craze for making campfires. They boiled eggs, and roasted potatoes in the embers for their tea.

On most evenings a column of smoke rose from the fire by the creek from where we could hear excited voices. The children were happy and filthy, and nobody got burnt.

Sally was now 13, a sweet-faced child with fair plaits. As a very young child she'd say, 'I want to be like Granny when I grow up.' And she is just like my mother. She was the peacemaker of the family, kind to those weaker than herself, wise and gentle, always making sure that any plans were honest and fair. She could be stubbornly confrontational, too, questioning everything, until she was satisfied everything was above-board. But I have always felt inadequate about living up to Sally's example.

Tim was ready to break in a horse of his own, and Lucky, Lassie's foal, was now a two-year-old and could be brought down from the back country. With Tony Sandall's book on horse-breaking propped up on a post in the yard, he set about it with success. It was to prove a valuable skill, with funds to be earned in university holidays, breaking in farmers' horses. Once, that we knew of, Tim was kicked in the head at Parnassus in North Canterbury. As always with gutsy Tim, we only heard about this from others.

SEVENTEEN YEARS AFTER WE TOOK ON ROCKLANDS' hard hills, 100 acres of flat land, a former dairy farm on our front boundary, came up for lease. Garry phoned me at the cement-works office to tell me he'd negotiated the deal. It was the best news I could have had. Now we had somewhere to fatten lambs and cattle and make lots of hay. Above all, a chance to survive economically. I left the cement-works job.

Six weeks later, a letter from my mother arrived. *It's nothing to worry about,* she began, *but I have this lump in my neck.* My stomach froze. I went looking for Garry to share what Mum had written. Whenever I face a crisis, I immediately go looking for my husband. He adored my mother, but was his usual optimistic self.

I phoned Ma's GP in Taradale. 'I am treating it as an abscess,' he said. 'Your mother is on a course of antibiotics.' The frozen lump in my stomach was not appeased.

Dear Ma, I wrote back, ***I am just miserable for you with that beastly lump in your neck, and no sleep with it. It sounds like some acute form of infection, and I am sure antibiotics will settle it.***

I was trying to be reassuring, but I didn't believe this – I was scared.

The GP phoned the next day to tell me that my mother was a lovely lady, and that the pain had lessened, 'but not the abscess'. He said Mr Fisher, a surgeon, would do a biopsy on Tuesday (four days away) and he would phone when he knew the result.

Your doctor sounds as if he feels the acute part of your complaint is being eased, which is a good sign, I wrote to my mother, while my frozen stomach screamed alarm. ***I gather the surgical ward is in the old part of the hospital with multiple beds. How ghastly. But it's only for one night, to have the biopsy, so I hope you get a knock-out pill and get some sleep.***

For years, as long as I remember, whenever my mother experienced stress in her marriage she had tummy trouble, pains in her stomach, for which she'd accumulated a vast array of prescribed pills.

A weekend intervened as I waited for the biopsy report. A gymkhana was being held in Upper Takaka. To distract myself I took the children to watch, but nothing could prevent my terror.

The GP rang. The lump was malignant. I was on my way to Nelson Airport, wearing sunglasses, despite the rain-darkened sky, to hide my tears. I told the airport officials I had to attend a funeral, in my effort to get a seat. The bus from Napier's airport left me on the northern side of the Bluff, from where I walked up the hill to the hospital.

There she was, my little mother, small and frail against the snow white of the pillows. The lump by now was a large sac on her neck. She had been given the choice of Auckland or Palmerston North hospitals for radiation treatment. She didn't choose Auckland, 'because I would be a nuisance to Jennie [my sister], having to cross the city to see me'.

An ambulance took us both to Palmerston North. Within minutes of our arrival my mother was swept away to have her first dose of radiation, before the growing lump could strangle her windpipe.

She was put in a ward where beds lay not just in rows at the side, but filling every gap in the centre, all with cancer patients. There was a preponderance of Maori women. Sad and jaundiced, they lay so still – not reading, not speaking, just lying there.

'Here, darling,' said Ma, pushing some cash into my hand, 'please buy me some Panadol.'

'But Mum, perhaps something should be prescribed for you? Perhaps you shouldn't be medicating yourself?'

'Just get them, please Robby.'

I didn't argue. And so my mother continued to take her own Panadol for the stomach pain. No doctor here, including the oncologist, seemed aware my mother had endured 20–30 years of stomach pain. Nor did a doctor at Palmerston North Hospital, I was later to learn, ever put a hand on my mother to palpate her stomach. If I had known this, I would have asked, but I was always chased from the ward when the doctors did their rounds.

Yes, she had all the tests. She was taken daily to one laboratory after another, searching for the primary cause of her cancer, as the lump in her neck was a secondary. Most of these tests were gruelling, and always required a jolting ride on a stretcher to the appropriate department, with a second daily ride to the basement for radiation. I accompanied my mother, grimacing as the porters chatted loudly to each other, while carelessly bumping the stretcher against the lift doors. 'Please, be careful,' I said more than once. And was ignored. My mother, of course, never complained about anything.

All the laboratory tests were negative.

My mother didn't respond to the negative reports with glee. Ma knew. After six weeks of radiation the lump in the neck had shrunk, but daily she grew thinner.

'Your mother can go home tomorrow,' the ward sister said.

'How?' I asked. After all, she'd arrived in an ambulance.

'I don't know,' the sister replied. 'That's for you to arrange. If you haven't a car, by bus I suppose.'

Bus? Palmerston North was two-and-a-half hours from Napier. My mother couldn't possibly sit up for that distance. Fortunately a visitor returning to Hawke's Bay was traced, who offered Mum a lift, spread out on the back seat.

Back home, in the flat she shared with Aunt Bet, we tried to tempt her with delicacies, but she had no appetite, and the stomach pain returned. It was worse than ever, now the effects of the radiation had worn off. I can still hear the little yelps of pain my normally brave, brave mother expressed from the warm bath, where she'd hoped to find some relief.

I sent for her GP, who apologised for not diagnosing the primary cause of her cancer. Months before. Years before.

I shrugged.

He admitted Mum to Napier Hospital where she was given a single room. My sister flew down from Auckland and together we met her Napier surgeon. He had put his skilled hands on Mum's stomach. 'There's a tumour there the size of a rockmelon,' he said.

'But the tests at Palmerston? They were all negative?'

The surgeon shrugged.

'Will you operate?'

'No. Why put your mother through that, when there is no hope?'

Four-hourly morphia was prescribed, and Ma had no more pain.

I visited daily, with the torture of wondering what she was

thinking. Was she scared? Did she know that nothing could be done? That she was going to die? My mother and I had never had heart-to-hearts, each of us always stoical and reserved, retaining our own problems. As a result, I was helpless at providing her with solace, or being the support a daughter should have been at this time.

Instead I would chat about mundane things. Pass on messages. Be endlessly cheerful. While weeping inside, for not knowing what fears, thoughts, my little terminally ill mother had.

Six months after her diagnosis my darling mother died. She was only 63.

Chapter 13

In 1975 a 14-bed geriatric hospital opened at Collingwood, and with school fees still to find I was taken on as a staff nurse – to find myself in a nightmare of consummate cruelty, such as I never imagined I'd ever see as a nurse in New Zealand.

Under instruction from the male nurse in charge, Mr K, the maxim was, 'every patient can be rehabilitated, no matter how incapacitated or paralysed they are'. Long-term multiple stroke and other paralysed patients would be showered on the toilet chair, then left to dry and dress themselves. This was impossible for most of them. For the sympathetic nurses among us, this meant darting in and out of the bedrooms to put on a singlet or do up some buttons, always on edge, in fear of being caught by Mr K.

Mrs C, an obese woman in her early sixties, with myocardial degeneration culminating in congestive heart failure, would be refused a wheelchair and expected to walk down the long passage to the toilet, cyanosed and breathless. If she collapsed on the floor she was abused for being lazy. Staff who wished to please Mr K would walk over her, and were encouraged to despise her, with jokes in the staffroom over this patient's obesity. The patient would be told she was digging her grave with her teeth. She fell in the shower, and was left on the floor, having been told to get herself up. I pleaded to be allowed to sit her up, to prevent her drowning from the congestion in her lungs. This was refused. A doctor later queried whether she may have had a further myocardial infarction. Mrs C's 'rehabilitation' only ceased when she became unconscious.

Mrs M, who was 87 and a long-standing stroke patient, had been a midwife in the district. She would be left on a chair in the day room from 9 a.m. until 8 p.m. – other patients were allowed bed rest after lunch, but not Mrs M. And the reason? According to Mr K: 'She is not walking and therefore not tired.' Mrs M would ask to be lifted up when she slipped down in her chair, but no one was allowed to help her. She had an indwelling catheter and would have been in extreme discomfort. If she appealed for help too often she was banished to her bedroom, to sit there alone for the rest of the day, as punishment for asking for help. 'I feel as if I'm in the dog-box', Mrs M would say in tears. Dr H, on visits, would prop this patient up with a cushion, which Mr K removed on the doctor's departure.

Captain W, another 84-year-old stroke victim, preferred to sit on the toilet seat to urinate. Mr K insisted he stood, which meant wet trousers for the rest of the day.

When Mrs B, a 75-year-old stroke victim, with an arm in a sling and callipers on one leg, fell in the day room, Mr K served her lunch on the floor. 'That'll fix her!' he said.

Mrs S, who was 80, arrived after a fractured femur had been pinned in Nelson Hospital, and was made to ambulate too quickly. Forbidden a stick or frame she had several falls, and complained of pain in her groin. 'Imaginary,' said Mr K. 'She is malingering.' The pain was real. The pin had moved. More surgery had to be done. The patient's daughter wanted to complain, but refrained at her mother's request, who feared being victimised on her return to Collingwood.

Mr K sent for me to accuse me of being *too kind*. He didn't approve of me delivering patient's washing to their relatives, or for steadying Captain W with a hand, or spooning up a piece of pineapple for a stroke patient; and I was to stop drawing the bedroom curtains during the afternoon rest to keep the glare off patients' eyes. 'Because it makes the place look dreary,' he said.

What kind of rehabilitation was this? Rehabilitation for certain patients, yes, of course, but there was a limit for most of the patients we received, whose lives had become hell because they were unable to walk without falling, do up tiny shirt buttons, or lift themselves back onto the toilet chair if they fell.

In one case a patient was jammed between the toilet chair and wall and left there for two hours.

Two other registered nurses were also concerned. We couldn't stand by and do nothing. According to protocol, complaints must go to the person directly above us in the hierarchy. This meant Mr K. Although tormented by the situation, we didn't have the guts to confront him. Instead we consulted one of the local doctors. He said he would look into the situation. Nothing changed.

Sister S travelled to Nelson to see a hospital board member, who sent her to see Miss G, who was charge nurse for the whole Nelson region. Sister S expressed her concerns. Miss G, who had appointed Mr K to his post, attempted to defend him. She made accusations against Sister S, wanting to know why she was so concerned about the care of patients, refusing to believe there was no other motive. 'What about your job?' Miss G threatened.

She told Sister S that she would deal with the problems in her own way, and in her own time. In the meantime Sister S had to do everything Mr K ordered, even if she knew it was wrong. Sister S left the meeting intimidated, feeling her job was in jeopardy.

SISTER S'S HUSBAND, ALARMED ABOUT THE THREAT to his wife's position, sought appointments with the Anglican Bishop, a Methodist vicar and another member of the hospital board, who sent him to see Mr W, the chairman of the board. The chairman asked Mr S why his wife hadn't gone through the proper channels, such as Miss G, before talking to a local doctor and then a board member. Mr S explained that Miss G was a friend of Mr K and had appointed him to this position. The chairman was told that on her six-weekly inspection visits to the Collingwood Hospital, Miss G came no further than the hospital doorstep, and spent the day fishing with Mr K.

Nelson's medical superintendent sent letters inviting

the Collingwood nurses, trained staff and aides to describe any atrocities they had seen at the hospital. Those who wrote 'would not be victimised or dismissed', he promised. Seven staff members wrote, including myself, detailing upsetting incidents observed. Mr K was summoned to Nelson to hear the contents of the letters.

He returned to Collingwood a shaken man, admitting to his staff that he had been somewhat overzealous. He wasn't sacked.

I was.

A flood of letters was sent to the board on my behalf. 'What is a nurse to do when she comes across cases of real or apparent cruelty?' Dr H addressed the board. 'What will happen, is that she will say nothing, for fear of losing her job. Mr K tends to be rigid and autocratic, showing surprising gaps in his knowledge, which I would not have expected to find in a ward sister.

'Rehabilitation,' the doctor continued, 'is impossible in patients whose strokes are of several years standing, as I have pointed out to staff. I would have thought someone with Mrs Robilliard's caring nature in such a hospital was fortunate. Apart from my concern about her, I am concerned that her dismissal may mean that other staff members may lose heart, if a similar situation arises in the future, and say nothing. I am naturally very concerned for the future of the hospital and the happiness of its residents.'

A relative who had complained to Mr K about treatment meted out to his mother reported to the board that Mr K had told him, 'We have to be like that because Mrs Robilliard is too kind.'

I was bewildered and incredulous that I could ever be in a nursing situation where the quality of kindness was considered wrong. This attribute had earned me four blameless years in the Christchurch Public Hospital, culminating in being appointed a staff nurse in the largest women's surgical ward. I had loved every minute in that hospital, with its estimable standards.

'WHAT A SET-UP!' A PATIENT'S RELATIVE WROTE to the newspaper. 'Nurses pledged to loyalty, relatives afraid of victimisation if they question or complain, and the patients with no one to appeal to. No helpfulness, warmth or compassion is allowed to be shown. An articulate group of patients would question this regime, but these patients are slow in thought and often slurred in speech, and indeed have nowhere else to go. So they are set impossible and even dangerous goals. And even untrained aides are allowed to initiate their own brand of punishing exercises.'

My departure was followed by that of others who had written to the board. Mr K had made them feel their presence wasn't welcome. Mr K remained. But the cruelty stopped.

I was 42 years old. Up until this age I had innocently thought justice always prevailed, that right would win over wrong when a situation was judged. How wrong I was. I was absolutely shaken.

But incredibly, unbelievably, within the four weeks following my dismissal from the Collingwood hospital, three miracles occurred, offering opportunities that changed my life.

Thank you, dear God.

FIRSTLY, I WAS OFFERED A FREE 28-DAY camping tour around the Australian Outback, by a company called Australian Pacific, if I wrote an article about it for the *New Zealand Weekly*. This was my first trip outside New Zealand. My eyes were out on sticks with the starkly coloured beauty of the outback. The second miracle was the opportunity to study other countries, with *The Dominion* newspaper taking all my work. The third miracle was an invitation to be the rural spokesperson on TV One's panel discussion, *Beauty and the Beast*.

By now our children were established in their careers, so my education could begin.

Tim was at Lincoln College studying for a B Ag degree, while

Sally was studying medicine at Otago. Mike, who hadn't known what he wanted to do, won a scholarship at the end of his second-to-last year at school, which took two pupils to Sydney for the summer holidays to stay with a patron of the arts. Here he met talented people of all nationalities, and decided he was going to be an architect, and study at Sydney University.

But Australian universities charged fees, unlike their counterparts in New Zealand at that time.

'Don't worry,' said Mike. 'I'll get jobs.' And he did.

All the children worked in their university holidays. Tim trapped possums, worked with shearers and broke in horses. Sally did gardening jobs, and joined a shearing gang in the North Island, where she was touched by the little collections of family photos each girl kept on a box carton beside their bed.

Chapter 14

My mentor on *The Dominion* was its deputy editor Frank Haden, for whom I will be everlastingly grateful, although I was terrified of him! Known widely as a hard-headed journalist of the old school who had worked on newspapers for half a century, he had a reputation for shouting a lot.

If the phone rang in his office he'd been known to hurl it into his top drawer and lock it in. 'Telephones are for me to ring other people. Not for them to ring me,' he would say.

He didn't shout at me. Perhaps he saw me as some little farmer's wife who was prepared to take herself around the world to dig out things of publishable interest.

I was happy with that. My pay was meagre, but had quadrupled by the time Patrick Ensor had taken over from Frank in later years. I was well used to living frugally on Rocklands, and with the help of rent from an old house I had bought in Nelson, thanks to a small inheritance from Aunt Bet, I would save all year for the annual trips.

I went everywhere, from Saudi Arabia and other Gulf States to Israel, the West Bank and the Gaza Strip. I travelled to four Scandinavian countries, the Soviet Union, China, East and West Germany, several times to Africa, plus India, Italy, France, Greece, Spain, Ireland and the United States. My big scoop was North Korea.

I just adored this opportunity to get behind the glass walls of usual tourist-type aspects. My passionate interest was in learning how the politics, economy, religion and varying cultures affected the lives of ordinary people. By writing about what I learnt, my sole aim was to create better understanding, in as objective a way as possible.

How did I come to be doing this work, galloping around the world interviewing people, untrained? God only knows! It was a matter of sheer enthusiasm and curiosity. The minute my feet hit the ground in each new territory I would be looking for a telephone to pack each day full with appointments.

While planning to study The Troubles in Northern Ireland I came across Dervla Murphy's book on the subject, *A Place Apart*. I was invited to spend two days at her home in Lismore, in the Republic of Ireland.

I felt totally inadequate beside this extraordinary woman, who was similar in age to myself. When cycling from Ireland to India and faced with an unbridged river in the Himalayas, she put one arm round the neck of a wild cow, with the other holding her bike, to get across. In a doss-house in Turkey, having woken to find a naked Turk on her bed, she calmly fired a bullet at the ceiling to send him packing, and went back to sleep.

What we did have in common, however, was our absorbing interest in other people and our curiosity about how they live. And an ability to travel rough.

In Europe I slept on train seats, stringing my washing from the rack, to seek material for articles by day, returning to a train at night. My food was a water bottle, a loaf of bread and a jar of jam. I once woke to see police frisking an Asian male, an illegal immigrant, sleeping a metre away from me in an otherwise empty compartment. He was carrying knives.

At times the planes I used were old and past their prime, with oxygen masks emerging unbidden from the overhead storage compartments. In the USSR a stewardess would come with a hammer and a mouthful of nails to hoist the masks back into the ceiling.

In New Delhi I was temporarily kidnapped on a motorised rickshaw, when an unsavoury, suited Indian got in beside the driver. I had asked to be taken to a city hotel where an interviewee was waiting. But the rickshaw driver, directed by the unsavoury passenger, headed out of the city. In response to my increasingly agitated enquiries about the driver's ability to find the hotel, the unsavoury one would reply, 'Yes, madam, this is the way.'

Soon we were in scrub country. 'Just be soothed please,' said the unsavoury one, when in fact the scenery was becoming increasingly rural. By now well alarmed, I leapt off the rickshaw and ran back in the direction we'd come. With luck, a policeman rode past on his bicycle, whom I flagged down, but not before I had recorded the registration number of the rickshaw, which had stopped and was unable to restart.

Served them right!

I adored gathering the material, but once home, with a suitcase of notes and film, I placed huge pressure on myself to get each series written before the facts I had learnt became out of date – and I wasn't a fast writer.

But I have never, to this day, forgotten the people who came to mean the most to me on my journalist excursions, such as those under communist dictatorships behind the Iron Curtain. I studied life under Soviet domination in East Berlin, Poland, Czechoslovakia and Hungary, and left in utter anguish for people who lived in constant fear, unable to trust anyone, with no freedom of speech or movement, having to barter for medicines and lavatory paper.

I'd met Anna of East Berlin on a train in 1981, when she was returning from a visit to West Germany to be with her dying father. This rare concession was due to recent negotiations made on East Germans' behalf by the department of Inter-German Relations in Bonn. But now the week was over, and Anna knew she would never see her father again.

Her grief was terrible. 'Our situation is inhuman,' she said. This was only the second time in 20 years that Anna had visited her childhood home. On that earlier occasion she had been refused permission to visit her dying mother, so she had crossed the border illegally, using some kind of desperate intuition to find her way. It was before the wall was built.

Before we parted Anna suggested I might visit her in East Berlin. This was both brave and generous of her. East Germans were not encouraged to receive visitors from the West. My article about this day, my first behind the Iron Curtain, launched my career in the New Zealand press.

In Poland, in 1986, I spent a day with Jan, a freelance photographer, and Aniella, a fine arts graduate, who had chosen to live 18 kilometres outside Warsaw with their two children 'away from the polluted air and dirty milk which parents are not advised to give their children until they are three years old'. Aniella had been asked to be an agent, one of every 10 Poles who were paid by the Ministry of the Interior to spy on their colleagues. 'Of course I refused. But if I had done something wrong they could have forced me to do it.'

When Jan was driving me back to Warsaw that evening we were stopped by a police car. They wanted to check Jan's identification and car registration. Laughing and teasing he invited the police to admire his battered vehicle, turning the lights off and on, tooting the horn and playing with the windscreen wipers. 'Why did you do that?' I asked, exhausted from the tension.

'Because I'm a bloody Pole,' Jan replied.

In 1987, in Hungary, I met Andre, a party member and part of the artistic élite. He'd had surgery for cancer. 'There's constant mental and physical strain in having to pretend approval of an ideology in which you don't believe, for the sake of your job,' he said. 'Many people crack.'

There were also the heroic figures I met and wrote about who had risked their own lives to save others. In France in 1988, I spent a weekend with Madame Carrive at La Girarde, her sixteenth-century farmhouse. She was born in Berlin of Jewish parents, and had met her husband, the French poet Jean Carrive, when he'd come to Berlin in 1935 to study Kafka. The poet had told the German girl's mother that he was not the marrying kind. 'Have you venereal disease?' the mother asked. 'No? Then you are engaged.' She wanted her daughter out of Germany.

Until France fell to the German invaders in 1940, and the Vichy government announced that no Jews or foreigners could be employed, Madame Carrive taught German to the shopkeepers in Bordeaux 'so they could sell to the German occupiers'.

She'd hidden her Jewish identity after marrying into a French Huguenot family, but then news came that an old Jewish aunt was arriving from Germany. 'My husband told me to keep her in bed, which I did for a year, but it was risky. The French delivered 76,000 Jews to Germany during the war. So the old aunt and I fled through the forest to La Girarde, my late in-laws' home. Then another letter came from a Romanian Jew who had escaped from the French army. "Only in the brothel can I get a bed if I wait until 3 a.m. – please take me or I will commit suicide."

'This was an awkward situation. La Girarde also now had the mother of Balthus, the famous French painter, and there was not much to eat. I told God He had to help us, and He did. The village secretary, knowing there were Jews at La Girarde, threw the incriminating papers in the wastepaper basket.'

In Crete, in 1987, I accompanied Alexandros Papaderos to a mountain village, surrounded by wild intractable country, where he had grown up. He was born in 1933. 'I am not sad for what I experienced,' he said, 'but I don't want any child in the world to repeat it.'

He was a partisan, aged seven, working with his father and brother under the instruction of two British officers who had been delivered by submarine to organise resistance to the German occupiers. Crete's refusal to surrender to Hitler caused the Germans to delay their attack on Russia for a fatal two months, and turned the tide of the war.

Reprisals came in October 1943 – with just enough time to ring the church bell to warn the village's men to escape, Alexandros, now nine, found himself the oldest male present when the Germans arrived to destroy the 250 houses and shoot the old and sick. Standing there in his shorts and bare feet he'd refused to put his hands up. 'I thought it wasn't honest.' A period in a concentration camp followed.

And nor do I forget the young Palestinian, with whom I shared the back seat of an Arab taxi on Israel's West Bank in 1989, who was just out of prison. The young man, a political science graduate, had learnt English during his five years of detention in the Negev Desert, where there were 2500 administrative detainees who hadn't been charged. What did he plan to do now?

'I was dreaming of planting my father's land. That was all I could think about – the soil.' The voice trailed off. His father's land had been expropriated to become a Jewish settlement.

And in North Korea, too, there were people who touched me, such as the old women minding their grandchildren in playgrounds, who walked bent almost horizontal to the ground, a relic of much harsher times when they carried too-heavy loads under the 35 years of Japanese colonial rule. They had wonderful faces. At a holiday park, while exploring alone, I joined three young soldiers sitting on some rocks. One was playing a guitar. They produced a handkerchief for me to sit on.

SO, HOW DID I GET INTO NORTH KOREA in 1984, only the second Western journalist to do so since the Korean peninsula was divided following the Korean war?

Knowing I would be close by while visiting China, I had written to the Department of Cultural Relations with Foreign Countries in Pyongyang, the North Korean capital, asking if I could visit the country. I was instructed to call at the North Korean embassy in Beijing.

From here a patient but persistent First Secretary put up with my constant phone inquiries for news, sending eight cables to Pyongyang over a period of 10 days on my behalf, until at last a reply came, expecting me on a flight in three days' time.

At the start of my programme Mr Ho, my guide, set out to show me what he thought important, and to tell me what he thought I should know. Marching with short, feet-turned-out steps from hotel to appointment, Mr Ho determinedly led the way towards museums, magnificent edifices, holiday resorts and parks, with me becoming increasingly vocal about my wish to visit a cooperative farm, a factory, homes and schools. I wanted to learn how the system affected people in everyday life.

Eventually, by packing more and more into each day, all my requests were granted, although of course of a selected nature. In my attempts to gain a less organised insight I would insist on going for walks on my own, in the hope that some unofficial person would speak to me. But when I entered a housing block, a police car would always arrive to chase me away.

Between Mr Ho and me, we sometimes reduced Miss Pak, my interpreter, to little whimpers of exhaustion, falling asleep as soon as she reached the car. Mr Ho would look at her in frustration, unable to continue my education with the lists of figures and percentages he carried in his pocket.

It was also Miss Pak's job to look after me in the hotels where she also stayed. 'Who was that?' she asked, when I emerged from the dining room talking to another foreign guest – this time someone from Guyana who was studying irrigation.

'I don't know,' I'd reply, with a ridiculous feeling of abandonment. 'In the West,' I'd explain, 'it's quite normal to speak to strangers.'

But there was no pretence about the class of gifted children we visited, with five-year-olds playing Vivaldi's *Concerto in A minor*, reading the music. A six-year-old boy stood on a chair to pluck the strings of a full-sized double bass. The eyebrows of a small girl almost reached her hairline with the intensity of swaying to the rhythm, smiling and playing her cello.

At Panmunjom, the compound in the demilitarised zone, where North–South discussions take place, there were six little huts. American soldiers, on a platform to the south, watched us through binoculars. I didn't see any South Koreans on that side, only Americans.

I sat at the negotiating table in the hut used for meetings, and thought how childish it all was, with a microphone cable dividing the room, including the table, exactly in half, to separate each side's territory.

The day before, the four-hundred-and-twenty-fifth talk since the armistice had been held right there, when North Koreans had summoned the Americans to complain about their deployment of 1000 nuclear missiles in South Korea. 'What was the reply?' I asked.

'The Americans told us they were moving their most up-to-date weapons to the border,' an officer told me. 'Phantom bombers, FA5 and FA6 missiles and A10 tanks. Missiles pointed against us now equal 390,000 tonnes. The enemy thinks we are preparing for war. But why would we want war with our own people?'

I was taken to an observation post, five kilometres from the high concrete wall the Americans had built across the Korean peninsula. Five metres high and 10 metres thick at its base, the wall had iron gates wide enough for tanks to pass through. The top was dotted with gun emplacements.

'Do you also send back shellfire?' I asked the North Korean officer.

'Yes. Why not? We show them what we are. If we are silent the Americans would look down on us.'

Not only was there continuous shellfire from each side, but

loudspeakers on top of the wall broadcast pop music to corrupt the North Koreans. In return, the North Koreans blasted back sayings of their Great Leader Kim Il-sung.

Silly, silly boys, all of them.

I WOULD RETURN HOME TO BE FRUSTRATED by the moans and complaints from my fellow New Zealanders, so rich in safety, democracy and luxury. Even the poorest among us were rich in comparison to so many of the people I'd met in corrupt and dictatorial police states.

I also came to realise, through these journalistic opportunities, that those who had suffered inhumanely, and who had been hungry, oppressed, cruelly treated and terrified, had enormous depths to their souls. They'd had to dig so deep within themselves in their efforts to survive.

And the music! I have never before or since heard classical music such as I heard behind the Iron Curtain, in Moscow, Warsaw, Prague, Budapest and Belgrade, where free speech, movement and writing were forbidden, and music was the only safe release.

But no matter where I had been, there was always a sense of lifting when I came home, to drive through the gate to Rocklands. Only in Golden Bay could I truly be myself, in old clothes, without make-up, with no social expectations to live up to – just total acceptance. Above all, I had a husband who was delighted for me to have had these journalist opportunities, even though it took me away for a few weeks each year. He encouraged me.

Today, thanks to these worldwide experiences, I have come to realise that the people who interest me most, whose values I most admire, have all, either in New Zealand or abroad, faced struggles or difficulties in some kind of way.

I no longer envy those who have had an easy life.

CHAPTER 15

To help Tim into a farm in Canterbury we sold off our lower hills, the mountain and most of the back country in lifestyle blocks. Townspeople, backed by their city earnings, and foreigners from overseas, seemed willing to pay for a piece of land overlooking the sea. Our drive became a public road welcoming half-a-dozen newcomers.

Even so, it was hard for Garry to part with land he'd slogged his guts over to develop, to then see it deteriorate with people only interested in the view. With the addition of the fertile flat land we'd leased and later bought, he'd developed Rocklands to carry 2000 ewes. But there was enough money left over to build us a house on the hill, so he had a new, absorbing interest.

We employed an architect, Ian Athfield, with Garry doing the building himself, taking four years to complete it. He would wake excited each morning, to pore over the plans and start work. The house was roofed with 40,000 native cedar shingles, each cut by hand. Massive boulders created the entrance, with more rocks forming the walls and floor of the hall. A cousin arrived from England and suggested we should wear goat skins to greet visitors at our cave-like front door.

Frankly, I'd had enough of rocks on Rocklands, and would have preferred a conventional house – it would have been easier to dust – but this was Garry's creativity, his chance to fulfil something special. With our architect nearby when at his holiday house at Awaroa, something unusual was created.

The house became a must-see for swarming locals and strangers. With deadlines for articles looming, I once ignored a door knock, but that didn't deter the couple. From upstairs I could hear them opening and shutting cupboards, showing themselves round the house. *Surely they won't come up here,* I told myself. This attic room was accessed through a stairway off the back porch.

Ha! Footsteps came up the stairs. I thought of getting under a bed, imagining their embarrassment when the intruders saw me. Instead I froze. Were the couple embarrassed? Not a bit. I was!

In desperation to slow the house viewers, I put a notice at the front gate saying *Robin working 8–4 p.m. Please ring*, and supplied our telephone number. Did that stall the arrivals? Not a bit. Some people, particularly city-based tourists, were furious. They wouldn't have welcomed interruptions to their offices, but writers were expected to always be on-deck. And if you have an unusual house, it seems you must always be open to the curious.

When I first came to Golden Bay I wasn't interested in reading the Nelson newspaper. I was not a Nelsonian. I didn't belong here. We were only going to stay on Rocklands in Golden Bay until we could sell and return to Canterbury. But as years went by I came to realise I couldn't live anywhere else unless the scenery was equally beautiful. And if anything threatened this remote and glorious district I was like a lion protecting her cub. I'd become outraged at any threat to this special place.

On a summer's day in 1981, there was a strange heavy feeling in the air outside our house. Not a smell, just a peculiar weight in the atmosphere. This was the day, we were to learn, that a kiln at the local cement works hadn't reached the required heat to destroy the polychlorinated biphenyls (PCBs) it was handling. Unbelievable as it sounds, this paradise was handling toxic wastes, supervised by the Health Department.

Rumours abounded, including that the local cement company was in deep financial strife, and doomed to close unless it generated extra income by commercially disposing of waste chemicals.

The general public knew nothing of this until things came to a head at a public meeting in Takaka, called by the Health Department and Golden Bay Cement Company, to assure people of the safety of the operation. The packed meeting in the high school hall, chaired by the Commissioner for the Environment, became an uproar when some cement workers broke the instructed official silence to tell of mishaps during the test burning.

They were angrily critical of what they described as lax precautions undertaken by Health Department officials during the initial trial. They spoke of spills, with cement dust thrown over one spill, and others being hosed into the harbour, where scallop enhancement was taking place.

We also heard that PCB oil had been injected into the kiln when it wasn't burning properly, resulting in toxic vapour sweeping the countryside. Full drums were being left in the open, with no signs attached to warn of their contents.

The imported toxicological expert responded by telling the meeting that PCBs were 'less harmful than common salt'.

At this the high school's chemistry teacher became alarmed. 'That man is either ignorant, duplicitous, or both,' he declared. Although admitting to being no expert on PCBs, this teacher's prowess in the classroom had made him a kind of scientific guru in the district.

While conceding that cement-kiln incineration of PCBs was safe, providing it was done properly, the teacher had no confidence in the Health Department's ability to conduct a 500-tonne burn at the local cement works 'on the evidence of their sloppy procedures during the trial'.

A committee was formed – a fisherman and his wife, the teacher and myself. We had no meetings, just conversed by phone, as we each frenziedly wrote or faxed scientists and environmentalists worldwide, to seek opinions about the situation we faced. With these replies we then sought the support of Federated Farmers, marine and conservation departments, the dairy company, horticulturalists, fishermen, orchardists and politicians, to oppose any idea of a toxic-waste disposal factory in Golden Bay.

Even if the process were handled impeccably, Golden Bay's reputation as a clean, unspoilt region would suffer by association with hazardous-waste disposal.

Health Department officials labelled our opposition hysterical and paranoid, and the media who supported our stand, both television and print, were accused of scaremongering and sensationalism.

A university-educated American, who had built his home in an isolated bush setting, first heard of the PCB burning during the initial trial, but did not think much of it. 'If it had been another department I might have worried more,' he said, 'but I thought the Health Department was in charge of people's health, and trusted them at that point. The September meeting opened my eyes.'

He predicted PCBs would not be the only toxic waste disposed of in the Bay. 'Once the system is working, then it's obvious they'll keep trucking it down here. Golden Bay will be known as a waste dump.' The American was reported in the press as threatening to take direct action to block the Takaka Hill road, to prevent PCBs being transported here.

Local incineration of PCBs stopped.

In 1988 the cement works closed, with the creaks and groans of machinery and belching silos silenced forever. With 125 workers losing their jobs there were huge howls from the established community about how the Bay would die. They'd been hooked on the big wages from that smelly, polluting plant for so long that they couldn't see the alternatives.

But the Bay survived surprisingly well. For a while Golden

Bay had more money on term deposit per head of population than anywhere else in the country, as former cement workers wondered what to do with their big redundancy windfalls, in many cases over $100,000. Some squandered theirs in the pubs, others set up marginal businesses like bungee jumping and quickly went bust. Quite a few established themselves in more sustainable businesses and exist comfortably today.

THE 1980S ARE REMEMBERED AS A TIME of turmoil for New Zealand's sheep and beef farmers. In 1984 Robert Muldoon's National government was defeated, and Prime Minister David Lange appointed Roger Douglas as his Minister of Finance, who set about dismantling the imposing mass of regulation with which Muldoon had shored up the country's crumbling economy.

With the crutch of farm subsidies kicked away, lamb prices plummeted, interest rates sky-rocketed, inflation ran rampant and indebted farmers were forced to sell. Those who stayed cut spending and saw their farms deteriorate. To rub salt into the wounds, some regions were hit by drought. Then the sharemarket crashed and any investments farmers had left were decimated. There were mental breakdowns. Suicides.

In the early 1980s, Leentje and Richard Thorpe on Glen Rannoch had taken up a development loan, encouraged by the politicians. Now their interest rates were going through the roof.

With the recession they couldn't sell their sheep. Old ewes, which they used to sell to flat-land farmers for $15 each, were now worth a couple of dollars. They raised calves, which sold well, but wool prices had also crashed. And the loan-repayment bills kept coming, with the bank overdraft getting ever bigger. The couple were desperate. The bank was charging them 27 per cent interest, with penalty interest added, and bankruptcy was a frightening possibility.

They told the bank they couldn't pay interest of $800 each quarter, and asked if their loan could be put on a longer-term basis, with smaller three-monthly payments. The bank refused.

'You must get a job,' a Ministry of Agriculture official told Leentje, a mother of six children. She started a correspondence course in teacher training, but a year later the course was cancelled.

In desperation she wrote to Prime Minister David Lange. 'I reminded him how Gandhi had said that it was the peasants who held a country up, and as long as the peasants were strong, the country would be at peace. I told him how during the war it was the farmers who supported the population in Holland. How there was no food in Amsterdam, and my father would ride out into the country, on an old bike with no rubber on its wheels, to buy a bit of wheat, a few potatoes from the farmers. If you have a lot of people living in the countryside, they can do that.'

She explained that Golden Bay had many small-farm families, with elderly parents often living on the place, with the children able to earn money on the farm, as her own children did: chopping manuka to sell as firewood, trapping possums to sell the skins, growing exotic fruit and vegetables.

'If we lived in the city,' her letter continued, 'our children would not have this chance. And other young people come here, from being unemployed in the cities, to ask if they can work for their keep, with many small farms in the district providing that same opportunity.'

Leentje's tears poured onto the paper as she wrote. 'Because everything I put down meant so much.'

A few months later a letter arrived from the Rural Bank. It

said they had reconsidered the Thorpes' situation, and would put their loan onto a different scale. They would not have to pay $800 a month. Other local farmers who had borrowed for development also had their loans reduced.

But according to Alan Wood, lecturer in agricultural policy at Massey University, the future for many hill-country farmers was bleak, whatever they did, even if they were free of debt. 'In a lot of hard hill situations, the only answer is to close it down,' he wrote in an article. 'If not this year, than the next. You can't afford to waste resources on such land. You won't get it back. If things pick up and they survive, they'll be in trouble again the next time round. The clever ones got out ten years ago.'

'Why not let the market take its course?' said an ambitious land agent in Golden Bay. 'Let the uneconomic farmers go out of business and realise their one real asset – the place. Send them off to live on the investment income and allow the commodity brokers and merchant bankers the pleasure of owning a place in the country. The real value of Golden Bay,' he added, 'is now effectively an extensive suburbia. Any other outcome would be artificial.'

Rage surged inside me. Why? Because the essential quality of Golden Bay had come from the rugged, independent hill farmers, who were prepared to live on the smell of an oily rag to stay on their land. Lose them and the Bay wouldn't be the same. It would be losing people of character. The old resilient farming life was changing before our eyes.

Some hill farmers hung on, but the question was being asked: was there a future for marginal land? Some said the land should never have been cleared in the first place. Hard-fisted Treasury economists suggested uneconomic farmers should die quietly. This was no comfort for farmers on Golden Bay's hard hills who knew no other way of life.

Garry, as provincial president of Golden Bay Federated

Farmers, had supported Peter Elworthy, the national president, in his stand to end farming subsidies. As its many critics pointed out, the policy flew in the face of economic logic and defied all principles of fair trade, and also encouraged farmers to overstock, cramming the hillsides with thousands of underfed ewes, skinny and worthless to the market.

But those who took this affirmative stand had expected the country's manufacturers to also have their subsidies removed, to provide a level playing field. That didn't happen.

The loss of the subsidies almost halved our income, but we worried more about indebted Tim. His dry, stony farm of 214 hectares at Southbridge in Canterbury, bought in 1981 with a large mortgage, was facing a big challenge. Tim knew the sandy and brown-top pastures would require work and money to bring them to a good productive level, but like other farmers he'd had no inkling of the bleak economic future to come.

Tim hung on, still in his early twenties, working so hard, fending for himself in a rough sort of home. He was once seen sitting at the back of a hall at a local Federated Farmers meeting chewing on a leg of cold mutton for his belated meal! He survived when many others didn't at that time. A 1988 article in Christchurch's *The Press* described Tim's success in re-grassing the entire farm with the lambing percentage now 100 per cent and wool weights up by one tonne a year.

Few of the original families remain on the Bay's tough ranges that fringe the productive valleys. Most of the lower slopes have become smallholdings. There were advertisements for seaside residences adjacent to native bush, or beside silted-up streams. Farmhouses and even old sheds were snapped up to house IT programmers, artists, craftsmen and growers of olives and other horticultural crops. Even grapes.

Every second person you talk to has a website, with technology making home-based employment possible for an increasing number. They have made a lifestyle choice and written off the negatives – the long distances to get anywhere else, the cost of freight, the two-hour-plus journey to get specialist health care – against the benefits.

It took a little time for Gordy to realise that his near-derelict cottage and hopeless farm was exactly what a newcomer wanted. He watched a man in a smart car drive slowly up and down the road, eyeing his land with all its potential for a lifestyle block. Gordy glared at him and hoped he wouldn't return. He didn't want to live in town. Even though it was said that another farmer, with land below his, had made a million dollars selling the property as lifestyle blocks.

'My brothers, who have a share in the place, always wanted me to sell, you know,' Gordy told me. 'But my mother would say, "Don't you let them! If you want to stay here, you stop here!" My father fought for the whole of his life to hold onto this place.'

The changes, with this urban influx, weren't always easy. There were problems with the new people's ignorance of rural rules about dogs and sheep-worrying, privacy, and courtesy, such as asking permission for crossing land. Over the hill one day came a man, standing on the seat of his old tractor, hair flying, as it raced towards a newly arrived lifestyler. 'Get your f– dog out of my f– land, you f– bastard.'

The new resident was terrified.

THE NEWER SETTLERS ARE OFTEN WELL-HEELED and can afford to drop out of the system. They've come to live a lifestyle they once dreamed about. A retired British Army major and businessman, Richard Penny, and his artist wife, Bardi Ivory, became near neighbours.

Richard had led a full and interesting life, firstly in the Punjab Regiment of the British Army, where he served with the Gurkhas, and in later years as a director of Rio Tinto, the multinational mining corporation. In Golden Bay, on holiday, he not only found Bardi, but a new and freer lifestyle.

'Ties and suits are out!' he gleefully discovered. 'And I can call everyone by their Christian names!' For a proper public-school-educated Englishman, this was a different world indeed!

In no time Bardi had their little house torn apart to convert it into a mansion. Flowers, shrubs and fruit trees sprung up under her hands. The builders would say 'No, it can't be done', and Bardi would say 'We'll find a way.' She just stuck with it. She knew it could be done.

Richard enjoyed women, good music, and the celebrations of eating, drinking and partying. He was an avid bridge player, but above all followed rugby and cricket. 'How lucky I am,' he was continually saying, 'to live in such a place.' The parties he and Bardi hosted, often with 60 people seated around the swimming pool, lifted our social lives to a new dimension.

But for Richard this Golden Bay life only lasted a few years. With chronic heart failure it became agony to watch him cross the street in Takaka, step by painful step, then grasp the roof of his car as he gathered enough breath to slip into the driver's seat. He delayed his admission to hospital until the Sunday, because there was a televised cricket test to watch. Instead he died at home on the Saturday morning. He was in his seventy-ninth year.

Bardi sold up and moved to the other side of the Takaka Hill.

A RUTTED GRAVEL ROAD LED UP TO A PLATEAU, on a spur that branches off our former mountain, where Sally's childhood hut was long ago replaced with a Skyline garage. It was the home of Jonathan, an Old Etonian. He had the most elevated house site in Golden Bay, with views south to the Dragon's Teeth Mountains, and across the Bay to Farewell Spit and the western ranges.

Socks hung from the rafters, with the bench cluttered with organic foodstuffs and various herbal teas, which are served with a dash of manuka honey. It took me an hour to walk from my home to Jonathan's, with the road getting steeper and steeper.

When his family's estate was sold in Northumberland, the only keepsake Jonathan wanted was a silver candelabra, to keep in his garage home.

WE ALWAYS KNEW WHEN OLLIE PHIPPS was coming up the road. Her cloud of dust sped faster than anyone else would dare, even in her eighties. Utterly fearless, she told us she would have liked to have been a racing-car driver. Whatever Ollie took on, it was 'harness your horse and go at it full tilt', always with flamboyance and style.

Widowed in her seventies, she'd then met and married Vice Admiral Sir Peter Phipps. But tragedy struck. On the day Ollie and Peter signed up to buy a 10-acre block with a small house on the Golden Bay coast, Peter was killed in a car accident, and Ollie seriously injured. She returned to her new home on crutches, with son Tony and his partner Kathy to live with her, ready to be issued instructions about making a garden. It was to have drifts of things: whole heaps of violets, floods of bluebells and water irises, no fewer than 50 plants of each variety. Massive plantings. Ollie did nothing by halves.

Tony bulldozed the gorse and drove it over the bank to the beach, which upset the neighbours. Delegations arrived, hoofing it over the newly laid lawn to confront Ollie. Hateful letters were sent and people complained to the newspaper. Not about the scrub being dumped on the beach to be taken away by the tide, but about the gorse being uprooted.

Months later Tony came across the main complainant in Takaka. 'I'm very disappointed,' he told her. 'You came and abused my mother, and you have never been back to see that sometimes removing gorse can lead to something beautiful.' When members of Canterbury's Horticultural Society toured the top of the South Island, Ollie's garden was the highlight of their tour.

Ollie never criticised anyone, or got into arguments. Vivacious, artistic and humorous, she would laugh at strange people and their strange ways. Even so, it must have been very hurtful to Ollie, who invited everyone she met to her parties, to be rejected by a women's lunch group. 'If Ollie comes, I won't,' insisted one long-time resident, who perhaps considered herself headmistress of the group, and felt threatened by Ollie's title.

'She doesn't fit in,' said another.

Not fit in? Well, how come the people you met at Ollie's house came from every walk of life, from hippy to farmer, from redneck to environmentalist, from old money to welfare beneficiary? There wasn't a snobbish bone in dear Ollie's body.

A farm worker, her next-door neighbour, was Ollie's regular companion when rugby tests were televised. He could never remember who won. 'We're so busy changing hats and blowing hooters,' he explained. 'Ollie had a different hat for every team.'

It wasn't until she broke a leg six years later that Ollie began to fade. Well, not entirely. Hospitalised in Takaka she still wanted her fingernails painted.

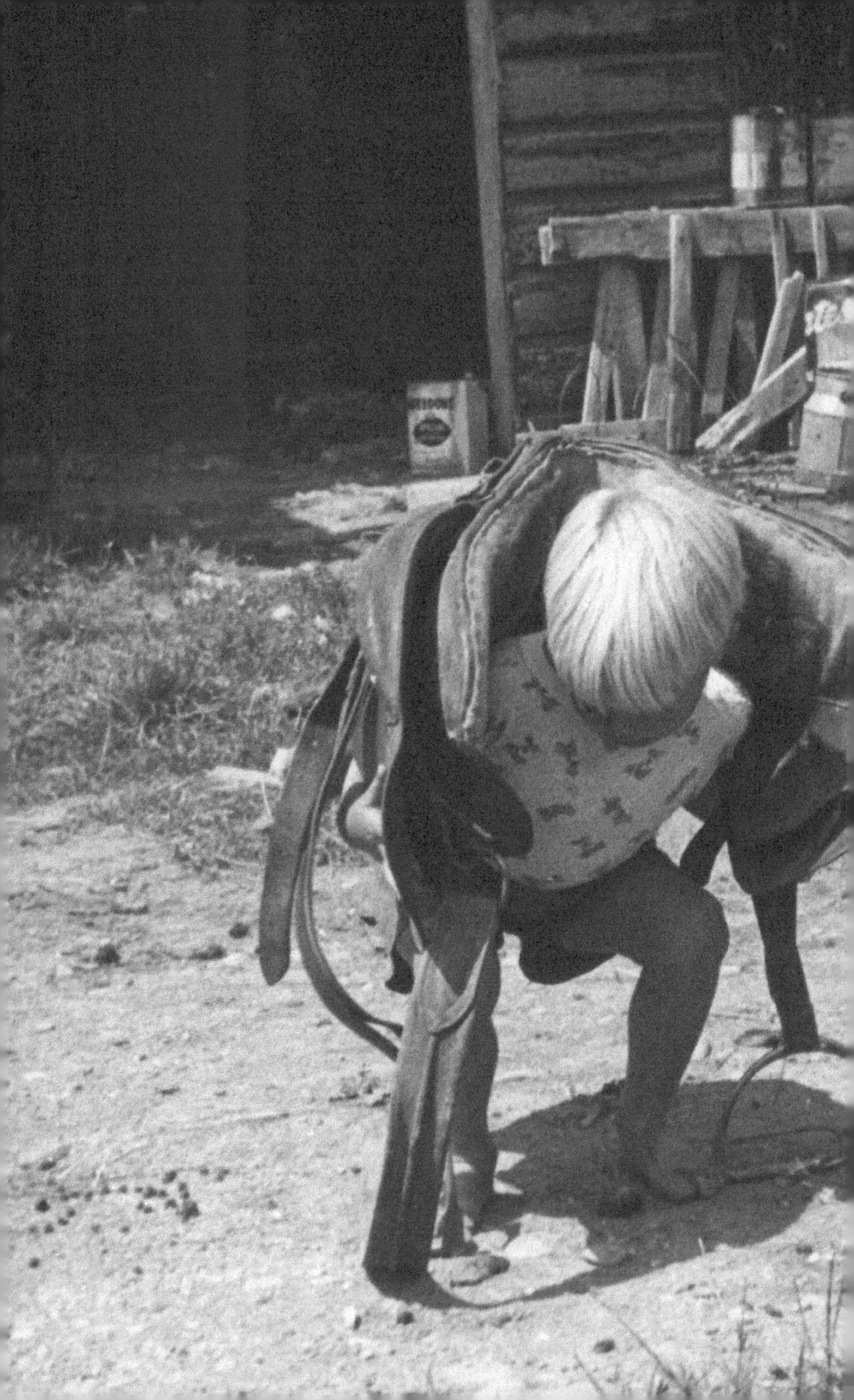

Chapter 16

I've watched the Bay change as the years rolled along. The alternative lifestylers, whose influx started as a trickle, now make up one-third of Golden Bay's population. Most are self-employed, utilising their many talents and skills. They've set up cafés, fresh food markets, an organic shop, endless fairs and community activities. Above all, their bright offspring have enlivened the schools.

Today the Wholemeal Café in Takaka is patronised by all sections of the community, having started out fully segregated. For almost three decades from the 1970s no one who considered themselves 'straight' would be seen there, even if it did offer the best vegetarian food in town.

People laughed when Jane and Andrew Dixon built the Mussel Inn in remote Onekaka, but not only did it survive, it's now famous as a unique institution. 'We have hippies, rednecks, old people, bikies and babies all mixed up,' says Andrew. Nearly every weekend there is live music. On the third Thursday of every month local poets meet here to recite their poems. 'Hell,' said one of the performers, 'we have more poets here than in the whole of Nelson.'

Established in 1973, the Rainbow Valley community, at Glovers Flat in the Anatoki Valley, in the foothills of the western ranges of Golden Bay, continues to exist. Today it's more a community of individuals, with most having jobs 'outside'.

'When we came here,' said Robyn, one of the founders, 'we obviously thought it was a good spot, but those who have stayed have had to fight real environmental adversity. Coping with sandflies, a shorter growing period, higher rainfall and the occasional threat of the Anatoki flooding to name a few.'

There are also the people politics. 'Living in a large group is not always easy, especially when most of us are strong-minded individuals!' There is general agreement that the community is a great place to bring up children. 'They grow up with confidence here and are held in high regard in the schools. They stand up for themselves. In their minds they are equal with adults.'

At least 400 hippie kids have been born in the Bay. Almost every week *The G.B. Weekly* reports the success of one of them, from winning first prize at Wearable Arts, to working at Weta Workshop on an internationally produced film – even gaining a place at Cambridge University to become a professor of anthropology.

What I find fascinating is that this younger generation, in contrast to their parent's values of the 1970s, want to earn money, with some even loving white bread and digital gadgets! A teenager living in one of the Bay's remaining communities has speakers in his bedroom, a PlayStation, a TV and a DVD player. 'I've got every set-up here,' he says happily.

The invasion of intellectuals among the alternative lifestylers has changed the Bay for the better. They spark lively debate. The locals enjoy the challenge, but we do get annoyed if our farming practices are questioned. Farmers bear an economic cost when a hippy neighbour stops a farmer spraying gorse. 'It's bloody medieval around here,' one farmer commented.

There wasn't a picture theatre in Takaka for many years. When Dalgety's farm store in the middle of Takaka was for sale, it was bought by Gerard Hindmarsh, who had been part of the homesteading movement. As he described in his book *Swamp Fever*, Gerard had no money whatsoever and the price was $115,000, so he claimed the GST back on the delayed payment and used it as a deposit.

For $1000 he bought the entire contents of a movie theatre in Auckland, just before the place was demolished. The power had been disconnected, so Gerard and his wife Melanie worked by torchlight to unscrew the seats and unbolt the projection gear. When heavy lifting was needed Gerard sought the help of passing pedestrians.

The Village Theatre opened in 1987. Gerard worked the projector and Melanie sold tickets while breastfeeding their first child. On their own they kept the place going for almost four years, but with high interest rates they were in trouble. They threw a big party and appealed to their supporters. An enthusiastic community took over the theatre as a trust.

Our Village Theatre is currently showing all 10 filmed operas from the New York's Metropolitan Theatre, as well as the National Theatre of London's filmed Shakespeare productions. How's that for what is said to be the smallest town in New Zealand to have a picture theatre?

Gerard is one of Golden Bay's most talented citizens. I've read *Swamp Fever* three times, to learn not only about his life, but also what was going on within the whole alternative community, which had arrived like an invasion of gypsies in the 1970s to enliven the district in so many ways.

He arrived here from Wellington in 1976, aged 19, having quit his public servant job as a cartographic cadet, to put his entire savings of $2000 down as a deposit on 14 acres of pakihi scrubland and swamp at Tukeroa near Collingwood. It was a swamp he came to love.

His career as a journalist began with his prize-winning article for the *New Zealand Geographic* about the heroic, and rarely attempted, five-day trip he did with three friends along a particularly rugged section of the West Coast south of the Kahurangi lighthouse. The 'to hell and back' trip followed the steps of Charles Heaphy and Thomas Brunner, the first Europeans to traverse this precipitous coast in 1856.

Since that achievement Gerard has published four books to date. His first, called *Angelina,* was based on his Moleta grandparents' pioneering life on D'Urville Island in the early 1900s. Gerard's mother's family, the Moletas, originated from the tiny island of Stromboli off the coast of Sicily.

Mike, now living in Sydney, had recently been to the book launch of another Moleta family history, written by a cousin of Gerard's.

'This Moleta author married my sister's husband's sister,' I tell Gerard.

'Then we're related,' he said. I wish we were.

LIVING BEHIND THE TAKAKA HILL seems to pressure people to expand, develop, dig deep and promote things that, perhaps, like me, they may never have dreamt of achieving before they came to live here. Extraordinary things happen here.

Perhaps it's the lack of criticism that gives people the confidence to do extraordinary things – this is not a judgemental society. Or perhaps it's because people are not spoon-fed with the comforts, temptations and ease of urban living, so they seek a sense of achievement by giving something, anything, a go. Above all, in a very small community, everyone can be someone. That's good for one's confidence.

If you'd suggested, when as a 23-year-old I first came over the Takaka Hill to live on an impoverished farm, that I would one day have the opportunity to study remote parts of the world as a journalist, flying away from behind the Takaka Hill barrier once a year, to return, grateful for the seclusion to write my articles, I would never, ever have believed it possible.

IN 1974 DICK NICHOLLS, A FORMER WELLINGTON LIBRARIAN, arrived in the Bay with plans to be an organic gardener. Then, from the car case he was squatting in near Parapara Inlet, his attention was drawn to an unoccupied block of sour Crown land on the coast, which appeared to be written off as useless. So he approached the Department of Lands and Survey, and under their auspices he undertook to reforest the area.

Within a year he'd established a plant nursery on the land and was successful in establishing natives in the sand-dune country. But by 1976 the true horror of the nature of most of the impoverished soils became apparent. 'Even gorse would not grow on most of it.'

So Dick started planting eucalypts, sending all over the world to obtain 90 different species. Some 50,000 trees were planted over the next two decades. The eucalypts thrived on the poor soil, broke up the iron pan with their roots, and enhanced fertility. With the attraction of nectar-laden flowers, native birds came to feed, and to disperse native seeds through their copious droppings.

Milnthorpe Park Scenic Reserve today is a glorious place, criss-crossed with a multitude of tracks through which our younger grandchildren compete at showing the way. There is a mailbox by the carpark from which maps of the tracks can be borrowed. People have donated wooden seats in memory of people who have died, where walkers can rest. Local sculptors camp here annually to produce beautiful objects constructed mainly from Nature. Children come dressed as fairies to dance in the shady forest.

On my last visit, there was Dick, now an elderly man, working alone to reconstruct a small bridge. It's people like him who should receive medals.

It was also in the mid-1970s that the Abel Tasman National Park went seriously green and magical things happened. Long hair was fashionable at the time, not only with politicians and All Blacks but also park rangers. Geoff Rennison, in charge of the park rangers, had the appearance, as he described it, of 'a small rodent peering out of the shrubbery'.

He put the staff at Totaranui, the park's campground, on bicycles, buying up old frames and wheels and painting them orange. 'They could get around silently without disturbing the campers, were non-polluting and dirt cheap to run,' he explained. 'The bikes were distinctive too, so they could be left anywhere, any time, without any risk of being pinched.'

Geoff revolutionised the rubbish system. The old way called for bulldozed holes in the ground, into which rubbish was tipped and covered over. 'Such a waste! What we did, instead, was to keep a hundred hay bales each spring when the paddocks were mown, to build a big dam, and into this went the pumping from the toilet blocks and the campers' organic rubbish. It would be stirred a few times by the tractor tines. The mature compost was used in the nursery where we grew a thousand trees each year.'

The whole aim was to 'tread lightly on the land' while not compromising standards. And in this Geoff's staff were streaks ahead of other national parks and enjoying themselves immensely. 'We were lucky, of course, that our boss of Lands and Survey Department was flexible, and probably bemused enough to let us play in our small corner,' he says. 'I doubt that today's Department of Conservation, hedged in with standards and procedures, would allow such an outburst of practical counter-culture.'

In 2003 Derry Kingston started his Heaphy Track Help business, so trampers can drive to one end of the track, and have their car waiting for them when they arrive at the other. After relocating a car to the Karamea end, Derry usually slogs back on foot to Golden Bay in a day-and-a-half, hence gaining the nickname of 'The Kingston Flier'.

Derry has now walked the track more than 300 times. 'It's fun,' he says, 'meeting people on the track, and having such a wonderful place to do my work. People are quite envious of my office.' One party was surprised to meet him coming towards them three times during their tramp. Of course this work keeps Derry fit for continual challenges.

At the age of 62, following a double bypass, he undertook a sponsored walk from Bluff to Farewell Spit, taking only 22 days. With the funds raised Derry purchased six wooden benches to install in different parts of the Bay for people to indicate they are waiting for a lift from a friendly driver. One dollar for 10 kilometres is the suggested koha.

And then there was Richard Bayliff, a graduate of Oxford University, who was not only a brilliant teacher at the Golden Bay High School, but prepared to work half the night spraying gorse on his hilltop land, with a miner's light on his forehead. He even had a desk set up on his farm bike, so when working on his land at weekends, he could mark his pupils' papers at the same time.

He'd told me 10 years ago that he was burnt out from teaching, but still he kept going, admired and adored by his grateful maths pupils. Known as 'Bayliff' or 'Uncle Bayliff', he'd spend intervals and lunchtimes in his classroom with pupils who dropped by, or were summoned or kept in. He was ferocious in his advocacy of mathematics, dogged in his pursuit of homework or correspondence-subject defaulters, and unwavering in his belief in the rightness of what he was doing. For 26 years he streamed his classes, whether educational orthodoxy said that was the thing to do or not.

Bayliff told outrageous lies about his own life, involving the content of his sandwiches. He neglected his appearance, stapling up the hem of his trusty walk-shorts as required, was intensely interested in his students' lives and, according to one ex-pupil, 'could spot a crush a mile off'.

As a solo farmer of his beloved piece of land near the skyline, Richard worked at both ends of the day and in the school holidays. One mode of transport to school in the early morning

– not many of the staff were there before him – was his blue farm truck. It would often leave at the end of the school day loaded up with posts or gravel. His muddy gumboots would sit at the classroom door.

In August 2013, aged 67, Richard died suddenly at his home. At his memorial service, school parents spoke of the devastating loss to the Golden Bay High School. He had put two, or even three, lifetimes into one.

WILLIE BUTLER, ALMOST A STORYBOOK CHARACTER, was yet another genius who'd come to live in the Bay, and benefit so many others. His whimsical humour first became noticed with his founding of 'Aunt Fanny's Sewing Circle', a club where men wore women's clothes and held annual battles on Takaka's main street with the Christchurch-based 'Alf's Imperial Army'. The locals kept out of the way as custard pies flew through the air.

On Saturdays there were hockey games, with Willie, his long hair flying, shouting encouragement from the back line to whatever team he was in at the moment. There were several. One game in the afternoon was never enough for Willie. He would often join in another just for fun.

But behind the frivolity he was concerned about society and where it was heading. Through the high school he set up a 'Challenge' programme, in which many youths pushed boundaries with him on a rock face, in kayaks and in caves. The council, with Willie's encouragement, built a skateboard park, and their 'Day Out' and 'Boredom Busters' holiday programmes bloomed with Willie involved. One Nelson judge attributed the lack of delinquents in Golden Bay to Willie's influence.

With a shy young grandson with us one school holidays, Garry and I decided to take him to one of Willie's rock-climbing days. We thought this would appeal to Sam, having heard of his prowess on indoor-climbing walls in Hamilton.

‘No thanks,’ said Sam, when this was suggested.

Garry and I decided we were going regardless. But I phoned Willie the night before to say we would like to bring a shy eight-year-old to the rock-climbing day.

So there was Willie, walking to meet us, to give Sam a special greeting, and of course, within minutes he had Sam climbing a limestone cliff with ropes under Willie’s careful guidance. Sam and a small girl were the stars of the day. It was an exhilarated grandson we took home afterwards.

ALBIE BURGERS, WHO CAME TO GOLDEN BAY from South Africa with wife Fill in 1979, collects unwanted computers from round the Bay, which he refurbishes into a simple operating system to sell cheaply or give away to local people. It was Albie, with infinite patience, who taught me how to use a computer.

When Albie gives a talk at the local library it’s packed, with people wanting to know what he has invented next, and to specifically seek his advice about how to get power cheaply.

When you arrive at the Burgerses’ Tugela farm in rural Takaka, the first unusual thing you see is a paddle wheel with blue sails. This is Albie’s latest windmill, a panemone, which is meant to generate electricity, but ‘only generates beauty at the moment’, says Albie. ‘It’s wonderful to watch it turning majestically in a good breeze with a glass of home-brew in hand.’

More reliable power generation comes from the ‘nano-hydro’ Pelton-wheel generator, made from a backing-gate mechanism from a cow shed, and powered from a spring in the hills behind the property. Albie calls it a ‘useful toy’ which runs all their reading lights. ‘It charges batteries at a low rate during the day, and we use it up over a few hours at night.’

Various generations of solar water heaters, each boasting refinements and increasing efficiency, provide hot water for the house. The materials were so cheap Albie reckons the savings on the power bill paid for them in less than three years. He diverts the surplus hot water to a spa pool he's built. 'This caused curiosity and amusement when Fill and I went to the rural supplier and sat in plastic stock troughs to test them for size.'

There's also the five-wheeled 'Quike', which is like a rickshaw with two sets of pedals, a solar panel and an electric motor. The solar panels double as a sunshade. 'Fill and I would like to go touring in the Quike one day,' says Albie. 'Well, to tell the truth, Fill's not quite as keen as I am about this idea.' More to Fill's taste is a solar-powered car called E-Hatsu. 'Because it's an electric Daihatsu, and it's impossible not to smile when you're driving it!' says the irrepressible Albie.

JOYCE WYLLIE, FROM A BEEF AND SHEEP FARM sandwiched between Westhaven Inlet and the wild western coastline, is a legend in the Bay. She is a vet, a farmer and a community advocate, and even finds time to home-school her children.

She is as pretty as a picture when glammed up, functioning as a celebrant at weddings or funerals, but never wearing shoes. 'I do have shoes,' she explains, 'but it's not easy to find decent ones to fit my feet. I grew up on a back-country farm on the east coast north of Gisborne, which is where the barefoot thing began.'

As the top of the South Island's representative to the Correspondence School's Parents and Supervisors Association, Joyce has been an important voice in the attempt to restore services to 'distant kids'. 'Unfortunately,' she explains, 'the Correspondence School now has a heavy focus on students considered "high needs", and so they get more attention.'

In 2006 she went to Government House to be awarded a regional achievement award, inaugurated by Rural Women New Zealand to mark its eightieth anniversary. This recognised her roles with the Plunket Society, Nelson Conservation Board,

Golden Bay Search and Rescue, Collingwood's Volunteer Fire Brigade, the Home-Schoolers group, the Aorere Valley church, Pakawau Rural Women and Federated Farmers.

It's Joyce who summons the Bay's dry-stock farmers for discussion groups and demonstrations, in someone's paddock or woolshed, something we always look forward to.

BUT IT'S FRANK SOPER, a born-and-bred local, who has perhaps contributed most to not only Golden Bay, but to the nation as a whole, with his slogging determination to have a large region in the north-west of the South Island protected.

Born in 1923, Frank was a conservationist almost before most New Zealanders had even heard of the word. He grew up exploring the countryside near his parents' farm at Puramahoi, and by age 11 was climbing peaks on his own.

By age 30, now with his own small dairy farm, Frank became increasingly concerned about the continual burning-off of the pakahi – the boggy mountain foothills in his area, characterised by their impermeable iron subsoils – which resulted in impoverished and leached ground fit only to be recolonised by acid-loving scrub. 'Under this scrub,' he explains, 'flourished a wealth of plants, and a perfect habitat for the pipit and fernbird, which the annual fires destroyed.'

He wrote letters to the New Zealand Forest Service, asking them to reconsider the way they issued burning permits, but his plea fell on deaf ears. Burning-off annually was standard practice on marginal country, in the belief that it facilitated new growth and made mustering easier.

For a larger voice Frank founded the Golden Bay Alpine and Tramping Club in 1960 with other bush- and mountain-loving friends. Together they pushed to gain protection for a large part of the region. Three decades later, in May 1996, after years of persistent lobbying to conservationists and politicians, led persistently by Frank, the Kahurangi National Park was officially opened.

It stretches from the base of Farewell Spit in the north to Murchison in the south, and from the Heaphy River in the west to Tapawera in the east. Over half of New Zealand's 2400 native plants are known to grow here, with 67 of the native plants found nowhere else. In addition, 80 per cent of all New Zealand's alpine species occur here.

The 18 species of birds in Kahurangi include the threatened great spotted kiwi, rock wren and blue duck or whio. It's a stronghold of the kea, the South Island kaka and the kereru. There are the *Powelliphanta* snails, which are a carnivorous throwback to a prehistoric age. Add to this the country's oldest fossils, rare bats, a showcase geology and New Zealand's largest spider.

There is no other place quite like it in the country.

In his two published volumes of poetry, *The Little Ships* and *These Small Fields,* Frank has tried to express the feelings inspired by living in this special place.

> A segment out of Eden
> Wide open to the sun
> Creations crowning glory
> When the world was just begun.

GOLDEN BAY IS THE PLACE where the unexpected is commonplace. Where sheep swim across rivers and humans survive on $4,000 a year. The Pupu power station was built by three men who mortgaged their homes to do so, and an

82-year-old woman went to a peace camp on the Iraq border to try to stave off a war. One man spent a third of his life trying to establish native trees on a wasteland, and an ex-sheep farmer collects cockles for a living.

In Takaka people take in sunshine lunches at outdoor cafés; they meander round the galleries, the organic shop and ethnic clothing stores, which sit beside agricultural suppliers, the hardware store and the big blue supermarket. The accents one hears range from German to American and even French. There are hugs at greetings, very seldom a worried face. There are no buildings of more than two storeys, no traffic lights, only a basic airstrip, and plenty of old cars.

I once saw a goat being walked through Takaka's main street.

On a Sunday afternoon each November Jane Bellerby hosts a women's afternoon tea in her garden at the end of One Spec Road. It's an afternoon with a difference, with fine china cups, delicate finger-food, even hats and gloves, with women, whoever wants to come, drifting around in floaty dresses having fun.

About 60 women turn up, and for a few hours in Jane's sheltered garden there is a buzz of women talking, singing, tea-drinking, laughing, with sometimes a few tears from those whose stories they shared. It's light and frivolous, and it pokes a little fun at the manners of yesteryear while holding onto the good stuff.

WHEN VISITORS FROM ELSEWHERE COME NOW, and meet the variety of people who live here, they return with others, with the sort of look on their faces which is curious, silently astonished, even envious, wondering what it is they had stumbled into. Perhaps their reaction comes from understanding that in planting our family's lives in this isolated region we have benefited from an immensely rich life. Not in monetary terms, but in the education, learning, stimulation and laughter provided by the people who live here.

The look on these curious, bemused visitors' faces is what I would have liked to have shown to those who had implied, almost 60 years earlier, that our purchase of Rocklands was a terrible mistake and doomed to failure.

Of course, for so many years, I also felt we were wasting our lives on Rocklands. The thankless land. But not Garry, ever. If asked that same question again he will still adamantly reply, 'I consider it has been an enormous privilege to have had this opportunity.'

So I've had to learn not to expect a productive farm as our goal, but to experience a situation, a district, that was not only one of New Zealand's most beautiful, but packed now with people of so much talent and fun.

But even the most vital of these newcomers cannot replace my affection for the hard hill people, as I call them. People like Richard and Leentje, Gordy, Leon Moleta, and others still hanging onto their difficult land despite everything thrown at them. These are the people with whom I feel most at home. We have shared so much together.

Chapter 17

In 2002, after 20 years on the hill, we sell the Athfield-designed house. None of our children are likely to live here – they have careers and homes elsewhere, and with house prices in Golden Bay booming it is sensible to sell at this stage of our lives, and enjoy some extra income. We buy our first new car – it's like being given a magic carpet, with confidence to know one could definitely get where one planned!

Where are Garry and I going to live now? 'Oriental Parade in Wellington could be fun,' I suggest quietly, but not much hope of that! We don't move far. Just to a little house at the other end of the farm, beside the Motupipi Estuary. It was a derelict building on our flat land which Garry had demolished and rebuilt on this site some years earlier.

I know, of course, when having one of my conversations with myself, that if I had a city home to regularly attend concerts, theatres and interesting lectures, I would, if it was permanent, soon hate the intensity of urban surroundings – the noise, close neighbours, and above all the lack of trees.

Within days of our move a white heron, or kotuku, appears at low tide, a very special welcome.

Two herons, standing at the edge of the estuary, seem to be doing the same thing. Wild sentinels in grey morning dress, their drooping crests like warriors' plumes.

This is the closest I have lived to the estuary – it was previously a distant view – and now I am unable to prepare or eat a meal without constantly looking out the window to note the estuary's minute-by-minute changes.

There are daily discoveries. The kotuku shares its domain at the mouth of the Motupipi River with spoonbills, black shags, white-faced herons, variable oystercatchers, pied stilts and the occasional influx of black swans. And there are little blue penguins further up the coast.

'A banded rail lives here somewhere,' Helen Kingston, a

friend, arrives on her bicycle to inform me. 'It's like a mini weka. Can you find out if it's nesting?' It's low tide, and we are skirting the quiet empty estuary that curls in from the sea, its bare channels sneaking along the sand, small scuttling creatures bubbling just below the surface.

From this house I am closer to our paddocks; so close I can hear stock breathing. From my bed I watch eight lambs frolick, then tease a young cattle beast who presses his nose towards the cheeky young things, unsure what to do; then the lambs giggle together, perhaps, and kick their heels in its face.

I'm closer to the weather. With a 360-degree view, I can determine at any hour of the day what clouds are being built up. On winter mornings when the valley is sometimes blanketed in mist, the mountains seem much closer, and when a northerly front is due they appear with a strange clarity, an intensity of colour, and one can see the patches of bush in detail and even isolated trees.

I start a birdwatching group for U3A – University of the Third Age – members. There is a breeding colony of spotted shags on the Tata Islands. It's 6 a.m. and five of us head pass the higgledy row of letterboxes and sleepy baches of Tata Beach to perch on the bank, some 10 metres from the water's edge, and watch the shags' behaviour.

Each day, just after dawn, but before sunrise, the shags fly to the beach. At first they come in single numbers, but soon the sky can be full with arriving birds. There can be as few as 40 or in winter up to 2000 – once there were 5000, or so I heard. 'Here they come,' someone whispers as the first shags arrive. More quickly follow.

They land on the water and vigorously flap their wings. Some swim along the edge between the sea and the beach, with their heads underwater. Then they move onto the beach where they may stay up to an hour, flapping their tails, before regurgitating little stones.

Then, as suddenly as they appeared, they begin to depart. At first a few, and then a constant stream, flying north-west towards the feeding grounds. Left on the beach are little piles of stones, perhaps 30 from each bird, sometimes with pieces of shell and bits of glass among them.

Why do they do this? Helen, now retired from her local medical practice, has been part of a group of people who have been counting and observing the shags for four years, which has meant constant early rising. 'No one really knows,' she replies. 'But the current thought is that it's to aid digestion, to help eliminate the worms the birds carry.'

This 'Dance of the Shags', as we locals call it, is a phenomenon that may occur elsewhere in New Zealand, but to date it's only known to occur here, with such numbers, at Tata Beach.

Also unbelievably extraordinary are the bar-tailed godwits. From a member of the ornithological society I learn one day in early September that the first of them have left their Alaskan breeding grounds. The fastest trip to one of their key habitats, Farewell Spit, is eight days, meaning the first birds could arrive in just over a week. Their mammoth journey is considered the longest non-stop migration in the world.

They will arrive exhausted and hungry, having lost more than half their body weight. They will then sit out the Alaskan winter on the Spit, feeding on worms, shellfish and crabs before they return to their breeding grounds in February or March.

Eight days later, while walking on Pohara Beach, as well as the hysterical shriek of the pukeko rising from a swamp, I hear the shrill grating call of the godwit. A few of these brave little birds have also arrived at our side of the Bay.

Not only that, but Jemima and Puddle, two paradise ducks, have appeared, tentatively edging across the lawn, Jemima in front, seeking a nesting place. 'Don't go there!' I silently remind them. 'You know the lawnmower will get too close and disturb you!'

They walk on, cautiously, towards the bottom of the lawn, where a steep bank drops down to the estuary. 'Be careful of high tides,' I whisper. I'm relieved to see the pair back, having survived yet another duck-shooting season.

The estuary closes in to the left, with historic Motupipi Hill towering like a natural bulwark above the water. On an ordinary day, the silence surrounding the hill's quiet presence is interrupted only by the odd cry of a seabird and the shuffling activity of the mudflat creatures. But some years ago it was threatened with an urban development of several hundred house sites.

Twenty-five of us went to the Environment Court in 1996 to oppose the development. We employed New Zealand's top coastal planner and a prominent ornithologist. There'd been months of fundraising. 'What do you think should happen?' the judge asked the coastal planner. 'Refuse the development,' he said. So she did.

Most of Motupipi Hill is now owned by the Rata-Tui Restoration Trust, which is restoring the forest and providing tracks for mountain biking and walking. What could be more perfect?

No one knows for sure when Maori occupation of Motupipi first began, but it's been safely suggested, according to recent carbon-dating, that at least 800 years ago Maori family groups made the estuary and its environs their home. With a population of 200–300 people, Motupipi was the largest Maori settlement in Golden Bay. Right here on my doorstep.

Nowhere else in the Bay are there finer examples of pits

used for storage of kumara and yams. They are unusually intact, deep and steep-sided and arranged in rows. Harder to interpret are the associated terraces. Could they have been level areas for buildings or gardens? Perhaps this ridge crest was the site of the 'three small hill pa' recorded by Heaphy in 1848?

And it was right here, at the foot of Motupipi Hill, that the first European child, Mercy Ann Lovell, was born in Golden Bay. Her parents, James and Ann, with a four-year-old daughter Mary Ann, had arrived at the Motupipi River mouth in 1842 after a two-day journey from Nelson in a whale boat.

It was the discovery of coal and limestone in the Motupipi area, by the New Zealand Land Company surveyors under Captain Arthur Wakefield, that had encouraged settlement.

Our grandchildren spend time on the estuary paddling about in canoes. One small headland, jutted into the water, is the site of the historic Clifton cemetery, where the Bay's first European settlers lie under a tall canopy of macrocarpa trees, with sea water lapping on three sides. Garry has permission to be buried there, but I don't want to be. It's low-lying ground, and with the sea rising I don't want my bones to be floating around. They could end up anywhere!

WHAT DO I DO WITH MYSELF THESE DAYS? Write this book. And walk. Part of the attraction of Golden Bay is undeniably its physical environment, with high mountains enclosing the valleys. With two national parks in the region, the Abel Tasman and Kahurangi, it's not surprising that walking is an important recreation.

I belong to three tramping groups, each with regular

programmes which take me to glorious places. I'm now in my eighties but still energetic, and I enjoy the younger company.

Parapara Peak is 1249 metres from the valley floor. We scramble up a little creek, which requires boulder-hopping for quite some distance. At the top we look across the great valley and into the back country; range after naked range with a glitter of snow on the big tops. There are other peaks to climb on day trips, such as Knuckle Hill, Hailes Knob, Pakawau Peak and Mount Stephens. Walking tracks have been developed on old bridle tracks up the side valleys, made by early settlers.

But it was rare on a tramping-club tramp to be so luxuriously hosted in a delightful house 600 metres up in the mountains, with solar-powered lights and a wood stove heating lashings of hot water. Jenny and Piers Maclaren own this house with 1048 acres of Moonsilver Forest. They'd lived here permanently in the 1970s, bringing up two children, Julian and Sylvia, with Jenny descending by motorbike on a rough track each Monday to teach first in Motueka, and then at the Golden Bay High School.

Twelve of us spent a night here, in the house and various sleep-outs. It was a magic experience.

I'd travelled up here in Jenny's 4WD, an hour's journey from Upper Takaka, with Piers in a second vehicle transporting the group's packs and contributions of food. I could be useful opening the gates on the carved rocky route, built in more recent years for power-transformer technicians. The main group of trampers were walking in from the Cobb Road, a nine-hour walk.

'No time to sit down,' said Jenny on our arrival. 'We will eat our lunch as we walk.' So off we charged, with the purpose of meeting the others. She wanted to show us the Tolkien-like entrance to a seven-kilometre cave.

Our trail was once used by gold miners, traversing cross-country with ripples of range curling up and down endless gorges – following creeks such as the Rupert Brooke and the Robbie Burn. There were limestone chasms and potholes, green with moss, with glimpses through low cloud of distant hillsides and limestone cliffs. So remote and otherworldly.

That night, after a feast of epic proportions, a blazing bonfire was lit outside. There were stories of possums and visitors who come and go. Starlight darted and winked behind the branches, and when the moon was high it looked as if it had been crackle-glazed with twigs. The open fire pulsed and faded. We went to bed hearing moreporks calling to each other, sounding very lonely in the silence that was compounded by small rustling movements, unnoticed by day.

Piers, who grew up in East Africa, bought Moonsilver in 1974 with the idea of establishing an alternative community. It was predominantly beech forest interspersed with a fringe of podocarp trees around the limestone outcrops. It was the hippy era. Jenny wasn't there. She was teaching in France following her Master's degree in English literature. Only later, in 1976, following Piers's research to find 'a mate with integrity' did the pair get together to marry.

As well as degrees in political science and economics, Piers had studied agriculture, which wasn't much use up here. It was predominantly pakihi land with no fertility for farming. In the meantime he was a 'sideline-ologist' as he called it, trapping possums, selling lichen to the US and potted ferns to garden shops. Eventually, wanting a more intellectual career, he did a degree in forestry, with jobs to follow in Rotorua and Rangiora.

Rather than being disadvantaged by his early years in a mountainous retreat, on graduation from high school Julian was offered 14 scholarships, including the Ernest Rutherford PhD Scholarship, with a chance to study at Cambridge University. Today, with a PhD in electrical engineering he is a researcher at Stanford University in the US. Sylvia, Piers and Jenny's daughter, has an Honours degree in ecology, and is helping Christchurch post-quake.

I woke early at Moonsilver, to walk the dew-wet grass. In the bush everything stirs at the first light. The dawn song of the bellbird is exactly like the tinkle of a very small, melodious bell. There is the smell of the honeydew, exuded by a tiny insect that sweats in transparent globules through a black, mossy parasite covering the trunks of native beech trees.

I've always felt happiest in beech-forest clearings. *One day,* I told myself, *I will build a hut beside our own beech forest on Rocklands' skyline.* That's another plan in my head.

I wished the others would hurry to wake up. But then most of them had walked twice as far as I had the previous day.

'Yes, I would like to walk out,' I assured my hosts, rather than accept a lift out as most of the main group were happy to do. But I did wonder at my choice, plunging through untracked bush, with two six-foot males for company. Stinging nettle and wild briar tore at my limbs, with fallen logs to climb over.

Bliss to see a rough hut, where Paul Kilgour, Brett Hutchison and I sat on its porch sharing sardines, rhubarb cake and chocolate. But however simple the food on a tramp, there is a special bonding that takes place, even with people who don't know each other well. A satisfactory feeling of exertion shared.

Paul's biodiversity work takes him predator monitoring and trapping to countless remote places. In December 2007 he departed Preservation Inlet to spend the next 48 days walking cross-country to Tekapo. 'Extremely challenging country; some days I walked 15 hours to avoid the sandflies.' He completed the unfinished part of the route, from Tekapo to Golden Bay, that same summer.

So why does Paul tramp? 'It brings me back to reality, makes me understand the importance of the little things that matter. Each day brings a sense of achievement and fulfilment, and reminds me of the beauty that is in everything and every moment.'

I was asleep by 7.30 p.m. that night, but woke on an exultant high about having walked so far. 'What will I do when I can no longer keep up with you?' I asked tramping friends. To postpone that time, I climb a hill daily to keep fit. When it's my turn to deliver Meals on Wheels I end my circuit near a walking track, leaving a note for Garry to say where I'll walk, in case of accidents.

On my daily walk up steep Rocklands Road I wear earphones to listen to National Radio, timing my walk for the 5 p.m. *Checkpoint* programme, or Kim Hill on Saturday mornings.

Kim is so important in our lives that if Garry is slashing thistles he'll string a portable wireless round his waist, having to slash in the direction where the reception is strongest.

We are outraged when people criticise Kim. 'She interrupts,' some complain. 'But of *course*!' we retaliate. 'She is so bright the questions just burst out of her. And please note,' we add, 'that in 2012 she was named Broadcasting Personality Worldwide at the Association for International Broadcasting awards in London, and has numerous other awards!'

When Paul leads tramps to the Kahurangi lighthouse I feel safe, with four rivers to cross on Golden Bay's far western coast. Once Big River is crossed, it's a further 45-minute walk to the former lighthouse-keeper's house, where DOC has provided accommodation for 20 people. Because of the tide times and the splendour of the scenery, it's necessary and desirable to stay one or two nights here.

This was the epicentre of the Murchison earthquake at 10.15 a.m. on 17 June 1929, causing considerable damage to Golden Bay. The lighthouse keeper, Arthur Page, and his son Alva, were cutting scrub on the hill when they heard a terrific roar. The men were thrown to their knees as the hillside heaved and cracked open, sending 200 acres down to the sea.

A huge slip had crashed down to their house, smashing it

against the lighthouse before flinging it over the cliff. But despite their fears they found Nellie Page, Arthur's wife, unharmed. When the quake struck she had been climbing through a fence to take some packages to the shed 20 metres away. Terrified, she ran just ahead of the widening slip as it crashed through.

The Department of Conservation also maintains Asbestos Cottage, 900 metres up a nondescript scrubby hillside overlooking the Takaka Valley. This humble corrugated-iron hut had from 1913 to 1951 been the home of Henry and Annie Chaffey, who were both hiding from former spouses. From Jim Henderson's book, *Asbestos Cottage*, we know so much about the couple's lives.

There, up in the clouds, without any neighbours, let alone electricity, running water or telephone, Annie had gone about her daily chores. Henry had often left her alone for one or two weeks as he went about his prospecting. She ventured out only twice, for medical reasons, during those 38 years. It could seem a lonely, desolate spot. But the distant view of the Takaka Hill road was apparently uplifting to Annie, when at night she could see the distant lights of vehicles making the crossing.

How could I possibly ever feel isolated, compared to this extraordinary woman?

I recently walked through the Milnthorpe Park Scenic Reserve, and then along the beach to Collingwood to take a friend, Gillian Jackson, to lunch at the Court House café. Now 84, her husband having recently died, she was moving to Wellington to be near a daughter.

In the 1940s and 1950s few women climbed mountains, but Gillian did, scaling most of the South Island's peaks. The last was in 1954, after the birth of her fourth child. But she hasn't forgotten what it feels like to stand on the highest point for miles around. 'It's the exhilaration of seeing the land springing away in an explosion of ranges.'

'I don't know where I'll walk in Wellington,' she said worriedly. 'I'll have to take the car to get somewhere suitable.'

After I'd returned from the café's counter with our coffee she remarked, 'I can see why you are a good walker. You have a short body and long legs.'

This was the first time anyone had found an advantage in my annoyingly high waist, which never worked with clothes. 'But I also have sticking-out ribs,' I complained, 'which means I have no bust.'

'All the better for your lungs to expand,' Gillian retorted.

Will she miss Collingwood? She'd been here eight years.

'It's been hard to make friends,' she said. 'The nine house owners beside me on the beachfront are all related. Born and bred locals.' As if that explained a lot.

'But there are several people who have retired to Collingwood from the outside world,' I pointed out, surprised that Gillian didn't know them. But she didn't encourage contact. When I phoned her, there would always be a sharp and impatient 'hello' perhaps because she'd been interrupted from teaching the piano or painting. Gillian also admitted to being a loner. Totally self-contained. Something I understand.

Yet each time I saw her, and it wasn't often, with our homes at opposite ends of the Bay, I was given a tiny watercolour she'd painted. At this goodbye lunch it was a delicate scene pasted onto a large-size matchbox. And I was given a *Wilderness* magazine – she drew my attention to the article on page 21 entitled 'Tramping Improves with Age'.

GARRY, NOW IN HIS EIGHTIES, ASKS NOTHING more than

to be able to put his boots on daily and have sheep and cattle to look after. He says he would die in six months if he had to stop farming. His routine is fixed. It's the same blue mug for tea, the same brown bowl for porridge, and I'm not to clean the porridge pot.

By 7 a.m. he is walking across a paddock to the barn, to let the dogs off and jump on the trampoline, while his coffee is brewing on a gas ring, before attending to farm work.

The barn is probably a health hazard! Dishes are never done. There are piles of the business pages from newspapers, and books on evolution, ecology and microbiology. There's a piano, a shower, a loo and a wood burner. The barn has no electric power. Water is heated by the sun on polythene pipes, which feed the tank in fine weather.

Once home in the early evening he has a medicinal glass of whiskey while he does the day's sudoku. He likes meat, potatoes and vegetables cooked in the camp oven on top of the stove, with fish on Fridays. Television doesn't interest him, not even rugby since it went professional, and he'd been a rugby star at school – in the First XV two years running.

We came down from our hills, but we didn't quite let go. We kept one block on the top of the range, bordering the Abel Tasman National Park, and due to Garry's continued efforts, even at his age, with a spray pump on his back, most of it is now in grass.

'No,' he replied to a hunter recently who wanted to shoot wild goats up there, 'the goats eat the gorse.'

Our flat paddocks beside the estuary are fertilised with fish fertiliser and lime, and the lambs drenched with cider vinegar and garlic, with most getting away fat before Christmas. We buy weaned buy calves from the Thorpes to grow for the beef market.

'As long as I'm fit enough, and feel I have something to

contribute to the land and stock, I'll carry on,' my spouse says.

Always the optimist, always cheerful, Garry is reluctant to spend a bean on himself, and has no desire to go anywhere, apart from Takaka for essential purchases on a Friday.

My husband is an expert at frugal living. He wears other people's cast-off reading glasses. He accompanied me on several journalist studies – to Nepal, India, France and Italy, with China blowing his mind – but that was enough, he said, of 'sardine-can planes where they won't let me smoke my pipe'.

Every month or so Garry meets half-a-dozen old farmer friends in the pub, driving his truck to Takaka at 40 kilometres per hour, holding up lines of traffic. Asked by a traffic officer recently why he was driving so slowly, Garry replied, 'Because I'm looking at my neighbours' paddocks, to see how their grass is growing.' The officer waved him on.

Once a year, reluctantly, he will travel over the Takaka Hill to Motueka, to the last old-fashioned clothing store in the province, to buy working trousers and singlets, both of pure wool, to wear year-round.

In a recent book about Golden Bay personalities, there is a page about Garry, saying he is the oldest sheep farmer in the Bay. And who else, I wonder, has built, with minimum cost, three houses on the place? The latest is a rammed earth house for the family to use on holidays.

But now that Garry is unable to do heavy work, it's Saint Jeff, as I call him, we turn to. At the time of the December 2011 flood, our sainted friend climbed over sliding hillsides to restore our water intake, a job that took 12 hours, with more work to be done on succeeding days, to ensure we and the stock had water.

Jeff is another of those gifted people for whom school didn't work. He left school in Dunedin as soon as he was legally allowed. He'd written an essay in the Third Form, so good the teacher didn't believe he was the author. Disillusioned, Jeff refused to write another essay despite the punishing strappings.

He will take on almost any practical job with extraordinary self-taught ability. A perfectionist, he built the two stone chimneys on our Athfield-designed house, plus a circular room of stone, which was as tricky as a giant jigsaw puzzle.

Jeff has built many houses in the district, with the building inspector photographing his work as an example for others to learn from.

And my right-hand man is Pete, who I phone when the lawn needs mowing, trees need pruning, a path is to be made, a brass doorknob is to be found, or pictures hung.

'It's Robby here.'

'Hello, Robby there,' Pete replies.

Pete, from Yorkshire, won a scholarship to a grammar school, but his family couldn't afford the uniform. But that didn't stop him getting a PhD in river periphyton. 'What's that, Pete?'

'The animal community in the slime that covers rocks.' Oh.

HE IS A TOUGH MAN, MY HUSBAND, the toughest around, but utterly honourable. I've never met a man I'd rather be married to. He is always there when I need him. When I remind myself of what he has put his body through on Rocklands, never giving up the absolute slog, for long, long hours, never ever complaining about the permanent aches and pains – standing up to eat except when we have visitors, because it hurts too much to sit – I love and admire him.

And Garry has loved our land from the start, even the worst of it. He has no resentment against its infertility. Once, and only once, I heard him say, 'after fifty years of farming sheep on difficult land, I realise in hindsight, this land we took on should never have been cleared of bush'.

Was I comforted to hear this? In a way, yes. It was the first recognition I'd heard about what I'd become aware of from the early years, that our battle to win back this hard country from regeneration was pointless. No matter how much of Garry's strength and our meagre income was spent on it, the land had one determined aim, to return to its former state.

But would our life have been better, more interesting, if we hadn't taken on this hard country in a remote part of New Zealand? I doubt it. Above all, surviving Rocklands had forced Garry and I to adapt to the situation and battle anything thrown at us. We'd had no other choice.

Not only that, but we've managed over almost six decades in Golden Bay to have led a vastly rewarding life, not in a material sense, but in the educational and philosophical insights it has given us; which perhaps, if our life had been easier, we would not have experienced.

Yes, I envy others who have inherited good land, and been able to improve it further to pass on to succeeding generations, while most of our hills have reverted since they were sold to lifestyle owners.

But a life wasted? No. The experience has made me strong. I firmly believe that you are never given what you can't cope with. The economic stringency and isolation have made me search for compensations in this beautiful valley, perhaps at times desperately, but I found them. Now 80 myself, I have grown up.

CHAPTER 18

I love being on my own. When I come home from shopping in Takaka, or from a Wednesday Walk, I love it that the house is empty. I sit at the kitchen table, with the estuary stretched out beside me, to read one of the newspapers that pile up here between infrequent 'tidying ups'.

I'll go days without seeing anyone but Garry, and be happy.

I cannot understand why people, usually women, won't attend a film or visit a café on their own. Heavens above, with Garry unable to sit for any length of time, and refusing to enter the Village Theatre here 'because it smells' he says – what rubbish! – I wouldn't go out at all. In fact an outing without Garry as a car passenger is less stressful, with his 'Don't gesticulate when you talk, keep both your hands on the wheel!'

Yet away from here I am different, eager to see people, hear their news, learn all about their life.

One day I will be able to regularly attend big-city events is another of the conversations I have in my head. I don't bother to check what's on in Nelson. Always, always, always it's that bloody Takaka Hill to cross, two hours to Nelson and two hours back, that is the forbidding barrier.

And then one day, in March 2013, I picked up a pamphlet that had fallen onto the kitchen floor, advertising the biannual Michael Hill International Violin competition. *I'm going!* I decided, and without reading the details I headed for the phone to book myself into the whole 10 days of the competition, starting with the semi-finals in Queenstown and the finals in Auckland.

Eighteen violinists under 30 years of age had been selected from videoed auditions and flown to New Zealand to be assessed by 12 world-class judges. Sir Michael told the audience of contestants, host families, trustees, judges, sponsors and supporters how he envied the 'amazing talent' of the violinists.

One evening there was no competition, but a dinner to raise funds for some charity. The waiter apologised for not having anyone to share my table. I didn't mind, because if there is only one person to talk to over a meal I am more likely to literally choke! And then a gentleman was produced, and before he'd even sat down I burbled that I tended to choke when talking and eating, so did he know the Heimlich manoeuvre?

'Yes,' he said. 'I'm a doctor.'

So that was comforting. I could enjoy his company. The times I've choked have been scary. The first time a teenage granddaughter knew what to do, as fellow diners at a Christchurch café stared in horror. On two other occasions – in Mexico's airport, and at a dinner in a French village – there was fortunately one individual who knew to get behind me and give a sharp punch to my diaphragm. More recently it was Garry who saved me, almost breaking my ribs in his effort!

I took Ana, a granddaughter, to the final concert. After putting her in a taxi afterwards I walked down Queen Street on an exultant high, longing to discuss the concert with others in the crowd, but knowing no one to talk to.

Next day, after picking up the car at Nelson Airport, I headed west towards the distant blue mountains, with my stomach clenching miserably, as it always does, at the sign at the foot of the Takaka Hill marking 50 more kilometres to Takaka, with the steep grind up and over the range, with 365 corners intervening.

And then, on calling at the supermarket in Takaka on the way home, I seemed to know half the people there, to be greeted with hugs and smiles. 'Hello, Robby, you're back.' 'How was the competition?' 'We missed you at the last Wednesday Walk, but told everyone where you were.'

Marvellous, wonderful Golden Bay people. This is where I belong.

The doctor, by the way, who'd been my companion at the charity dinner in Queenstown, was sitting four seats away from me at the final Auckland concert. 'Good to see you,' he said, grinning. 'No choking lately?'

IT'S PEOPLE WHO HAVE STRUGGLED, not had an easy life, with whom I feel best connected. When I meet people in new places, I find myself consciously looking to see if they too have had times that haven't been easy.

I recently undertook Walk Gisborne, a three-day farm walk, with a chance beforehand to meet old school friends, and hear about their tough struggles on the steep and isolated hills of the East Cape and beyond. Immediately there is an understanding about experience shared.

Six months earlier, 10 of us from the Bay drove south to do the Hurunui High Country Walk in North Canterbury, where a young couple had given up well-paying jobs in Australia to take on this very hard property, the third generation to do so, spending their first two years developing a walking track to provide extra income. Not only has there been 30 kilometres of track to maintain, and accommodation to check daily as trampers' packs are delivered, but there have been young children to transport to and from the school bus, as well as normal farm activities to cope with.

People who farm hard country are the people I admire the most; especially those in back-country areas, who are self-contained, who don't take on this life for riches – most not earning a living wage – who are not ruled by clocks, who are not parasites living off other people's efforts but are totally independent, and go about their hard and exacting tasks according to the seasons.

So much has changed in the Bay since our arrival in the late 1950s. It's an exciting place, but always at the back of my mind is the loss of most of the hill families who lived their stoical, hard-working lives on the reverting ranges fringing the Takaka and Collingwood valleys.

There was a wisdom and rightness about the old ways and the old life.

By the gate into Eddy's we meet him working on his old tractor, broken down again. 'It's a bearing problem,' he says. 'I rang the engineers and they told me not to use it until it's fixed. But they haven't come and rain is threatened. They do the big dairy farms first, and then me.'

Eddy turned up in his rough old clothes at the local A&P Show, to which the tourists flock in their shorts and bikini tops, 'because I wanted people to know what real country people look like'.

CHRISTMAS DAY 2011, AND OUR CHILDREN and seven grandchildren are with us. Tim suggests we take a picnic to our land on the horizon. So off we go in 4WD vehicles. It takes some effort to get there, up a zigzagging unsealed road for an hour, and many a gate to open. And then the silence is clear of traffic noise, the cicadas roar and an occasional hawk can be seen.

We stroll to a knobby eminence and climb to the top for a better view. The morning mist has almost gone, with just a few big cumulus clouds blowing by, chasing their shadows up and down the range. We look across Golden Bay to the dark brooding hills of the Whakamarama Range behind Collingwood, with the distinctive peak of Mount Burnett dominating the skyline.

Then, looking east, the view opens up to the vast Wainui Bay, with mussel farm buoys bobbing about in a tidy grid, and, faintly, there on the horizon, is the perfect pyramid of Mount Taranaki.

Looking at this peaceful scene it is hard to imagine that this was the very spot the explorer Abel Janszoon Tasman, who commanded the Dutch East Company expedition to discover more about the great southern continent, which included the already chartered coastline of much of Australia, lost four men to warlike natives on 19 December 1642.

It was at the hands of Ngati Tumatakokiri, the tribe which was in occupation at the time, that these Dutchmen met their death, and the area became known as Massacre Bay.

It's been suggested that cultural misunderstanding was at the heart of this first contact between Maori and European. Maori may have challenged the ship because they feared the white people were patupaiarehe (fair-skinned fairy folk or ghosts), who were feared because they took women and children away. Or perhaps the Maori were simply guarding their territory from attack.

By the late sixteenth century Ngati Tumatakokiri were strongly established around Golden Bay and on the West Coast of the South Island, but subjected to successive raids from other tribes throughout the seventeenth and into the eighteenth century. It's also a fact that Tasman had arrived in the middle of the kumara-growing season, and kumara was a vital food source.

Today, most of Wainui Bay remains in the hands of a European family who have been dairy farming here for four generations, with Jim and Marie Robertson occupying the homestead.

In 1897 Francis Robertson, Jim's grandfather, bought 200 acres from Paramena Haereti, the Ngati Tama chief who lived at Wainui, leasing a further 1000 acres from him later. The old chief was still living in a whare at Wainui. 'He wasn't very popular,' Jim told me. 'A savage, wild old devil. He would tell people he used to eat small white girls.' The chief continued to live at Wainui Bay with about 20 of his people, but soon after he died in 1902, the men and canoes departed.

Jim, in his eighties, has noticed plenty of changes in the farming scene and in local society generally. 'It's certainly a different ball game now,' he said. 'In my grandfather and father's day farming was something you did for the lifestyle. Nowadays it is very much a business. Dairy farmers are still busy of course, but in different ways. I'd say there's nowhere near the amount of hard work, and nowhere near as much satisfaction now.'

He has cautionary words for farmers currently enjoying the current dairy boom. 'There's always a leveller,' he says. 'If you get a boom, such as dairy earnings now, you can bet your life that something will crop up to flog some of it.'

Tim is cooking our chops over an open fire. The youngest grandchildren, Giulio and Filippo, roll in the grass with one cousin and then another, the rest of them now university students or graduates.

'Don't ever sell this land,' says grandson Sam, who is soon to take up postgraduate jazz studies at Queens College in New York. I tell him I plan to build a hut up here. 'That's good,' he says.

After lunch Mike leads the way over a previous possum beat, remembered some 20 or more years later, where he and Tim had set their traps. 'Are you sure you know where you're going?' I ask, as we disappear into thick bush. He does.

It is a lovely walk, up through open beech forest with its carpet of leaves and small ferns following the ridge until we reach the top and our boundary with the National Park. Tui sing. Robins fly to the footprints we leave, seeking insects.

Overall, there is a sense of peace and solitude, of the perfection of growth and renewal in the untouched New Zealand bush that are part of our 150 acres here.

Back at the picnic spot, fresh tea awaits us. And a recognition comes, with the happiness of the day, that Tim, Sally and Michael have a fondness for Rocklands, this rough tortured land where they grew up, with happy memories of working up here as kids, helping Garry fence, doing stock work, or on a possum beat.

Rocklands' value to me, as their mother, is that its challenging environment, and particularly the lack of money, has been the *best* possible start for our children, providing them with not only a work ethic, but a strength of character that has enabled all three of them to reach their individual potentials, and live happy successful lives.

Nothing else matters.

BEFORE GOING INDOORS THAT EVENING I STAND for a short while on the steps at the front door and look about me. There are sheep and cattle grazing nearby, and across the estuary a drifting pool of sun, as it dips behind the mountains.

Maybe there is something uncanny in the summer air, but as I stand there, looking about me, for a moment in time it seems that I now belong to this place, to this Bay, and it to me – in eternity.

My country, I think.

The extraordinary beauty of this Golden Bay region feeds my soul daily, and the many talented, selfless and creative people who live here provide endless inspiration. There is total agreement among us that living behind the great Takaka Hill has forced us to do things, achieve things, that we may never have done in a more conventional area.

I grew up in Hawke's Bay and spent my early adult years in Canterbury and still, today, find myself changing to 'fit in' when visiting both provinces. Only in Golden Bay can I truly be myself. We know each other so well here that there's no point trying to be anything else. That makes for a very comfortable and honest environment.

And now, with the grown-up grandchildren wanting to visit each summer, always with some tramp as part of the holiday, how could I ever regret that we established this base? We hung onto it, despite years when I, but never my hero, Garry, sometimes considered it sheer hell with the worry and stress. This tough, tortuous Rocklands, in this glorious district, has turned out to be the best possible place to offer each member of our family somewhere very special to include in their lives.

There is nothing like writing a book about one's life to force you to look back at the tough times, and the many, many times when life didn't seem fair. But in almost every single situation, I learnt something I needed to know. Bit by bit I gained the strength and ability to tackle what came next, to make the very best of my life. It's given me a drive, and focus.

I wouldn't change a thing.

Acknowledgements

While the vast majority of this memoir is my personal story with my family, I wish to acknowledge with gratitude the sources that provided some background information: *Swamp Fever* and *Kahurangi Calling* by Gerald Hindmarsh, *Asbestos Cottage* by Jim Henderson, *Yesterdays of Golden Bay* by Pauline Blincoe, *Stangers in Mohau* by Robert Jenkin, the *New Zealand Geographic* magazine, *The G.B. Weekly*, *The Takaka Hill* by Cliff Turley, and Carol Dawber and Cheryl Win's histories of Golden Bay. And a special thanks to my friends who have agreed to be in my book.

For more information about our titles please visit
www.randomhouse.co.nz